this
day
in
the
life

DIARIES FROM WOMEN ACROSS AMERICA

Copyright © 2005 by This Day, LLC.

All rights reserved.
Published in the United States by Three Rivers Press, an imprint of the Crown Publishing Group, a division of Random House, Inc., New York.
www.crownpublishing.com

Three Rivers Press and the Tugboat design are registered trademarks of Random House, Inc.

Library of Congress Cataloging-in-Publication Data
This day in the life: diaries from women across America / created, compiled, and edited by Joni B. Cole, Rebecca Joffrey, and B. K. Rakhra.—1st ed.
1. Women—United States—Diaries. 2. Women—United States—Biography.
I. Cole, Joni B.   II. Joffrey, Rebecca.   III. Rakhra, B. K.
HQ1410.T57 2005
920.72'0973'090511—dc22   2005013646

ISBN-13: 978-1-4000-8232-2
ISBN-10: 1-4000-8232-3

Printed in the United States of America

DESIGN BY ELINA D. NUDELMAN

10 9 8 7 6 5 4 3 2 1

First Edition

this
day
in the
life

Edited by

JONI B. COLE

REBECCA JOFFREY

B. K. RAKHRA

 THREE RIVERS PRESS
NEW YORK

For Stephen, who makes it possible
Joni B. Cole

For my amazing and generous mother, Judy
Rebecca Joffrey

For my family
B. K. Rakhra

Contents

Resilient, Even as a Kid

Eleven Number-One Hits on the Country Music Charts

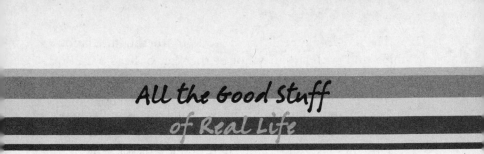

All the Good Stuff
of Real Life

On Tuesday, June 29, 2004, the United States government had just returned sovereignty to Iraq. The future World Series champions, the Boston Red Sox, were in the midst of a three-game losing streak against the New York Yankees. And TV sets across the country were tuned to *Jeopardy*, thanks to then nineteen-day champion Ken Jennings, a polite, teetotaling Mormon who appeared unstoppable, even in the category of "adult beverages."

But June 29, 2004, also proved meaningful in ways that didn't draw public attention. That evening, for example, a pilot flying over northern Maine appreciated the loveliness of a fireworks display 35,000 feet below. In Brownsburg, Indiana, an exhausted mom managed a few hours of uninterrupted rest when her one-year-old baby slept through the night (almost). At the Olympic Training Center in Colorado Springs, a blind athlete received some friendly advice from her teammates on what to wear on an important first date. And in small-town New Hampshire, a seventy-seven-year-old woman celebrated a happy birthday with her family, who baked her a white cake with Dream Whip and strawberries and gave her four new dessert plates and a bracelet engraved with her initials.

The day-to-day realities of work, motherhood, relationships, and birthdays may not be the stuff of headlines. But this, too, is what matters—these moments both quiet and dramatic, funny and serious that occur throughout any given day and illuminate who we really are as individuals, as women, and as Americans.

On Tuesday, June 29, 2004, hundreds of American women created a "day diary" for this book project. In suburban neighborhoods and on family farms, in uptown lofts and in homeless shelters, on U.S. battleships and on summer vacations, women from every state in the United States and from fourteen other countries chronicled their activities, thoughts, and feelings on this single day. The result is *This Day in the Life: Diaries from Women Across America,* a collection of thirty-four complete day diaries, plus a diversity of first-person perspectives, intimate details, meaningful moments, and laugh-out-loud truths—all the good stuff of real life.

While it was impossible to include every contribution in the book, it is important to note that every day diarist informed the pages you see here. Each woman lent a unique voice to the project. Each perspective broadened our own. Who knew, for example, that a ninety-one-year-old nun could be so sweetly funny in her prayers? Who knew that even the most "together" of moms could be driven to the brink of insanity at mealtimes, when none of her kids will eat the same food and, heaven forbid, the sauce touches the meatballs? Who knew that a female soldier in Iraq would go to such extremes to remove a camel spider from her workstation without squishing it?

On an individual scale, these may not be grand revelations, but they speak to a collective truth. All of us hold misconceptions about other women, perpetuated by the labels society assigns us and reinforced by the limitations of our own experiences. Nun. Stay-at-home mom. Soldier.

While these labels may be accurate, they are always inadequate.

The goal of *This Day in the Life* is to offer readers a way to see beyond those reductive labels, to understand the individual behind the woman's circumstance, job title, skin color, stereotype. We are all burdened with so much ridiculous divisiveness, most of it grounded in false assumptions—feminists aren't feminine; abortion supporters aren't pro-family; working women are at odds with stay-at-home moms. By sharing the perspective of another woman, even for just one day, we gain not only a greater understanding of who that woman really is, but—equally important—how much we all have in common.

We would like to express our heartfelt appreciation to the 493 women who volunteered their day diaries for this book project. You have shared with us your home life, your work life, and your inner life, and we can't thank you enough for your generosity and remarkable honesty.

Enjoy *This Day*.

Joni B. Cole

Rebecca Joffrey

B. K. Rakhra

On the Home Front with a "Type A" Television Reporter

Amanda Lamb, 38, Cary, North Carolina

A crime reporter for WRAL television in Raleigh, she loves her job—the investigative aspect, having sources, getting tips, getting to know the families on both sides of the case. The job also appeals to the writer in her. "Every day I'm telling a story." She's comfortable in courtrooms (both her parents are lawyers) and loves a good mystery, real or fiction. Outgoing. Organized, "sometimes to a fault." Goal oriented. After graduating from Northwestern, she drove up and down the Eastern Seaboard with a box of tapes in her car, knocking on station doors. She landed her first job three months later, gradually advancing her career with an eye toward the bigger markets. Halfway there, she adjusted her goals when she fell in love with a metals recycler and drummer. "My life happened here in Raleigh." Married eight years and mom to two daughters, ages four and one, she feels lucky to have a career and a family. "Raleigh is a medium market—a good place to do TV and still have a life." Like most working moms, balance is the big issue. Her strategy? "I don't think you can achieve it. The closest you can come to balance is being in the moment. When you're with the kids, be there 100 percent and don't think about work. And when you're at work, focus on that instead of feeling guilty."

1:09 a.m. I hear the baby, Chloe, flailing around in the playpen, the rustling of sheets, the rattling of toys, the heavy pacifier-sucking noise. She reminds me of a live fish, still hooked on the deck of a boat as she arches her back and wriggles on the thin mattress. In my sleepy fog, her sheets sound like someone crumpling wads of crisp newspaper. I do not usually sleep in the same room with my daughter, but we are on vacation. "Vacation" is a funny word for what this is, two endless weeks with children in constant, close, needy proximity.

3:00 a.m. Chloe is snoring now. I need to go to the bathroom, but if I wake her I'm sunk. If she realizes I am here in the room with her, she will want me. Her head will pop up over the edge of the playpen and she will lift her arms, the universal "hold me" sign for babies. Then comes the scream, piercing, impossible to ignore. I decide to hold it.

5:44 a.m. Our rooms at home have blackout shades that let in very little light. On the other hand, rental homes at the beach are built to let light in. The early morning light dapples the bedroom comforter. This looks good in the rental brochure, but is not good for young children. It wakes them up, and in turn wakes us up. This morning, day four of vacation, is no exception, although I hoped it would be. I whisk her out of the crib into my arms to keep her from waking her grandmother and sister in the room across the hall. My husband is joining us for the second week of vacation, so for now I'm on my own. I don't know how single mothers do it.

6:00 a.m. You can hear my other daughter, Mallory, coming from a mile away. She is loud, brazen, disturbing to us and the tenants in the condo below. The man who is staying downstairs with his family asked me yesterday whether we had hardwood floors in our unit because it was "so loud!" Mallory jumps onto the bed and begins her passive-aggressive ritual with her baby sister. She makes her laugh and then sits on her head. Mallory is four and a half. She is beautiful, difficult, funny, smart, and complicated. One minute I adore her, the next minute she makes me want to get on a bus and leave town.

6:15 a.m. I give up. There is no possibility of sleep. Eating is next on the agenda. I am a schedule person. I believe kids and adults function better on a schedule, even on vacation. You might say I'm a little obsessive-compulsive, but it has served me well. We head to the porch to eat. Mallory, who eats virtually nothing ever, has a donut and milk. Mostly she drinks. This would be a concern, except for the fact I was the same way and somehow survived, albeit with a limited palate. Also, I am too tired to fight about it. Chloe is a good eater, but this morning she decides to throw small pieces of waffle on the floor beneath the high chair. Amid the noise, my mother wakes up and wonders out loud repeatedly why the children are awake so early.

7:15 a.m. It's too early and too cold to go to the beach, but it's never too early to exercise. I have a double baby jogger. Before I had kids I looked at women pushing these things and pitied them. Why would anyone want to push such a ridiculous and heavy-looking thing? But now the jogger equals freedom. I need to exercise. It's my sanity. Some people take drugs, I run. Granted, I'm an adrenaline junky, but I'm at peace with my choice of obsession. The jogger allows me to GO. Anyone who laughs at the sight should try it. Pushing sixty-five pounds of children at a high rate of speed should be an Olympic event.

7:35 a.m. The New Jersey beach town where we are staying is breathtaking. The homes here in Cape May were built in the 1800s and are surrounded by wraparound porches, iron fences, and wildflower gardens. Many of the old homes have been refinished and made into shops, restaurants, and bed and breakfasts. There is a boardwalk that runs the length of the downtown where I take the jogger, bordered on one side by the beach, on the other by the town. The only problem is that I have a lot of pent-up envy. Envy of the people who are not with young children, who can sit and drink wine on the verandas, browse in the cute boutiques with lots of breakable items, and stroll the boardwalk after dark. And then there are the memories. Like the restaurant where I had to dress like Martha Washington in college, or the spot on the beach where my first real boyfriend, a lifeguard, and I had a fight because he played volleyball with a girl.

7:48 a.m. I am wearing an MP3 player, listening to a mixture of hip-hop, chick ballads, and seventies disco. Mallory keeps trying to talk to me, but I can't hear her because of the music. It makes me feel a little guilty to be ignoring her, but then I think it could be worse. It's not like they're playing with matches while I'm passed out on the couch.

8:00 a.m.   I get two cups of coffee and balance them on the top of the baby jogger. The coffee shop has detailed descriptions for each blend. One says "dark, brooding, spellbinding." Another says "distinctly complex." I never realized coffee, like everything else in my life, seems to be an emotional choice. I'm feeling more complex than spellbinding today.

9:15 a.m.   Getting two kids ready to go to the beach is almost so exhausting it's not worth the trouble. But being a Type A working mother, with all the guilt that goes along with this role, I plan for every contingency to make the day at the beach a scene out of a Disney movie. The list includes bathing suits, hats, sunblock, sunglasses, diapers, changes of clothes, toys, towels, chairs, drinks, and snacks. The planning is the easy part. It's the execution that's hard. After watching me do this, my mother says instead of "a village" it takes "a city" to raise children.

10:00 a.m.   We arrive at the edge of the beach. The Jersey Shore has big, wide beaches, so pushing the baby jogger across the sand is a bit like crossing the Sahara with a rickshaw. People stare and say things like, "You've got your hands full!" Or "What a workout!" I politely smile and imagine running over their feet. Upon arrival at a good spot, the setup begins. There are two kinds of beach people here. The people who bring their own chairs and towels, and the people who stay at hotels and inns where the staff sets them up for you. We are the former; my mother longs to be the latter.

10:15 a.m.   We have the beach almost to ourselves as it is still a little cool. In an unlikely turn of events, the baby has fallen asleep in the jogger, so Mallory and I have a rare moment to ourselves. I am taking pictures of her as she does cartwheels by the water. I want to remember her like this, her skin the color of toast, her blunt short haircut falling into her eyes with every tumble. She gets bored and decides we need to build a drip castle. It's the only kind of castle I can build because it's meant to be abstract instead of perfect. My mother never built castles with me because she didn't like sand. So by doing it, I kill two birds with one stone, complete my working-mom-guilt Disney fantasy and one-up my mother.

10:35 a.m. A little boy and his family set up camp next to us on the beach. He looks about Mallory's age. She begs me to make an introduction. She is always afraid to approach new kids, but desperately wants to meet them. I see a lot of myself in her insecurities. Because I understand, I always try to help her. We introduce ourselves to Daniel and his family. While the adults make small talk, Mallory and Daniel become fast friends over a drip castle. I am proud of her. I think she's a lot braver than I ever was.

11:06 a.m. Going to the beach carries a different meaning when you have kids. There's no reading, no dozing, no idle sunbathing. It's busy. The baby wakes up. She is in a cute bathing suit that matches Mallory's. I vowed I would never buy my children matching suits, and I didn't. My mother did. Like buying a minivan, I felt like matching outfits of any kind on my children was admitting I'm no longer cool. The truth is, at thirty-eight with two kids I'm not cool, probably never was, and the suits are damn cute. Of course, the baby has peed through her swim diaper and totally soaked the suit. I dig into my bag and change her into a white onesie with a snap missing in the crotch. Within minutes she is rolling in wet sand and is soaked again. I feed her raisins and Goldfish. She picks up the ones that drop with her sandy hands before the seagulls can get to them. I turn my head. I'm a lot more laid back about parenting the second time around.

11:17 a.m. Mallory sees some girls she would like to play with and quickly ditches Daniel. After negotiating with their leader (the big sister), she grabs a shovel and begins to dig with them, leaving Daniel to sit at a distance and stare at his feet. I call her over and quietly explain she must include her old friend with her new friends. There are so many things I want to teach my daughter, and compassion is very high on the list. I remember how mean kids can be, the sting of rejection, real or perceived.

11:47 a.m. My dad calls on the cell phone. The reception is awful. We keep yelling at each other. "Can you hear me NOW?" After several disconnected calls, we can finally hear each other if I stand in one position and don't move my head from a slight tilt to the east. My parents are divorced; we are spending the next week with my dad. He is calling to tell me he has bought me a case of Dr Pepper and wants to know the girls' shoe sizes so he can buy them flip-flops. Seems trivial, but with my dad the love is in the details.

12:00 p.m. The problem with bringing a baby to the beach is that she must nap not long after you have made the BIG effort to get there. Neither of my children has ever napped on the beach. My mother stays with Mallory, and I take Chloe back for a bath. She has sand in every nook and cranny of her pudgy little body. I wash her, nuzzling her soapy wisps of blond hair as she bores her tired head into my shoulder. She is a cuddly baby; it's one of the things I love about her. Mallory doesn't give or seek such affection easily. But when she does give it, it makes me feel like maybe I'm doing something right.

1:00 p.m.　　Against my will, my mom hires a babysitter for the afternoons to sit at the house while Chloe naps. This frees her up to do whatever, and it frees me up to do something with Mallory. It is a good idea, as are most of my mother's ideas, but I feel guilty, for what I'm not sure. Mallory and I meander our way back to the beach, ducking into little stores like girlfriends with nothing but time on our hands. I buy myself a sash, one that I will probably never wear because I've seen it on too many teenagers. I buy Mallory a dusty shell necklace, one that I'm sure has been in the shop storeroom since I was a little girl. We run into Daniel at an outdoor lunch place. He tells Mallory he is getting a big shovel. Suddenly, I am shelling out $3.17 for her big shovel.

2:45 p.m.　　Mallory and Daniel are playing near the water as I sit under the umbrella. I want to give her space and independence, or at least the perception of independence, but I am terrified of her drowning. Mallory is a risk-taker, plus when she was a baby she got bacterial meningitis and almost died. I try not to be overprotective, but I know what it feels like to almost lose her, and I never want to feel that again.

3:00 p.m.　　Mallory is now playing with two girls she calls "the six-year-old twins." I realize that Daniel has once again been banished from the play, not intentionally, but when the cartwheels begin, he falls back. This time I don't intervene. Maybe this is the age when boys and girls begin to part ways. Mallory is tough and energetic, but she is also a girl; a cheerleader, a dancer, a wannabe rock star. I realize as I watch her with other children that I will have a big role as navigator in her life, if she lets me. It seems like a daunting responsibility.

3:20 p.m.   The twins' father comes over to say hello. We have exchanged polite smiles this week, but have not yet met. He is clearly either a divorced parent or a widower. He is alone with his three girls. At first we make pleasant conversation, and then I realize he's wondering whether or not I am single. I am at once flattered and uncomfortable. I tell him I have a baby. The conversation ends quickly.

5:37 p.m.   We're trying to get ready for dinner. Chloe is whining, eating toilet paper, digging in the trash, pulling out the night-light, and putting her finger in the socket. To keep her amused we play peekaboo with the shower curtain as water sprays all over the bathroom floor.

6:05 p.m.   We're ready to leave for dinner. Chloe cries unless I hold her. Mallory is asleep on the couch. I try to wake her and she moans and curls up in a ball. Alternately, I carry both of them, crying, to the jogger.

6:15 p.m.   Mallory refuses to eat. She drinks chocolate milk and runs around the courtyard of the restaurant with two kids she knows from the beach. Chloe is happy as long as she has pasta to throw on the floor. The small Italian restaurant has no liquor license. My mom goes around the corner to the liquor store to get a much-needed bottle of wine. When we finish the meal, we clean out Mallory's plastic milk cup and fill it with the rest of the wine. We drink it through a straw as we shop.

7:30 p.m.   We take turns going in the stores and watching the baby. The take includes a pair of purple leopard-skin slides for Mallory, a red leather purse that looks like a bustier for my mom (chosen by Mallory), a white sweater with pearl buttons for Chloe (to replace the one that got moldy in the washer), and assorted toys for Mallory, including a magic wand. We are spent in more ways than one. At one point, I am waiting for my mom and Mallory to come out of a toy store, and I decide my butt can fit in the extra baby jogger seat. Chloe loves it and laughs uncontrollably. It's actually not that uncomfortable. I get a few looks, but I don't care. I can't believe this is the first time I've ever tried it.

9:00 p.m. We head home, put the kids to bed, and put on season six, part one of *Sex and the City*—a guilty pleasure like *People* magazine or coffee ice cream with sprinkles. When you spend so much time analyzing everything to death, it's important to have a mindless release. This is mine.

11:30 p.m. I always plan to go to bed early. It never happens, life gets in the way. But that's okay. Another full day, another full night, likely to be followed by more of the same the next day. I wouldn't have it any other way.

Flavor of the Week

10:50 a.m.   Drive by Culver's Frozen Custard (yes, the very same place that also has Butter Burgers). I need to avoid this establishment like a bad virus, especially considering I'm headed to the Y. They post their Flavor of the Day on a board outside and, every day, I check it with apprehension because they just might have a flavor I can't resist. Today's feature is Raspberry Royale and I almost shout with joy in the car. This flavor does not intrigue me in the least.

Marilyn Weigel, 36, Grayslake, Illinois; book reviewer,
Romantic Times Book Club Magazine

Porn

1:45 p.m.   I hear some news on the piped-in stereo system, something about Iraq and then some other story about porn. I think of my mother. When I was away at prep school I took an ethics class. I had to debate this guy (whom I had such a crush on) that it was important to fund all art. The topic of Mapplethorpe and pornography came up. The night I prepared for the event I called home to get some help. My mom couldn't understand why I would not argue against pornography. It never occurred to her that I was assigned this position by my teacher. She thought that I really backed porn. To this day, she still believes this and tells people that I support pornography.

Laurie Ballentine, 29, New York, New York; jewelry sales associate

Helmwige

11:30 p.m.   I put Gabriel into bed. Ah, finally a quiet house. I go into my music studio, pull out *The Ride of the Valkyries,* and sing out my part, the role of Helmwige. I have to watch out not to sing too heavily, especially in the high range. Besides that, nothing is very hard except those tricky entrances. I put on the recording, fast-forwarding the orchestral sections, which are so heavy they almost make me laugh. It will be some work to memorize the German, but it will be worth the effort. Midnight comes and I am deep into finding the higher meaning of the Valkyries' dialogue about their horses.

Valerie Williams, 41, Bremerton, Washington; voice teacher/singer

Happy birthday

4:00 p.m.   The cast of *Friends* is on with Oprah. That was one of the few shows I watched every week. I liked it because it wasn't a show that revolved around a family. I know at the end they were all getting married, but it was still different. I have seen all the episodes now. My real friends suck. Not a single one called me on my birthday.

Kim Olsovsky, 31, Darlington, South Carolina; teacher

Crystal Wilkinson, 41, Bloomington, Indiana

She was raised on her grandparents' tobacco farm in rural Kentucky. As an African American who grew up in Appalachia and became an author, the label she identifies with the most is "country"—a cuss word to her city cousins and a headache for her publisher. "I write from that Affrilachian perspective. I'm proud of my rural heritage." Her short story collections have earned honors (Atlanta's Creative Loafing *magazine named her one of the South's best writers without a bestseller), but "country" can be a hard sell at the bookstore.*

The first in her family to attend college. A single parent to teenage twin daughters and an adult son. A creative writing teacher. Reared as a Southern Baptist. "I'm always worried about going to hell." She's much in demand as a speaker and reader but still shy in the spotlight. Uneasy with compliments. "If someone says 'I love your outfit,' I'll give them a big explanation about how it's cheap and how it has a spot on it." She took a year off from teaching to finish her novel. Instead, she got married, got divorced, became a grandmother, and needed to take every paying gig that came down the pike. *"The light bill had to be paid."* Her agent and publisher are having conniptions. *"Crystal, you've missed three deadlines!"* She recently landed a dream job at Indiana University, but the opportunity meant leaving Kentucky. Homesick. *"Bloomington is only three hours away, but it feels like it's across the country."*

1:35 a.m.   Even wine is not helping me sleep, and three window air conditioners and a floor fan aren't cooling me down. My mind is swirling. The move. The kids. My twin daughters met their boyfriends again last night in the park where they work and "talked." When I place myself in their fifteen-year-old minds and bodies, I know they are thinking and feeling like this is the best summer of their lives.

Their perfect summer is my summer from hell. I've been fifteen before, and sixteen-year-old boys "talk" with their hands and their peni. (I wonder if it's called "peni" when there's more than one.) I'm giggling. Is it the wine? Or is it that there has to be *one* frigging thing to laugh about in the midst of all of this. I'm sure that my daughters will grow into the powerful, educated, outspoken black women that I have wished them toward being their whole lives, but right now I just picture them being kissed and gyrated on by these two little white boys who are still wet behind the ears. Of course, away from my daughters, I could imagine these boys as nice kids. They are always polite: "How are you, Ms. Wilkinson?" but I glimpse something else, slight, but far from "right," when I glare at them and their eyes shift down. "They are up to something," my brain says. "Stay the F away from my babies."

3:00 a.m.   I could go into the living room and watch TV, but eleven years of my life is in there in various stages of being packed. Going in the living room would only make me more depressed or stressed or whatever I am. I decide to stay in the den that used to be my son's bedroom. My own bed is filled with things waiting for boxes or the trash. I hate making those decisions—papers from ten years of teaching, pictures of my grandparents, spiral notebooks filled with journaling about the marriage, the divorce, and everything that came before and after. The movers will be here on July twelfth, but I can't tackle my bedroom yet. I can't tackle any of it. Yet.

6:00 a.m.   I managed to get some sleep. It feels like only a wink. My country girl instinct, paired with the ringing of the phone, lets me know that it must be 6 a.m. My mother is my alarm clock. She calls at exactly 6:00 every morning, even though I've been waking up on my own for twenty years without an alarm clock. The daughterly thing to do would be to answer the phone. The motherly thing would be not to call so damn early.

7:00 a.m.   I promised myself. Me and I had a pact that we would start on either packing or critiquing my students' writing first thing this morning, but when I reach the living room, peeping through the piles of packed and unpacked boxes is *Mystic River,* one of the unwatched DVDs that I need to return. It begs, "Watch me. Watch me."

I put it in and flop on some floor pillows, because the living room is nearly furnitureless. I moved the living room couch into the den long before the packing began. My twenty-four-year-old son's room is now the den—a signal to him to grow up and move on. It's not working. My den is filled with his clothes. He doesn't quite still live at home but keeps his territory marked by oversized jeans, sweatsuits, and tennis shoes. This so-called den is also full of my granddaughter's toys, which is the only indication that this room is semioccupied by a father. "I love you, Gerald," I say out loud. Someday he'll get it together.

I'm watching *Mystic River* thinking that Sean Penn is old. I remember him young and James Deanish at Madonna's side in the eighties. Of course, this gets me to wondering if people who saw me twenty years ago would think I look old, too. Of course they would. My grandmother said, "Black don't crack," but I'm feeling like one worn-out sister right now.

10:00 a.m. The movie? Melancholy, but I liked it. I'm becoming a fan of all things dark and gloomy. Depression?

10:30 a.m. I imagine myself eating whole wheat toast, multigrain hot cereal with soy milk, and a bowl of organically grown fruit. I am sitting on the patio of my new residence in Bloomington. I am prepared to teach one of my classes. My novel is written. My dreadlocks are catching the wind. All boxes are unpacked and discarded. Everything is neat and tidy.

My reality is two bowls of cereal (a sugary brand that my kids love), which boasts a whopping twenty-nine grams of carbs per serving. (I must have had at least four servings). My low-carb friends would be appalled, but I enjoy my comfort-food breakfast. I don't even bother to wipe up the dribbles of milk on the throw pillows. Maybe I'll get rid of the pillows, too. I need new ones.

10:40 a.m. I'm folding clothes. A mother shouldn't be jealous of her daughters' size six jeans. Well, jealous is not the word, really. I'm just amazed that someone can actually get their hips in such tiny clothes. Even at my smallest, before the twins, I was a size ten. But even at a size six my girls have womanish hips. They should make a pill for fifteen-year-olds that depresses hips and breasts until age eighteen, maybe twenty-one. I'm still mad about the boy situation, so I fold the girls' clothes up in a big stack in the den. I vow to leave them there until they rot.

11:00 a.m. The girls are waking up. They have to be at work at noon. This may be my only chance to get in the shower first, so I dive in.

Noon Sometimes I think it's magical that all three of us can be ready in less than forty-five minutes. I guess we've perfected our ritual after all these years, even with one bathroom. And since both my husband and my son are gone, we are a male-free society except for the occasional intrusion. And then there is the new issue of "the boys."

In the car we are all quiet. The girls arrive at work on time. I want to demand that they don't wear shorts, but this would be ridiculous since they work at a pool. I just say, "Pull your shorts down, please." I've been giving them my lukewarm shoulder. Dealing with "the boys," on top of moving, on top of starting a new teaching job, on top of being about to miss my fourth deadline for my novel, on top of turning forty-two is not my idea of fun. Who the hell said that the forties were the most enjoyable? Well, one of my friends said that. Pat, I think. I make a note to discuss this with her later. The girls kiss me good-bye, which breaks a tiny chip off my frustration. At least we still have *love* even without *understanding*.

12:10 p.m. I'm here at the local Mediterranean restaurant to meet three writing friends for lunch. My first goodbye party. I've been selected by Atlanta's *Creative Loafing* magazine as one of the South's best writers who is not on the bestseller list. This is something to share, something to be excited about. But I don't want to go in and face these women. They are friends, but I don't want to recount the moving experience, the unfinished novel, any moments of my life. Maybe I'm a drama queen today, but I feel as though it's too hard just *living* in my skin right now. "You should be packing," I say to myself and apply lipstick. My daughters have told me the color is too dark for me. "Smile!"

3:48 p.m. The food was delicious, although spots of it landed on my blouse. Look at Miss Fiction Writer, grease spots on her boobs, lipstick eaten off. I didn't tell them my good news about the article. I smiled, chatted, laughed, and even cried at the end, which was my cue to go. I cry too much. Pam and I stood for another hour in the parking lot. I couldn't stop talking. Maybe I needed the outing more than I thought.

4:00 p.m. Time to pick up the girls. I haven't done any packing, any cleaning, haven't read my students' papers.

4:15 p.m. I'm a citified country girl. I think I'd just die without my cell phone. Joan calls, makes a joke right away, "What's up, Big Head?" She always manages to make me laugh. I tell her we need to go out before I leave. There is a sadness in me nearly as strong as death every time I really think about leaving.

There is still silence among the Wilkinson girls in the car on our drive home. I glance at them, one in the passenger seat, one in the backseat—earrings flopping, hair looking too stylish. I want them to be ten again. Where in the hell are my little girls, my babies? I turn the radio from NPR to the R&B station. A familiar hip-hop tune fills up the car. We are still not speaking, but the music is a tiny compromise.

5:00 p.m. A friend calls and we talk about our kids, our lives, our careers as writers. We try to discern if we are "in a funk" or "in transition," and decide that we should meditate as soon as we can. "You have to be in the moment. The moment of peace has to begin now," my friend says. "You should bottle that shit and sell it," I say.

6:00 p.m. The packing still haunts me, but I decide to cook dinner instead. More comfort food. My grandmother's recipe for stuffed green peppers—turkey (instead of hamburger), rice, onions, and ketchup.

6:45 p.m. "Mom, Ben and Anthony want to meet us at the park." I don't say anything. "Mom." Silence. "Moma." "Mommy." They are savvy enough to know that "Mommy" reminds me of my babies, who are buried somewhere in these womanish bodies, all hips and breasts and lip gloss.

"I'm tired of these boys every time I turn around," I scream so loud I can feel the burn in my throat. I go back to the kitchen and then into the den. The stack of folded clothes has disappeared. I leave the issue of Ben and Anthony unresolved. I look at them with a look that says, "I f-ing dare you to ask me to go out with them little boys again!"

7:25 p.m. One daughter asks, "When will the peppers be done?"

"Soon." I am perfectly fine talking about food—anything and everything, but don't ask me about boys.

named "one of the south's best writers . . ." 19

7:30 p.m.   I have avoided the bill collectors all day, but one catches me on the phone. "She's not here," I say. I know it's not the right thing to do, but I'll be damned if I tell them the "my ex claimed the kids and messed up my income tax return and I just got a divorce and I'm starting a new teaching job in August" story even one more time this week.

7:45 p.m.   I give in and let the twins go to the park, knowing that "the boys" will be there. They abandon my stuffed peppers, without any regard for their great-grandmother, and head out. I immediately scarf my peppers down with a diet pop. I am eating on a Styrofoam plate and even that nearly brings me to tears. My dishes are packed away. The people who think that black women are all superwomen would be surprised not to see even the slightest hint of an *S* on my chest.

These days I have lots of moments when I long for the past. Perhaps it's the move. This is the first house I have owned. I remember how proud I was. A single mother, black, country, and proud. Gerald was thirteen and Elainia and Delainia were four. I didn't have my first book published yet, and I was a nine-to-fiver in public relations. I wasn't a grandmother. My life is indeed in transition. I'm leaving my son, my mother, my granddaughter, my friends, my writing community, my state, eleven years of my life in this house. Am I too old to reinvent myself?

9:00 p.m.   The girls are not back yet. They have fifteen minutes. I don't give them their fifteen minutes. Instead, I drive to the park and find them. Innocent, of course, sitting on the bleachers, talking. No Anthony. Ben, lanky and nervous, but doing nothing wrong, other than sitting beside one daughter, with her sister 'close by. "Ben needs twenty-five cents to take the bus back home." They are all

this day in the life   **20**

scared of what I'll say or do, but I do and say nothing, except agree to drive Ben home on the other side of town. I want to rip Ben's little, pointy head off.

On the way home I break my mad silence. I explain to my daughters that I don't understand this desperation to see these boys every day, every night. "We are moving away," one of them yells (the one devoted to Ben), tears threatening behind the crack in her voice. "Ben is going to visit his father in New York and we are moving." My head hurts. She cries. The other twin is silent, but I feel her comforting her sister. They will always have each other.

Soon we have all returned to our silence. I want to talk. I want us to return to our norm, but I don't know how.

"I don't understand why you are mad at us all the time," my daughter says, being more of a woman than me in that moment. I say nothing. I never wanted to be this kind of mother. We are supposed to be the most communicative frigging family on earth. That's how I planned it, but I can't find words tonight to make them understand that I want to keep them safe and secure forever. Why aren't they happy watching cartoons? Read a book! Go spend the night with a girlfriend and paint your toenails. No words. Silence.

9:30 p.m.   I write. They reheat and eat their peppers. The girls watch a movie. I worry and pout.

9:45 p.m.   My mother calls again. "Do you need my help?" she asks. Maybe that's the heart of my problem, too. Maybe none of them *need* me so much anymore.

"No, Mama."

"What's wrong?"

"I don't feel good," I say, trying to be truthful and evasive, but I sound childish.

"Oh," she says, drawing out the *O* like she's talking to a five-year-old. "Are you doing okay?"

"I'll call you tomorrow," I say, then follow with a forced cheerful, "Okay?" hearing my ex-husband's voice in my ear: "You are borderline cruel to your mother." But it works; the concern eases from her voice. We exchange I love yous.

10:00 p.m.   I hear them in the other room, talking first to a friend (I can tell by their voices, exchanging the phone back and forth and giggling loud), then I hear these new, serious, more grown-up voices they seem to reserve for "the boys." I am wallowing in something I can't even identify. Self-pity? No. Loneliness? No. Just wallowing to be wallowing?

10:45 p.m.   My friend Daundra drops in. "When you don't answer the phone calls," she says, jutting her hip out like Daundra does, "then I just have to drop in." I am both happy she's there to distract me and wishing she'd leave to let me wallow. I don't invite her further into the house where she can find a place to sit. We stand beside the door and talk, but don't really talk.

I love Daundra. She's one of my best friends, at least she was. The stress of our lives has created a gap. I hate the awkwardness. She catered my wedding, and I took photographs at hers. My marriage lasted less than a year and hers is just beginning. I still owe her wedding pictures. I promised she'd have them before I leave. Another thing on my to-do list. Daundra and I vow to spend a day together, maybe Saturday. Maybe we'll take a day trip to Louisville or to Cincinnati. Something we haven't done in a long time.

11:00 p.m.   The girls are in bed. Safe. I have packed nothing. Nothing on my list is checked off. The movers will be here on July twelfth. I need to lie down and try to get some sleep.

The Stakeout

8:30 a.m.   At my desk. It's covered in overdue police reports, arrest folders, and other miscellaneous stuff left over from yesterday. I hate paperwork more than anything. I'd much rather be on the street making arrests, which I know inevitably leads to more paperwork. It's such a vicious cycle!!! I just sit here and frown at the pile on my desk.

10:10 a.m.   Snuck out of the office at headquarters. Couldn't take it anymore. It's such a beautiful day outside. I don't even notice the syringes, empty vials, and other trash that surround me as I sneak down the alley. I'm making my way to a burned-out vacant house that backs up to this basketball court. Pretty soon all the dealers will come out and the addicts will swarm the court to get their fix. Hopefully, I'll be able to identify some of the major players in this drug organization I'm investigating.

10:17 a.m.   My sarge just called to let me know we're doing mass raids on Thursday. I'm supposed to start my vacation, but I would rather postpone for one day. Can't miss out on all the fun!

11:00 a.m.   I'm sitting on the edge of a broken desk, looking out the window at the basketball court. Still no activity. They're late today. The smell of this house is starting to give me a headache. The walls are covered in black soot. This room looks like it used to be someone's bedroom. There's a stained mattress on the floor. The furniture is mismatched and worn out. Piles of dirty clothes are scattered about the room. It's depressing.

11:20 a.m.   Someone yells, "Five-oh!" to warn the drug dealers that a police car is driving through the block. The basketball court is getting crowded. One of my targets is yelling, "Twenty-four-seven out!" advertising his heroin product. Junkies are flocking to him with their money in hand. He points them to another guy standing at the rear of the court, holding a plastic bag filled with blue-top vials of heroin. I can feel myself getting an adrenaline rush. I love this part of my job. They don't know I'm watching. They don't realize that soon they will be under arrest and headed downtown to our booking facility. I'm smiling to myself . . .

12:30 p.m.   Driving back to headquarters to submit the money and drugs I seized from the two dealers I arrested. I'm glad I shut them down for today. I am not naïve enough, however, to think that they won't be out tomorrow.

> *Marjorie M. German, 32, Baltimore, Maryland;*
> *narcotics detective, Baltimore City Police Department*

Jennifer Foth, 23, Lauderdale, Minnesota

She landed her first real job at a homeless shelter, as a volunteer coordinator and fund-raising assistant. Her degree is in anthropology, "but if I could have majored in everything, I would have. I wish I could have every job for one day." Her future is hardly settled. She wants to travel. She's "totally up for meeting people," but puts up walls. "I get really scared when I date that I'm going to like someone too much." She's considering a career in sales—six years selling shoes part-time has convinced her she has a knack. "I like playing that game, seeing that instant achievement." She moved twice as a kid, the first at thirteen, one of the roughest times of her life. No friends, big pubescent changes. She immersed herself in playing the piano and clarinet to escape the pain. The second move came after her parents divorced, in her senior year of high school. "I wasn't going to slip back into that scared little girl. I saw how upset my mom was, and I needed to be strong." She still talks to her mom every day. Motivated. Organized. Crazy about music. Her pet peeve is a dirty kitchen. Friends say she can be intimidating, blunt. "I'm really direct, and it freaks them out. They feel threatened by someone who, even if she doesn't have it together, appears like she does."

7:32 a.m. Alarm clock time. (Real time 7:15 a.m.) Two text messages. Why do my friends only send me messages when they are drunk or horny?

Coordinate movements around tiny bathroom—the kind where the door hits the toilet and you have to move just right to make sure your belly fat doesn't get squished between the door and the one shelf that holds all your bathroom things, and inevitably there will be a hair-dryer cord, and you'll either trip on it or it'll get stuck in the door. The challenge is to avoid getting frustrated EVERY morning.

I must say, my roommate and I are quite good at this. Amanda leaves the bathroom upon my arrival at the door. I pee, she gets dressed, I hop in the shower, she applies makeup. By the time I'm out of the shower, her hair is fixed and I can start on mine. It helps that she has to get to work a half hour earlier than me.

8:02 a.m. Last-minute dance around the house. Cell phone, keys, water bottle, Nutri-Grain bar half in mouth. Say g'bye to my cat, Angie, remind her that she'll get fed after I get home. I feel guilty because I know I can't predict when I'll be home. Today it is hot, so I am worried that I should have turned on the air, but I should have been on the road two minutes ago. She'll be fine.

8:17 a.m.   Traffic. What is this? I drive out of the city into the suburbs, so in theory I shouldn't sit in a mess of cars. What kills me is I know that if I would have left literally two minutes earlier, I wouldn't be stuck in traffic. So now I have to decide if I have time to get a chai. Do I even have $4? No.

9:05 a.m.   I make it to the shelter. Open donations from Target—shampoo bottles, ripped boxes of Kleenex, dented canned goods. Thank God. Now I'll have less scrambling to find random projects for the volunteers. In fifteen minutes, twelve thirteen-year-olds wearing lime-green T-shirts will arrive, filling the last crevices of open space at the shelter. I run a list in my head. Four of them can assist with child care. Two will sort clothing donations. Two will clean windows. Four will organize Target donations. That should keep them busy for at least an hour. These mission groups always have good intentions, but inevitably I will have to chase down two or three kids using Windex like a squirt gun. Be patient. I know. Remember, Jen, you don't communicate well with children.

9:45 a.m.   Volunteers are working on individual tasks. Quickly check voice mail and e-mail. Ah, trusty horoscope— will it influence my actions later in the day? I only have ten minutes before running back downstairs to grab the Windex kids and start them vacuuming.

11:30 a.m.   Lunch is only a half hour away. Starving. Lunch is the one meal I eat regularly because it's free and I am NO cook. My desk is right above the kitchen, so when residents start cooking, my stomach starts growling. I hope it's good today.

12:15 p.m.   No. It's big sausages. I'll skip it.
    I'm just going to take a minute to gloat. I have a date on

Wednesday. Yippee. He's tall, and that's good because it means I can wear my tall shoes. I could never wear my tall shoes with the paramedic. He felt intimidated by them. Speaking of the paramedic, I'm sure that I saw him on the highway yesterday (red Suburban with a paramedic sticker on the back; the driver was wearing his baseball hat backwards).

After we passed each other on the road, I got really angry. I think what hurts the most is that he just walked away. We had one awkward night, and then he just stopped calling. After all that time as friends/more than friends/ friends, he couldn't be a man and say g'bye. So, like any rational person, I yelled "fucker" as I was sitting at the stoplight waiting to get on the highway. Then I channeled my anger into working out. Sweat out the toxins.

That wasn't gloating. It was bitching. Or, as my mom would say, "processing." I think I process too much. Concise. I keep trying to talk less, feel less, be calm, but I can't put myself in a box. I don't even know what would go in the box with me. I'm too verbal sometimes. Make me shut up.

1:53 p.m. Laboriously tallying and entering silent auction donations from the softball tourney we had this past Saturday. How many hours left to work? It should be a crime to work on the one sunny day we've seen in weeks.

3:00 p.m. Seriously, ADD.

Okay, I couldn't handle it. I spent some of the afternoon making fund-raising phone calls, trying to get businesses to give us money. Explaining our shelter over and over to people who don't know it well gets so tedious. You'd think saying "HOMELESS SHELTER" alone would be effective at pulling a heartstring. Apparently not. So I left early. I've never done that before. I think I might be losing it, but legitimately I have bad allergies and I have overtime.

5:53 p.m. I spent the last hour sunbathing. I read an article that said Americans don't get enough sunshine, so I felt it was my duty. Stupid, because my allergies are kicking my ass. But we only get a handful of beautiful days in Minnesota before it gets cold, and even less of a handful that aren't spent working.

6:40 p.m. At my mom's, watching cable. Where is my roommate? I'm hungry! Amanda is coming over for dinner and to do laundry. Whenever we have laundry, we joke about heading over to the "nursing home," or my mom's condominium. Common conversation in the hallways revolves around hospital visits and who just died. It's depressing. Anyway, we have to be careful about doing laundry here because my mom lives in a condo full of older people who are curious. I often have to lie, saying I still live here. Seriously, people, we're twenty-three, we have no money, we're still learning to budget, paying off loans, and we just want to use free laundry facilities twice a month. Can't you look the other way?

Amanda arrives. My mom has a big financial test tomorrow, so we wanted to make her dinner, but we decide she probably isn't that impressed with Jenny-O Turkey Burgers and a bag of chips, so we order Chinese. It amazes me how smart my mom is. She changed careers three years ago from social work to financial services. While all I can think about is dinner, she's busy balancing being mom, financial planner, and student. I wonder if I'll ever be that smart and successful someday? I know my mom is proud of me, but I wonder if she realizes how proud I am of her.

7:00 p.m. I chat online with my friend Mike from college. I used to chat online all the time, but then again, I had a working computer. Mike calls me J. Fo. I am even entered in his phone as J. Fo.

Someone else at work called me J. Fo today. It weirded me out. Only Mike calls me that. My coworker, being the only male (the maintenance guy stereotypically) in a woman's nonprofit organization, said it. My immediate thought was, Do you really think my butt is as booty as J. Lo? And then, realizing that our maintenance guy is equivalent to being the grandfather of the shelter (and is a real father himself), I thought, No way. It's got to be innocent.

7:30 p.m. We're watching TV at the dining room table and eating cheese wontons. I could live off cheese wontons. I would die of a heart attack, but it would be worth it. I wonder, How do people come up with these ideas? Cream cheese, fried? Mmm.

9:00 p.m. My roommate and my mom used to have their Tuesday *Queer Eye* night. I was almost always working and so I never participated. But tonight, both Amanda and I are off, so instead of cleaning our own apartment, we're messing up my mom's and engaging in some good gay TV. Tonight it's *Queer Eye for the Queer Guy*.

As I watched, I found myself feeling annoyed by the gay guy who was getting "queer eyed" because he didn't act gay enough. And then I thought, That's dumb that I would hold the stereotype that gays are only "gay" if they act flamboyant. And even more dumb of me, because I have a friend who is gay, and he is a paramedic, and he is so *not* flaming, so why would I assume gays on TV would have to be flamboyant?

10:30 p.m. Amanda and I just got home from my mom's. There was a notice under our door about vacating our apartment next month. We're not losing our deposit for August. We are so excited!!! We just signed a lease on a three-story house in Northeast Minneapolis. I can't wait! I haven't lived in a house in five years, since we lived at my grandpa's when I was in high school. We'll have our own washer and dryer!

Around this time I start thinking about bed. I never thought about sleeping before midnight in college, but these days I think I am bored, so I go to bed. I keep working, because I think the more time I put in, the closer I'll get to knowing what it is I want. But how does exchanging time for money help me realize what I want out of life? All I have learned so far is that I don't want to do that—I don't want to exchange time for money.

I also start thinking about bed earlier now because night is when I feel the loneliest. I think about boys a lot late at night. I wonder if I'll ever fall in love again, if my college love was real love, or if, magically, I'll find that "someone." Mostly, I miss having that comfortable snuggle and someone to say good night to. And then I usually tell myself to stop being selfish. Maybe I just watch too much *Sex and the City*?

I think I'm nervous for my date tomorrow. Not because I don't know what to wear or because I might get something stuck in my tooth during dinner, but what if he's really amazing and then I start liking him? I am scared of letting someone in. (I let the paramedic in; that didn't work out.) But I can't let my emotions about love completely control my actions about life. When I was eighteen, I couldn't wait for my emotions to get out of control, and now all I can do is try to keep my life in control. How stupid. I should listen to my own advice. What happens, happens. Just go with the flow.

11:45 p.m.   I'm going to bed. This is much later than usual. Tomorrow starts another day of work. I'm scared of this cycle. Are people really happy sleeping, eating, working, eating, working, sleeping?

12:05 p.m. Finally I'm done. No more work e-mail. I'm on vacation for God's sake. Doesn't anyone get that? Or is it me who doesn't get it?

I. Javette Jenkins Hines, 37, White Plains, New York; program director, IBM

4:17 p.m. I have a major food hangover. I should get away from the computer and do something that will get my blood flowing. I wish all the piles would become more manageable. I also wish I would quit whining. Oh, poor me, my life is full of a job I like, family, friends, but still I'll find something to whine about. If people could read my mind, I'd be very irritating. Maybe I am anyways.

Maret Orliss, 29, Pasadena, California; assistant promotional director, Vroman's Bookstore

8:00 a.m. I check my work e-mail and find a response from my boss on the document I sent him last night. He said it was "very good." What does that mean? I thought it was excellent. Maybe it's just the way he talks. He's a new boss for me, and I haven't really gotten a good feel for him yet. Perhaps it was just "well done" and I'm way too over-analyzing.

> *Lisa Muth, 22, West Charlton, New York; software*
> *engineer*

11:00 a.m. I head to the elevators for my lunch er-rands. My first stop is Victoria's Secret to pick up some lo-tions on sale. There are four separate bins full of girly boxer shorts, which are supposed to be sorted by size. If that is the case, then I can't tell. I immediately begin to sort them and put them in their appropriate bins. I'm thinking, Hey, I'm doing their job, but that still doesn't stop me.

> *Sharon Bragg, 28, Houston, Texas; marketer*

6:12 a.m. I'm up early to clean before the cleaning ladies come. My husband reminds me how stupid that is, but I insist on having the house clean before anyone comes. Of course, my husband will never understand that our home (and its state of cleanliness) is a reflection of me personally. Okay . . . that is stupid.

> *Michele Dortch, 31, Pasadena, California; owner,*
> *Acacia Leadership Consulting*

3:40 p.m. Wow, I love *General Hospital.* Twenty-five years of the same soap and they are definitely in worse shape than I am—yeah!

> *Ann Gaillard, 58, Pelham, New York; owner, Breath of*
> *Spring Landscaping*

Jolee Lautaret, 29, Kingman, Arizona

A barrel racer. The competition course is three metal barrels set in a cloverleaf pattern. The average run is sixteen seconds; her best time is 13.78 seconds. An only child in a rodeo family, when she went away to college, she missed the horses and the life. A true cowgirl. "It's a lifestyle; it's more than just someone who slaps on a pair of boots and a hat and goes on out to the dance hall." Her mom is also a barrel racer, and she and her dad occasionally team rope. "One does the head, the other does the heels." Competitive. She enjoys performing to crowds that can reach thirty thousand. "It gets your heart rate going, gets you cranked up, all those people cheering for you." Her mom sews her competition outfits: "Lots of sequins and feathers, fake fur, beads, pretty flamboyant. Looks great going by fast." Single, "but I definitely would like a family of my own someday. Most rodeo competitors have families, and they all seem to manage it pretty well." Right now, she's on the road or rodeoing or training, trying to make a living competing. "The money can be good, but you're not going to get rich. You have to do it because you love it."

12:01 a.m. And we're off! Not just the start of another day, but the start of the busiest week of the rodeo season, Cowboy Christmas. We left Greeley, Colorado, about an hour ago after our first competition for the Fourth of July run. We have to be in Prescott, Arizona, tomorrow morning, but, luckily, that's just three hours away from home, so we'll get to sleep in our own beds tonight. They call this week Cowboy Christmas because there are so many good rodeos and so much money to be won. My best Fourth of July came two years ago when I put together about $8,000 for the week. I am sure hoping to top that and feel pretty good about my chances.

Greeley has not been good to me in the past, but this year I am leaving in a solid position, sitting fourth in the first round of competition and third in the two-head total (we call it the average). The best twelve times in the average will return on Sunday for the short go—the final round, which will be televised. Greeley is not a rodeo that my mare, Belle, usually likes. I feel pretty content with my performance but am excited that my traveling partner, Mom, is winning the rodeo.

We were supposed to be well rested for the drive home tonight but had truck problems getting to Greeley. We were broke down for several hours trying to get there. Mom and I spent a lot of time popping the hood and looking the engine over. Course, we don't have much clue what we are looking for. The Ford guys in Greeley worked at replacing stuff all day in order to get us ready to go. Radiator problems.

ranked tenth in the pro rodeo world standings   **35**

12:35 a.m. Made it through Denver, just barely. Will they ever actually finish the roadwork around here? I promise you when they set up those concrete barriers, they are thinking of people in their compact cars and not my 8' by 29' horse trailer. Driving in these conditions just zaps me. Time to pull her over and wake up the next driver.

On these all-night trips, Mom and I try to switch off every couple of hours and, hopefully, we will make it without being too exhausted. We are trying to get home; got some things to take care of before hitting the trail again. Need more hay (prefer to get it from home), need to do laundry, showers would be nice.

I stretch out in the backseat of the truck. It would be a little easier to get some rest without the muffins, our three dogs. The big boy, Spanky, is a bichon-Maltese-Lhasa apso mix and, I can say without prejudice, is the best dog ever. Then we have the "rats"—Mickey and Minnie, our Maltese puppies. They seem to think my head is a playground as I am trying to catch a little snooze.

1:48 a.m. Time to fuel up. We have made it to Pueblo, and I feel better for a little rest. I hate stopping for diesel. It's $80 every time we pull in. The high gas prices are killing us. I don't know how other rodeo competitors are doing it. We are lucky to have a steady paycheck (my dad is president of Mission Bank back home in Kingman), so even if we lose, we will always still eat. But it seems that less and less of my winnings are making their way into the money market account.

While we're stopped, I check on the horses. We put an air-ride system on the trailer to give them a smoother ride. I give them some more hay to munch on and check their water. We let the dogs out here at the gas station, since there is no traffic. They are running through the water puddles.

2:11 a.m.   Back behind the wheel. I'm taking over for another shift while Mom sleeps. Time for the radio and some really bad singing. At the top of my lungs. Lucky for her, Mom doesn't hear that well.

3:38 a.m.   We're cruising right along, headed up Raton Pass, when the truck overheats again. I was getting really tired and just hoping to make it over the hill before trading drivers when I looked down at that gauge. Had a few choice words for those mechanics who sent us on our merry way this morning, after collecting $500 of course.

Once again we throw open the hood and there is smoke and steam billowing out. I have this incredible sense of dread because the next two rodeos we are trying to make are the most important ones to us. I really can't bear the thought that we might not make it and am so tired and frustrated I could just about cry (except of course that I am too pissed to break down into tears).

We know from experience that it will take at least an hour for the engine to cool and that AAA doesn't tow trucks with twenty-nine-foot horse trailers. So we figure there is nothing we can do but crawl back into the living quarters of the trailer and get a little sleep. Luckily, there is not much traffic, but I hate when those big rigs blow by and rattle your teeth.

4:52 a.m.   It wasn't easy, but we've drug ourselves out of the bed and crawled back to the engine for another look. We decided we'll add a little water to the radiator and ease down the hill to get some help. Thankfully, we are just about to the summit, then we should be able to coast on in to Raton. Mom is driving because my eyes are refusing to stay open. I am not sleeping though, but doing the jerk awake every ten seconds with visions of horrible wrecks running through my brain.

5:10 a.m. Mom decided we needed the breakfast of champions at McD's, since there is no way to know when we will get to eat again once we hit the Ford dealer. The people taking our order are having some issues, but at least they are friendly. Nothing aggravates me worse than being waited on by people who act like you did some injustice to them by wanting whatever their business has to sell. I don't mean to sound old either, but it sure seems like lots of them are teenagers.

5:32 a.m. Barely made it through the meal. I need to peel my contacts out. They're not made for overnight use, but that's the way it goes. The friendly McD's crew gave us directions to the Ford dealer and a couple of garages, so we hope we are on the right track. Yesterday, the main problem seemed to be a radiator hose that kept coming loose and leaking antifreeze. Maybe it will be something that simple again.

5:45 a.m. Had a nice little snooze in the passenger seat and missed beautiful downtown Raton. Mom found the Ford dealership and learned they don't open until 8:00. We are at the rodeo grounds, which we were told no longer existed. Maybe they thought that because it looks like three days after the flood. At least there are some big pens and an arena for the horses to stretch their legs.

Clogs are not good shoes to lead your horses through knee-deep mud. I walked right out of them. Or got drug out of them. Chloe is a new horse for us. She is young, just five, and on her second road trip. She is not used to being locked up for so many hours and is ready to run. The shoes were just a bad idea all around. (How many times have women said or thought that one before?)

Another bright spot through the frustration is those little rats. Mickey and Minnie are so funny, taking turns throwing each other into the mud. I should be thinking, Geez that's going to be a pain to clean up, but it is really too cute. After all, dirt does wash off, thank God. Off to bed again, for two hours this time. At this rate it will take us a week to get our proper eight hours.

8:31 a.m.　Now here's the trouble with small towns. No one can help us. They don't have time. They don't have a diesel mechanic, blah, blah, blah. I live in a small town, wouldn't trade it for the city ever, but this is one problem. We have seen the full range during the many times we have been broke down over the years—one dealership owner even drug our trailer out to his house where he had pastures for the horses to stand in while they worked on our truck. That was in McAlester, Oklahoma.

Then there's this bunch. The one guy who would at least look at it told us, "It's hot." Well no kidding, you think? I realize we are just women and so therefore must know nothing about cars and engines, but I think the steam and smoke blowing off were a good indicator of the temperature. One thing I can't take is for people to talk down to me.

They told us to call the dealer who fixed it. What's the dealer going to do from three hundred miles away? Worse yet, we have two trucks, but the other one kept stalling as we were leaving town last week and is currently in the shop at home. We are in my dad's truck, so he doesn't even have a way to come rescue us.

9:16 a.m.　We've had it. We can't just sit in Raton, getting no help eternally. So here's our plan. We hit the Kmart and loaded up on antifreeze. We filled a bunch of water jugs. We topped off the radiator and are hitting the trail. If we keep an eye on the temperature and take a break if it starts to get hot, we should be okay. We have some friends in Albuquerque, and if we get close enough, they would probably come rescue us.

10:34 a.m. We may just make it. We have to keep checking the temp gauge, but I feel better just heading in the right direction. We had a great lunch of pb & j while fueling up. Couldn't take any more grease. It doesn't take long to hit my maximum fast-food quota. Worst part about being on the road is the junk you end up eating.

11:43 a.m. Time to pull over and switch to the passenger seat. We're between Las Vegas and Santa Fe. Making progress, albeit much more slowly than we expected. We thought we would be to about Winslow, Arizona, by this time. A worker for the New Mexico Department of Transportation pulled over to see if we were in trouble. We had the hood up again, just checking the hoses and fluids. It was nice of him to take time to offer help.

12:00–4:14 p.m. ZZZ

4:15 p.m. Dragging myself awake as we are coming into Albuquerque. The truck seems to be working all right, so we are going to just keep going. We've only had to pull over twice to let the engine cool. The worst thing about being broke down is that it always happens when you're far from home. I think Mom and I both have this desperate sense that we would skip the whole run of rodeos if we could just make it home. We're only about seven hours away.

This day was supposed to be about rest, since the rest of the week is tough—two runs in Prescott on Wednesday; one in Window Rock on Thursday; an all-night drive to Cody, Wyoming, for Friday; Saturday at Oakley, Utah; and wind up back in Greeley (we hope) for the finals on Sunday. Today has not been what we needed to gear up for that.

this day in the life 40

4:19 p.m.   Why is it that no matter what time we leave, we always hit rush hour in some city?

4:22 p.m.   Since we're going nowhere fast at five miles per hour, and worried about overheating, we decide to stop for a nice dinner. Dad says we know the best restaurants in every city in the West. Rodeoing allows us to see many places we would never think to visit on a regular vacation, but one drawback is that you tend to go to the same places from year to year, especially with the changes in pro rodeo making certain rodeos more valuable.

I do enjoy the "city folk" watching us pull into a mall parking lot. The looks are classic—like we must be aliens recently landed on earth. We put the windows down for the horses so they can do some people watching, too. I wonder what is going through their heads, watching the cars and people.

I made the mistake of looking in the mirror. Driving cross-country certainly isn't any beauty show. Mom and I both do a pass at cleaning up. Brush the hair, or at least find a hat and a scrunchy. Splash water on the face and for the love of God find some deodorant and perfume. Now we are just like eighteenth-century aristocrats.

5:15 p.m.   We're feeling like humans again after some fresh food. Sometimes you need a little detox from all the junk you eat while driving—boredom food. I'm sure I couldn't drive an hour without cheddar Goldfish, peanuts, sunflower seeds, or Hostess anything. Traffic's still bad, so we are navigating the surface streets. Don't know if it's any faster, but it makes us feel better.

5:30 p.m.   Once again, gassed up and ready to go. I do my usual "it's a total rip-off" speech regarding gas prices. I'm sure Mom just drowns me out, but it really amazes me how gas prices always seem highest when people are driving the most. I understand supply and demand; just don't go there. Fact is, there is a finite supply of the stuff and jacking the prices up in the summer isn't going to make it last any longer. Hello, how about synthetic fuels? I wouldn't drive (out of protest) if I could rodeo from home.

5:38 p.m.   Great, now it's raining. Two years ago, our truck hydroplaned and the whole rig was totaled. I still don't feel comfortable behind the wheel in the rain, but I'm getting better. I used to have to pull over immediately. The rain always reminds me of that day and how lucky we are to be alive—dogs, horses, and humans.

5:59 p.m.   We've decided to go straight to Prescott. At this rate we won't make it home before 1:00 a.m. and would have to turn right around and leave about 9:00 a.m. Plus, Dad is really busy with the bank right now, so he is stressed, too. We don't want to add to it. Prescott is just three hours from home, so he can come rescue us after work, whenever the other truck gets fixed.

6:03 p.m.   I can't believe how green everything is here in New Mexico and Colorado. Everything is so dry at home. It makes for a much prettier drive. It looks to me like we are going to make it fine, and as long as you're within a certain distance from home, you just feel better. One thing about troubles like this—you really realize how great good friends can be. When we broke down a few days ago, our good friends from Cheyenne brought us their truck to get us into Greeley.

6:18 p.m.   We've made it to Acoma. There is an arena with big pens and water behind this casino that makes a nice rest stop for the horses. We are going to feed them and let them relax. In the meantime, we are cleaning the trailer. There is quite a bit of dirt and mud on the floor from the happy little muffins and their adventure in Raton. With such a small space, you have to clean every day.

7:12 p.m.   Everyone got a nice break, so we are off and running again. Guess we have about six or seven hours to go. I am so ready for this day to end.

8:30 p.m.   Don't you just feel better finally being in your home state? We cross the border, still three hundred miles from home, but I just feel a little happier. Ever wonder how your mind gets from one subject to another? I mean, you leave somewhere and you're thinking of the movie you saw recently and an hour later you're on to cloning or something. Sometimes I try to track back through my thought process and figure out how I ended up where I did. I just wonder if other people do this. Maybe I'm just totally weird. Definite possibility.

11:38 p.m.   We are about two hours away from Prescott and sleep in a bed! Since I'm starting to see pink elephants dancing across the highway, I better turn it over. Wow, what a day. It was supposed to be ordinary, boring. So glad we are almost to our destination. Hopefully, things will turn around for us tomorrow at the rodeo.

P.S. We got there at 1:30 a.m. and were so happy to get in the bed in that trailer!

1:18 *p.m.* We're at our meeting place and the bus was supposed to leave at 1 p.m. sharp. I'm still waiting on two bridesmaids. Where are they? I hope they're okay—they were flying over from London. My fiancé, Brian, is calling all over on his cell phone to find out if they left a message with anyone. What if their flight didn't arrive? How will they get to the wedding if they miss this bus? How long should we wait for them? I'm seriously getting stressed out. Everyone sees me in my sheath dress and keeps offering me a jacket, but I am generating enough heat with my nerves to fuel a small village.

> *Nataly Kelly, 28, Nashua, New Hampshire (in Ireland on the eve of her wedding); translator*

4:23 *p.m.* A former coworker just called to ask a question and brought up the wedding. I had an uncomfortable moment when she said she hoped she got an invitation. Eek. Not planning on inviting her.

> *Amy Wirdzek, 29, Franklin, Tennessee; marketer*

8:45 *a.m.* I was looking in the mirror after my shower and I thought, You know, I have not lost any weight for this wedding, which is in FIVE days, but it's hard to get upset about it. I mean, I know I'm pushing forty, I'm the heaviest I've ever been in my life, and my dress isn't going to look as beautiful on me because it's a halter and my shoulders will be showing, and they're kinda flabby, but I still feel beautiful, you know? And I just started dancing, standing there naked in front of the mirror. Randy just makes me feel so beautiful.

Susan Forrest, 38, Phoenix, Arizona; foundation associate director

11:59 p.m.   I am waking up once again and I see Mac sitting up in bed and looking down at me. I'm thinking, what's wrong? But he smiles and says, "I thought we'd invite the kids out in a week or two so you can meet them. You'll want to come out to Utah later this year, maybe we can make a quick trip to Vegas; we need to get married." Then he kisses me and I think, Am I awake or am I dreaming this?

Sharon Lambert, 54, Bear, Delaware; payroll administrator

10:50 p.m.   First the gel, then the lotion, then the cream. For a blemish-free complexion for my wedding day, I'd apply Borax.

Catherine Myman, 25, Los Angeles, California; teacher

On June 29, 2004 . . .

81% of day diarists said, "I love you."

~~~~~

When Love Comes Full Circle

Connie Linnell Ambrose-Gates, 79,
Northwood, New Hampshire

She grew up during the Depression, in a musical family with three brothers. "We struggled, but were better off than many others." In high school she fell for a boy everyone called Sonny, but her mother disapproved, wanting her only daughter to go to college, open up her possibilities. "My mother's hopes were that I'd go on to be a great singer somewhere." She and Sonny dated briefly, but then he went to war, and she went to the University of New Hampshire, majoring in music until the music director enlisted. There she ran into another fellow whom she'd also dated in high school, just back home after serving overseas. They fell in love and got married, raised four children. Both became teachers. Welcomed six grandchildren. Five days after she turned sixty, her husband died suddenly. This blow was quickly followed by another: her ninety-year-old mother suffered a stroke, and so she moved back into her childhood home to care for her. That's when she received a letter out of the blue. It was from Sonny, her long-ago sweetheart, asking her to meet him at their fortieth high school reunion. Like her, he was newly widowed after thirty-nine years of marriage. "A miracle," she says of their reconnection. "I can still picture the first time we saw each other again. It was instant. I knew this man, his smile, his gentle, loving manner." They've been married eighteen years now and counting. "It's a neat fairy tale, and fairy tales do come true."

4:15 a.m. Awoke early for a quick potty call. Have a commode next to the bed now, as I can't walk fast enough to get to the bathroom in time. I can just sort of roll out, do my thing, and roll back in. I miss having Sonny in bed beside me, often reach over to touch him and am saddened to not find him there. The only place he seems comfortable enough to sleep since he fell a month ago is in the recliner in the family room. It works for now, but I hope it won't last forever.

6:25 a.m. I dozed a bit, I guess, as the next thing I knew, I heard Sonny wheeling his chair into the bathroom. I would like to lie here awhile, but our new day has begun. A quick prayer to the Lord to help me make this a good day.

6:30 a.m. I am first aware that it is raining quite hard, then that I am sore and stiff—probably a combination of weather and the work I did in the gardens yesterday. I am so glad I found time to get rid of some weeds. Now the rain should spruce up the area by the clothesline and the flowers in the big pot over the old well. It is a neat feeling to be living in the house where I grew up and planting my mother's favorite flowers in the same spot she used to all those many years ago. (Sonny and I bought my mother's house after she passed away at age ninety-five.) This year I put in nasturtiums. Have had to cut the gardens way back, as I can't care for them anymore.

I quickly realize it is Tuesday and there is much to be done. Grab my sweats from the bench where I piled them last night and make up the bed.

6:45 a.m.   Sonny is doing okay this morning; had a good night's sleep for a change. Was able to get from the wheelchair to the toilet more easily and with less pain. I encourage him to do everything he can for himself. Sometimes that is hard, and I wonder how I would react if I were the disabled one. Not good, I am sure. I do like to be in control and it's hard for me to accept help.

We go to the kitchen and I test his fasting blood sugar and bring water, etc., to the table so he can brush his teeth. I really miss one of my favorite rituals of the day, having a cup of tea and half a bagel in bed together while we watch the early news. He just can't get up in the bed anymore, so he has tea at the table while I watch a quick few minutes of news and weather.

What good news to hear of the transfer of power in Iraq, two days ahead of schedule. Hope things improve quickly over there. Weather sounds like it should clear up. I'm glad, as I hate getting groceries in the rain! Let our beloved cat, Tigger, out, but she won't go far in the rain. She still isn't used to that big old wheelchair!

7:00 a.m.   Draw the insulin, then inject it. This is the beginning of our fourth year of dialysis, and I am glad I learned how to do this comfortably way back, before Sonny needed me to. Now it is a piece of cake! Seem to have a hard time remembering morning medications lately; we both take quite a few and it keeps me busy just keeping our supply current. Breakfast is hot cereal and juice, and the best part of all—a good cup (really only a half a cup) of fresh-brewed coffee!

While we eat, I read little bits and pieces of the newspaper to Sonny. He slowly but devotedly reads the sports section and the back page. When he could see well, he devoured the whole paper. On dialysis day, there isn't a lot of time, so we skip over the editorial page except for cartoons, but always read obits! Watched the Red Sox game against the Yankees last night, so already know that they lost, but he reads a few more details, anyway. We are sure they will win tonight! Believe me, our lives are a constant challenge in positive thinking!

7:30 a.m. Clean kitchen while enjoying the natural beauty of our backyard through the picture window in front of the sink. Late spring flowers were at their peak this week. Hate to see them go, but others will follow. A few brave goldfinch and house finch are looking for food at our many feeders, but I don't think the hummingbirds will come until it stops raining. I find rain and cloudy weather restful. Sonny is resting, maybe even snoozing.

I put up his lunch, so we don't have to rush later. It is sometimes a challenge to find interesting, nutritional foods he can open easily with his left hand, as his right arm is strapped down for four hours or more for his treatment. His choice today is potato salad with low-fat turkey meat cut up in it, cucumber and cut-up apple to help give his mouth a little moisture, cookies (for quick sugar if he needs it before he returns home), and water. I zip it into his insulated bag and set it by the door, glad to have that done!

Wish I could do a load of laundry, but there just isn't time this morning.

8:10 a.m. Now time for me. Toiletry, check the computer for e-mail from grandchildren and friends (just love hearing from people), then begin to get dressed and put on a wee bit of makeup. When I look in the mirror I am distressed at this old, tired face looking back at me. Wonder if I could find time for a facial/massage today while in town. Haven't done that since my birthday last September. If I look at our needs (house needs painting, new roof, furnace repair, etc.), I would know I can't afford it, but the amount I would spend isn't really going to make much difference. Will see if I can squeeze in an appointment.

Had to take my pain pill early today (hate to do that!) and pain is always reduced following a massage. I am excited about going to town *all by myself.* Being a full-time caregiver, the thing I miss the most (and I am sure he feels the same) is having time away from the house alone. Have many errands to do, but will try to take them as they come and not worry about what doesn't get done!

9:15 a.m. Okay, time to get Sonny (and me) ready to leave. He needs help with socks and shoes. His feet and ankles seem badly swollen this morning. He has gotten so that he can partially dress himself. I had to do it all when he first came home earlier this month after his fall, but he keeps trying to do more. I am so blessed that he is even-tempered, appreciative, and still loving—even pats my derriere as I walk by sometimes, so I make sure I get close enough for him to do that!

We have a small cup of tea and muffin before he leaves for dialysis to keep his sugar in balance, read a bit more of the paper, and wait for the volunteer driver. This is perhaps the hardest part of the day for me. During the past three years I have driven him in once and sometimes twice a week. Now that he is in a wheelchair, I haven't driven at all, but I try to be close by so that we can chat and he won't feel too left out of things while he waits.

I have a hard time just sitting, so I try to think of light stuff I can fill in the time with—sorting old photos for albums for the kids, checking on bills, etc. Sonny often likes to reminisce and this is a time when he can do that. It is so nice we both knew the same people growing up. This morning I sort a few medical forms, and soon his ride is here. We never know just when they will come, but are always ready by ten and grateful for the help of volunteers from the VFW, our church, and community members who drive him back and forth. What would we do without them?

10:05 a.m.   I fasten his seat belt and give him a good-bye kiss. He NEVER leaves without one! It has nearly stopped raining, so check the rain gauge. Not a lot, but certainly better than nothing. Won't have to water plants today. Good.

10:15 a.m.   Am on my own. Call café for soups of the day, so I will know beforehand what is good, call spa and get an appointment for 1:30, finish dressing, grab a couple of tapes for music in the car, put ice in cooler to keep food cold, make sure I have all of my lists, and leave for Concord, about twenty miles from here.

This is the first time I have gone off by myself for many weeks and I feel free as a bird. The rain has stopped, traffic is light, and I put in the Three Tenors tape and sing along (rather loudly at times, I'm afraid). How I do love my music! As I approach Concord I am treated once more to the most fantastic cloud formations. Being a river town, this is not unusual, but I never tire of seeing them.

10:50 a.m.   Decide to go to café early to find a parking space. I am lucky, there is one left. The soup choices are good—lemon chicken, vegetarian chowder, and split pea, so I get three of each and pack them in ice. Comforting to have quick meal choices. I have gotten so that I do NOT like to cook anymore.

11:10 a.m.   Ten minutes late for my appointment with the foot doctor to pick up shoes I had ordered two months ago. Actually, didn't need to fret about being late, as I waited for twenty minutes! I was born with a club foot, which was partially improved as a baby and again as a nineteen-year-old, but it left me with one foot size eight, and the other size five. Try as I might, I could not find stores to accommodate me, but then I learned I could special order shoes from a regular manufacturer. I am so excited about having comfortable shoes!

I am at the foot doctor for forty-five minutes trying them on, walking in them, adding an inner sole. One concern for me: As a senior with a foot disability, there is no funding from Medicare. Only diabetics are covered. So it is an out-of-pocket expense of $145. Seems like we need a little leeway there!

12:30 p.m.   Decide to stop at the park to have my liquid lunch. (I often don't take time to eat a healthy lunch, but with V-8 or Ensure I can grab something quickly.) I know this park well, as it is near the dialysis center. Mothers with small children, seniors, teenagers, all are here. It's fun to watch and listen and guess. Have gotten so I don't really mind being alone, but would much rather share with hubby. Will tell him all about it later.

Need a few staples, so stop at a small market on the way to the spa, then pack them in ice. I really miss having help shopping. Before Sonny fell he could push the cart and reach things from high places. He misses not being able to get out, and I am sad for him, but I cannot lift the wheel-chair.

1:20 p.m.   Finally reach the spa. For the next HOUR I am pampered, petted, lotioned, and massaged. Her hands are magic, finding all of the places that are tight and sore. The mood music is gentle and soothing and I love it. I learn much from the operator about diet, exercise, and even fibromyalgia, which I have had for over twenty years. I am so glad I made the choice to come here today. I only wish this option of therapy were open to all and not just those who can pay the bill!

2:30 p.m.   Have one more stop to make and am glad it is on the way home. I feel pretty laid back. The physical therapist has advised a commode for my husband, and I need to stop by the medical supply store to pick it up. Un-fortunately, there are so many rules and regulations for Medicare coverage, I sometimes wonder if it is worth all the trouble to get it! The salesperson tells me the commode will not be covered because Sonny's arms are strong enough to push himself into the bathroom, so we will see what we can rig up at home. That's it for now. I need to head for home.

3:15 p.m.   Arrive home, pick up mail (have learned how to get it from the car so that I don't have to do so much walking), and find Tigger waiting. We have a snack to-gether. I look at the mail (nothing but advertisements and a bill) and then I lie down with the cat and my book, Dan Brown's *Deception Point*.

3:30 p.m.   Need to start watching for Sonny. He can ar-rive anytime in the next hour. I try to begin our evening meal, but still keep an eye out the window. He is always exhausted when he gets home, more so now than ever. I help get him into the house and washed up, then do a blood sugar. Both readings are good today. He is ready to rest while I finish supper. My son called a short time ago to see if everything had gone well today. It is comforting to know he is right next door.

5:00 p.m. This next hour is tiring. I try to fix meals that are nutritious but light, as Sonny is never very hungry. Tonight is a quick chicken stir-fry. He seldom has room for dessert on dialysis days, so we'll wait until later to have fruit. After dinner, I help him get cleaned up for the night, then roll him in to watch the news. I listen as I clean up the kitchen. I have never minded dishes or housework—something rather soothing about it. I find messes stressful, so I try not to let them get ahead of me.

6:15 p.m. I go outside to close things up and drop down in my chair for a few minutes. It is just lovely out in the backyard. I listen to the evening birds and the gentle fall of water from the fountain, and then return to the house to be sure all is well.

7:05 p.m. Make sure we have the right channel for the Red Sox game and the TV control where he can reach it. Check the computer one last time (long e-mail from granddaughter in Virginia), run bathwater, and be sure to take book and phone into the bathroom. I am tired; hope I can soak awhile.

8:00 p.m. Soaked a long time. Didn't read, but did think back to my life as a caregiver. I don't mean to make it sound easy; it is not. I began at thirty-one when my first husband was hospitalized for many months with a nervous breakdown and needed much care when he came home. I had four small children at the time. Later, I helped care for both Mother and Father in their declining years. Then Sonny had a massive heart attack ten years after we were married.

I have learned much through these experiences. I may have given up part of my life for others, but there is no greater satisfaction than helping another who needs you. There have been instances when I hear an inner voice saying, "I just can't do this anymore," but then somehow I find a better way to manage things. I still contribute whenever and however I can to church activities (potted a dozen perennials last week for the fair), donate books to the library book sale, save stamps and send them to veterans organizations, and donate crafts to the Women's Club Christmas Fair.

When I can do more, I will. For now it has to be enough. I have learned a lot about baseball and the Red Sox by joining my hubby in watching the games. I sit with him during parts of each game so he will have someone to talk to (or complain to). Tonight's game is a tough one to get through.

9:45 p.m. A snack of crackers and milk, washing up, then tucking Sonny in for the night. He always seems cold these days. Lately, I have heated a warming pad for his feet, and cover him with a couple of blankets. We have always kissed good night and said I love you. Who knows what tomorrow will bring? He usually settles down quickly and may even be asleep before I am in bed.

10:15 p.m. I turn on night-lights, check doors to be sure I locked them all, and go to the bedroom. I usually watch a little of the 10:00 news. Not much new happening tonight. Sometimes the cat joins me (if not now, later). I cozy down under the covers, thank God for this very good day, and bless those around us.

1:17 *a.m.* The phone rings and I'm letting my voice mail catch it. I'm awake but that's not the damn point. The person calling is the kind of guy I used to really like but can't stand anymore. He has a husky voice, a New York accent, a record deal, a nice car, and he used to be part of the entourage of a dead rapper that I had a major crush on. He just thinks he's so fascinating, and he's always calling me to come hang out at his house or come over to the studio and watch him work. He must really think that I'm going to give him some just because he raps. I don't have time for that kind of nonsense. And really, who wants to go and watch someone work? Unless you work in a circus, then leave me the hell alone.

> *Rochelle Spencer, 26, Atlanta, Georgia; graduate student*

6:25 *p.m.* Lining shelves and filling cabinets for the guy I'm seeing. On to the silverware. Matt tells me his grandmother gave it to him for when he gets married, but he's going to use it anyways because he doesn't want to go out and buy another set. For some reason that changes how I feel about the silverware.

Becky Horowitz, 22, Framingham, Massachusetts; intern, NFL Films

2:29 p.m. I need to take a shower and change my clothes. We've already received today's mail, and I didn't get a letter from Baba. I really didn't expect to since I got one yesterday. I really miss him. I can't wait until he's released and has his life back. Reintroduction into society won't be a problem for him. He's such a people person. But, for now, I'll have to settle for letters and periodic, long-ass drives to the desert to see the man I've come to love over time.

Leontyne C. Sloan, 46, Long Beach, California; substitute teacher

2:00 p.m. Risk Insurance Management Society annual meeting. At lunch I notice something—there's only a handful of women in the entire room filled with a sea of about eighty men! You'd think I would have noticed this at other meetings, but then again I wasn't single before. I doubt many of these guys are eligible since a good deal of the table talk is about children. Disorienting moment. The two men to my right are discussing potty-training techniques for their two-year-olds. At length. In the old days, these are the guys who would have been the good old boys. Now they seem so, well, DOMESTIC. The irony is, I wasn't thrilled about this. Part of me longed for the glamour. It's like, you wanted to belong to this exclusive club with all kinds of excitement and then, when they let you in, it's not like that at all. It's actually no more glamorous than where you came from—the kitchen and the laundry room.

Stephanie Giancola, 49, East Hampstead, New Hampshire; risk manager

6:00 a.m.   I change my VMail ringer from four to two rings. No one has been calling, especially not Quentin, this guy I met two weeks ago. Of course I envisioned him as my future husband and us having two cats and a dog and the whole nine yards. He was so cute.

Sharon Bragg, 28, Houston, Texas; marketer

2:45 p.m.   I watched a movie this morning. One character asked another, "Are you happy?" It made me think of my own life. I *am* happy, but now and then I wonder what it would be like to have a husband. I know I don't want children, but I would like for a man to love me. Maybe I just want a boyfriend. I'm not sure. It seems as if, at my age, I would know. I don't. I'm still a work in progress, I guess.

Bobbie Trowbridge, 46, Statesboro, Georgia; teacher

Midnight   Falling asleep over an old *New Yorker* article about Raoul Felder, a "high-stakes" divorce lawyer. Why am I reading this? I am already divorced, the stakes weren't so high, and I'm tired.

Judith Strasser, 59, Madison, Wisconsin;
producer/interviewer, Wisconsin public radio

The First Female Firefighter
in the FDNY

Brenda Berkman, 52, Brooklyn, New York

She started her career as an immigration lawyer but was intrigued when she met FDNY firefighters through the Uniformed Fire Officers union. "It was a way of serving the country without joining the military." In 1977, she took the firefighters exam with five hundred other women. Not one passed. "It was beyond belief that there wasn't a single woman qualified to be a firefighter." She brought the lawsuit that resulted in the hiring of the first women firefighters in NYC, including herself in 1982. Now she's captain of Engine 239 and the second highest-ranked woman in the FDNY, despite a long period of relentless harassment (death threats, refusals to train with her). "The job is all-consuming. You have to spend the time and energy to be accepted, become part of the team." Outspoken. No nonsense. She's one of the most famous firefighters in this country, as much for her advocacy as for her time on the job. The first firefighter to serve as a White House Fellow, her speeches inspire women toward nontraditional employment. She's been profiled in a PBS special on gender in the workplace and was the subject of an off-Broadway play. A shit-stirrer with a purpose. "It's not a bad thing to question the status quo, but you need to do it for a positive reason."

0000   I am in Engine 239's office, simultaneously listening to the Brooklyn fire dispatcher on the department radio and paging through an office supplies catalogue. I'm wondering why I am still awake after being in the firehouse for the previous seven and a half hours (I came in early). It has been a relatively quiet shift so far—a couple of runs—nothing serious.

Only two firefighters assigned to this firehouse are working tonight. The other two that make up my crew for the night shift (6 p.m. to 9 a.m.) have been "detailed" from other firehouses, including a "probie" (with less than a year on the job). At emergencies, probies need to be closely supervised, so having one on my crew, and from another firehouse at that, gives me something else to think about.

Earlier we drilled on a new piece of equipment, ate dinner, and then I went back up to the office to do paperwork around 10 p.m. Now I have an upset stomach from dinner, and I'm still doing paperwork—paperwork that seemingly hasn't changed much from the nineteenth century when the FDNY was founded, although a few years ago they did give us computers (but not access to the Internet).

0030   I am ready to wind down, watch a little TV to put myself to sleep. One advantage to being promoted is that I have my own bunk and don't have to listen to anyone snoring, although the wall between me and the firefighter bunkroom is pretty thin. There's nothing on TV (despite having one hundred channels), so I turn it off.

0200   The sound of a window shade banging in my office (where my bunk is) wakes me. Most firefighters say they never really sleep well in the firehouse. We always have one ear listening for a run to come in. The traffic noise from the road in front of the firehouse is loud and constant, but I like to keep the window open, anyway, rather than use air-conditioning. I am lucky to be able to sleep almost anytime and anywhere.

I sleep in my clothes, all except shoes. It gets uncomfortable, but it's a habit I picked up from my start on the job when I slept in a bunkroom with nine men. Now, even though I sleep by myself, I keep my clothes on, so I don't fumble around for my pants when I'm half asleep and called to a run.

The computer screen gives me enough light to find my way to the bathroom. I often get up in the middle of the night to use the bathroom. New firefighters should be told in recruit training, "Always use any available bathroom. You may not have another opportunity for a long time." Bathroom logistics are tough in our protective gear (bunker pants and coat), especially for women.

The weather is changing. Rain starts to make the streets slick. I start to think about whether we might get called out soon to go to a car crash. After more than twenty years as a firefighter, I find I think differently about most things than "civilians." When I think about the weather, I think about how it will affect fighting a fire or whether it will cause more runs. When I walk the city streets, I look at buildings constantly to think about how fast a fire could travel, or how many people might have to be evacuated or searched for, or how the firefighter assigned to the roof will get there.

With the rain now, people tend to go home or stay home. The rain might make it a quiet night, or not. After all these years, I've learned not to take anything for granted. All hell can break loose on the nicest day.

0215   The rain is really coming down now. I need to grab some more sleep, because I have to work another sixteen hours. As I go back to bed and turn toward the wall next to my bunk, I see over my head a framed poster of thumbnail pictures of the 343 firefighters who died at the Trade Center on September 11, 2001. Hell, I'd never noticed that poster being there before. How could I have missed it?

I can't decide if I like having that image being the last thing I see when I go to sleep and the first thing I see when I wake up. It's not that I want to forget those who died, but I don't need that poster to constantly remind me. After almost three years, I still think about them every day, the hundreds of guys I had actually worked with over the years who were killed. A lot of guilt and anger and sorrow and frustration. Not much hope. For now, I decide that the poster was simply meant to be there and I stop worrying about it. After all, it's now 3:30 a.m.

0625   The alarm tones go off in the firehouse. We have a call for a fire in the housing projects in Red Hook. The dispatcher tells the companies we have a "child caller." A lot of these kinds of calls are false alarms. We use lights and sirens to try to stop the traffic racing past the firehouse (our own Indy 500), so we can pull out. Few civilian drivers seem to care about the safety of emergency vehicles or how long it takes us to get to an emergency call.

As we get to the address, one of the officers already on the scene announces on the portable radio that the caller is an "EDP" (emotionally disturbed person). The chief gives the radio signal for a false alarm. The six units that re-sponded (including us) return to our firehouses.

0640 Back at the firehouse, the biggest question of my day becomes, Is there coffee? We have an on-again off-again coffee machine. Sure enough, the machine is making sludge. The firefighters know the captain needs her coffee immediately. One firefighter puts the backup coffeemaker into service while another tries to fix the sludge-maker. The *Rugrats* are on the kitchen television and I am tempted to linger, but I go back upstairs with my coffee to the office.

0715 The junior (least experienced) member of the fire-house comes into the office to report to work. He has a reputation as a big eater and is just back from a cruise. I ask him to turn sideways so I can gauge how much he "en-joyed" his vacation. He tells me he put on fourteen pounds. I offer to help him lose weight by having him eat the same amount I eat. I tend to eat less than everyone else on the crew; firehouse meals are traditionally enormous and not particularly healthy. He considers this for a millisecond, but decides the suggestion is completely unworkable.

0745 The department radio announces an alarm for a "helicopter down" on the Brooklyn Bridge. Oddball calls like this grab my attention. I flip on the television. If there's a copter crash, one of the TV stations might have their own copter covering it. Nothing on TV for now. Then the first responding battalion chief reports to the fire dispatcher that he sees police units on the bridge with an apparent "jumper." Nothing about a helicopter.

0755 In the course of flipping channels to find the copter crash, I find some "news" program showing a woman reporter doing a human interest story at a New Jersey firehouse. She

the first female firefighter in the fdny **63**

is wearing some guy's firefighting coat. The reporter is being urged by the male firefighter to climb a raised aerial ladder (the big one on the fire truck). In a giggly voice, the reporter is demurring—she doesn't have her "safety gear" (wink, wink. Real reason implied—women can't/don't like to climb scary ladders). So with all the firefighter guys watching her, she is given a helmet (does it fit?) and told she can climb now. After she climbs a couple of rungs, the real firefighter with her on the ladder turntable tells her to stop, to her enormous relief (feigned or real). And the television audience learns what? Women firefighters hate these television segments.

0825 The day crew is coming into work. This is one of the most confusing times because personnel is changing over. I'm in the kitchen preparing to write a "roll call" in the company journal. Firefighters have checked over the equipment on the fire truck, and we take turns teasing a newly arrived firefighter who recently transferred to a nearby ladder company. A call comes in for a fire on the first floor of a multiple dwelling thirteen blocks away. We are assigned as the first engine company to the alarm.

As we arrive, we see people on the sidewalk mid-block waving us in and pointing at a building. I see a small amount of smoke coming out of the first-floor apartment window. A passing car almost runs me over as I get out of the fire truck. As I go up the building steps and in the front door, adults and children, including people with babies in their arms, are pouring down the interior stairs and out of the building, nervous and upset. It is hard to avoid bumping into them.

After I try the entrance door to the fire apartment and find it locked, I call on my radio for my company to stretch a precautionary hoseline to the apartment door while I wait for the first ladder company to force it. I don't want to give the radio signal for a "working fire." Given the conditions—light smoke, no heat—it's likely the problem is "food on the stove" (pots left on the burner, which overheat, burn, and cause light smoke but don't extend to the rest of the apartment). But the battalion chief who is on the scene gave the working fire signal after I told him we had smoke in the building.

After the ladder company members force the door, I go into the smoky apartment and find a flaming pot on the stove, which I put in the sink and douse. Emergency over. Now we have some routine issues to take care of: checking the stove and adjoining walls for any other burning; opening an illegally locked door in the hall; putting our equipment away; finding and questioning the fire apartment residents. They were sleeping when the fire started, and they had a baby, but no working smoke detector.

0902 Immediately after we return to the firehouse, we are called out for smoke in a nearby subway station. Probably rubbish burning. This time we are not first on the scene, so we are held in reserve as other companies extinguish a small fire on the tracks.

After we return to quarters, I begin an endless cycle of telephone calls, part of the time-consuming officer routine for a day tour. The calls relate to:

Problems with parking our cars in front of quarters. Not enough spaces means conflicts with civilians who want to park there. We had given out a couple of tickets and someone was scratching our cars.

The unusable seat-belt setup for the officer seat on the new fire truck.

Breathing protection for the fire truck driver at hazardous materials/terrorism incident, so s/he doesn't have to get out of the truck to put it on.

Repairing the firehouse emergency communications power backup.

Trying to find a way to get fire prevention law updates at the firehouse.

Figuring out (in June!) what winter weather supplies I need to order for the firehouse.

Updating our daily diary showing who is working, on vacation, has overtime tours—a truly time-consuming task.

Ah, the life of a firefighter is thrill-packed.

1230 We took the fire truck to a takeout place for Mexican food. (We pay for our own meals, but we have to be able to respond to calls, regardless of whether it is time to pick up food or eat.)

1300 Lunch eaten, I went over several drill topics with the firefighters. We watched a pretty awful training tape on our new defibrillator. Then we repacked our life-saving rope (for when we have to rappel down a building) and our search rope (used in large areas where visibility is limited or nonexistent). And finally, I discussed our operations at some recent calls.

1430 We are called out on a medical run for an unconscious person at a bus stop. We find a transgendered person who claims he is only waiting for a bus, but he keeps nodding out. He claims he is still "hung over" from the Pride Parade (two days earlier!). A private ambulance service shows up and takes him to the hospital. We really do get to meet all kinds of people.

1530 Back in the firehouse, I'm feeling pretty drained by now. It's definitely my low-energy part of the day.

1630 My relief, a relatively young and inexperienced lieutenant assigned to the company, comes in to exercise in the firehouse gym. We go over all the calls and issues I have dealt with during the previous twenty-four hours. We talk about an interpersonal conflict one of the firefighters is having with another; mainly people getting on each other's nerves. All the officers (myself and the three lieutenants I am in charge of) are working mightily to keep this situation from becoming a disciplinary issue.

1730 I take a shower and dress in my civilian clothes to go out to dinner with friends. On the way into Manhattan, I drop off at home some of the stuff I brought to the firehouse, then hop back on the subway.

1800 With time to kill, I wander into Urban Outfitters, a clothing store generally aimed at the younger generation. I see some items they are selling as "vintage." They don't seem so vintage to me and I feel old. I think firefighting has kept me a lot more active than most of my age group, but sometimes working with kids young enough to be *my* kids makes me feel a little ancient.

1830 I don't have the restaurant name or address where I'm supposed to meet my friends, but I know the block, so I wander along until I see one of the other people, Laura, standing outside the restaurant. We chat until the third member of our party arrives, my ex-partner. The three of us haven't gotten together for a long time. Or rather, Laura and I haven't seen each other for a long time. It turns out Laura is a big fan of Venetian food, as am I, so ordering *cicchetti* and other Venetian specialties quickly becomes the topic of conversation.

We talk a little bit about the New York City street

dedication to Susan B. Anthony and Elizabeth Cady Stanton that my ex-partner just marshaled through the City Council. Then we talk mainly about politics. I give her the Al Gore autograph that a friend of mine had gotten for her. We discuss the Kerry campaign. Laura tries to convince me to do some phone banking (I hate the telephone) for Kerry. There is some brief discussion about Laura's current girlfriend, films, and the theater. After dinner, we walk over to a fancy chocolate store, and I buy some chocolate as a gift for my current girlfriend.

2000   I hop back on the subway and in a short time I am home in Brooklyn. It is an absolutely beautiful evening, perfect for sitting in the backyard listening to the garden fountain, hoping to see a firefly. I call my girlfriend, but she is too tired to get together. I go in the front door and discover I have missed a package delivery (love surprises). I think about what errands I have to run tomorrow and look through my mail. Mostly junk. Think about whether the new plants I have put out in the backyard are doing okay, despite a squirrel infestation.

2030   Turn on the television and there is some obnoxious reality show. I hate that junk. Who cares about these people's lives? What are they doing to make the world better? What is this stuff other than televised snooping/gossip? I hope for a *West Wing* rerun, but some other program I have absolutely no interest in is on instead. I am too tired to read or write letters. So I immediately go to sleep.

11:15 a.m.   I went to play my harp in the CCU. It's usually frantic here, but I go in, anyway, knowing that it's doing both staff and patients good. I heard a story about a patient who had heard my harp in the CCU and asked a hospital volunteer, "Am I in heaven?" The volunteer told her, "Oh, no, dear, that's our harpist Verlene playing right outside the door." Later she asked the patient, who was in the process of dying, if she was afraid. The patient answered, "No. Ever since I heard the harp music, I'm not afraid."

   Verlene Schermer, 48, San Jose, California; harpist

10:17 a.m.   My intern is copping a major attitude because I totally ripped apart his work. Serves him right for doing a half-ass job. He's been here over a month and I correct the same crap every damn day. Damn pretentious college kids. I hope I wasn't like that a few years ago when I interned.

   Adrienne Katzman, 24, Bethesda, Maryland; researcher

4:45 p.m.   Went to the break room to buy Skittles. They got stuck in the machine, and without thinking I asked a nearby male coworker to help me get them out. After about twelve times of him almost knocking the machine over, I realized it was fate's way of keeping me from eating them. I told him this, but it obviously struck his male ego. (Maybe he thought that I didn't think he could get them out?) He had to continue to shake the machine for five more minutes until the Skittles fell out.

Annie Wood, 24, Port Richey, Florida; technical writer

Noon I am fortunate on this job to have an indoor bathroom with sinks and toilets. Most jobs have portable johns with no running water. They smell really, really bad in the summer. Did I mention how bad they smell? Really, really bad. But they're a fact of life in this field, so I've gotten used to them. Besides, their walls are usually filled with graffiti of all sorts to entertain you. Some construction workers are quite the artists and comedians. I keep liquid hand sanitizer in my lunch bag for those job sites.

Irene "Rocky" Hwasta, 50, Parma, Ohio; carpenter

8:00 a.m. I compile my list of things to do today as I wait on sales calls to trickle in. There is chatter all around, and by 8:11 I am bored. I pull out my new binoculars and look around the floor. We have an open cubicle layout with low walls. Zero privacy. My binoculars were my five-year anniversary gift from the company. It was that or a pen, picture frame, or toiletry bag. I chose to be different. They may come in handy one day.

Sharon Bragg, 28, Houston, Texas; marketer

On June 29, 2004 . . .

41% of day diarists gossiped.

57% swore.

〜〜〜〜

this day in the life 70

The Only Brothel Madam Who Was Never a Working Girl

Laraine Harper, 48, Las Vegas, Nevada

She'd been semiretired for three years after a long career in casino management. Then the new owner of Sheri's Ranch, a legal brothel outside Las Vegas, invited her to be the general manager. She paid a visit. "It was atrocious, dark, dirty. Three double-wide trailers connected by hallways with blood-red carpeting. I wouldn't even put my purse down." She reconsidered after seeing the plans for renovation but consulted with her family first. Her husband, a former cop, was supportive. Her daughter, twenty-one, asked, "What are you going to do there?" Her son, twenty-three, couldn't pick up his cell phone fast enough. She says she made the right decision. "I love my job. I'm running an X-rated day care. I get more Mother's Day cards now than in all the years I was raising my own kids." Her attitude is can-do. Live and let live. In public talks, she pushes the message, "Don't be so

*naïve to think if legal prostitution was outlawed, there'd
be no prostitution. So why not legalize it, control it, keep
it safe?" An activist. A registered handler of therapy dogs.
A clotheshorse. Her husband describes her fashion taste as
"Queen Amidala from* Star Wars." *Scarves, capes, faux
fur. Rings on almost every finger. "Everyone has precon-
ceived notions about what a madam looks like. I want to
live up to their expectations."*

7:10 a.m.　I stumble down the stairs to be greeted by
my doggies: three beloved Saint Bernards, my pit bull, and
two new pound puppies. My Saint Bernards are my alternative to dieting. The bigger they are, the better I look!

7:15 a.m.　Coffee with my husband, Kevin, on the
patio; him reading the paper and me watching the dogs
play.

8:00 a.m.　Shower and get dressed. Normally, I am
dressed to the nines for work—flowing outfits with sequins,
a lot of jewelry, and, of course, heels. However, these days I
spend more time on the construction site, so jeans it is!

9:00 a.m.　Held a meeting with all the dancers (forty-
eight to be exact) at our strip club, Sheri's Cabaret. There
is camaraderie between some girls and friction between
others. Day-shift dancers complain about the swing-shift
dancers who complain about the grave-shift dancers.
"Some girls are always late to the stage . . ." "Some dancers
approach the customers as soon as they walk in; let them
sit down and get a drink before you converge on them . . ."
"The bartenders show favoritism . . ." But all in all, the
meeting ends on a good note.

10:15 a.m.   I'm leaving the Cabaret now, on my way to the Ranch, located in Pahrump. It is a fifty-five-minute drive, as I live in Las Vegas. There isn't a day I don't enjoy the desert scenery, the warm air blowing through my hair (when I drive with the top down), and the wild horses and burros I see along the way. It's like the calm before the storm.

11:15 a.m.   Here I am at the Ranch. I say hello to our shift manager, Candi, and several ladies (working girls) in the hallway. Kayla gives me a kiss on the cheek. Mya gives me a hug. Monica gives me her usual greeting, "Hi, Mom!" I gather my messages taped to my door. As I'm walking in, my phone is ringing. It's Mark, my dearest friend from my hometown in New Jersey. We chat a bit about the upcoming party at the Ranch, which he is flying in for. Our annual summer party is July 24. This year we are expecting about twenty-five hundred people. The party is our way of saying thank you to the town of Pahrump for their support. It's a great time, lots of food, drinks, bands, DJs, and tours. Everyone loves the tours! I check my e-mails—197. Wasn't I just here yesterday?

11:40 a.m.   After answering about eighty e-mails, I go through the daily reports. We track everything! Customer counts, the daily transaction report for brothel business, shift reports from the shift managers, housekeeping, security, limo reports, cab reports, bar revenue, gift shop revenue, and soon we will be adding hotel and spa revenue.

Noon   As I head out to the construction site, I hear the shift manager making the announcement, "Ladies, you must be floor ready by 1 p.m." Construction is coming along well, but I'm really worried that it won't be complete by the party. Our expansion consists of the spa and ten hotel rooms, three of which are themed suites: Egyptian, Pirate, and the Suite of Romance. Electricians, plumbers,

the only brothel madam   73

painters, and other trades are scurrying around. A lot of landscaping needs to be done, and I'm sitting here with about four thousand rose bushes, trying to keep them alive until they can be planted.

1:00 p.m. I'm meeting with a gentleman named Don who wants to set up a luncheon and a tour for his group, the Royal Order of Jesters, a division of the Shriners. We sit in the bar and discuss menu particulars. Don thinks his group will be about one hundred attendees. I tell him we'll break them up in smaller groups for our extensive tour of the brothel—the Jacuzzi and bubble-bath rooms, the S & M dungeon (which is everyone's favorite), our commercial laundry facility, one of the ladies' rooms, and our five themed VIP bungalows. I explain how the brothel works, from lineups to negotiations to the actual booking of the party. The ladies wink at me as if to say, Glad you got one!

1:30 p.m. Answer some more e-mails from prospective ladies interested in working at the Ranch and interoffice e-mails from both the Ranch and Cabaret, etc.

1:40 p.m. Another one of my many walk-throughs of the property. I see the red lights flashing. These notify the ladies that we are having a lineup and they should gravitate to the parlor. Just as I approach the pool (we even have a red light here), one of the ladies dives in. When she surfaces, I ask, "Why are you getting your hair wet; we have a lineup." Part of my job is to make sure everyone is front-line ready—hair, makeup, and attire perfect. "I'm going for that active look" is her response. I'm amused because, even with her hair wet, she looks great!

2:00 p.m. Brock, our general contractor, is here and we go through the punch list: the Jacuzzis in the suites need to be hooked up; countertops need to be installed; the parking lot still needs to be striped; and of course, the landscaping. Where are the landscapers? The party is less than a month away. Brock assures me it will all get done. He asks, "Who are the guys digging the trench?" I say, "Aren't they your guys?" Evidently not. It seems they just showed up on the job saying I hired them. The only people I hire besides my staff are the ladies, and these guys definitely do not fit the criteria! Brock throws them off the job. Another problem solved!

2:45 p.m. I pop in the Ranch salon. Kristy (a six-foot beautiful redhead) is getting her nails done, and I complain to Lu, the stylist, that my natural highlights (which used to be red and are now gray) are taking over my head. Lu is great. She can make you look ten years younger in about thirty minutes. As Lu tends to my hair, I catch up on all the Ranch gossip, one of my favorite things—who's going in for a boob job, who is dirty hustling, and so on. So many different personalities under one roof 24/7 certainly makes my job interesting!

3:15 p.m. I leave the salon. Lu has redone my highlights blond, texturized my hair, and styled it. Oh yes, I'm young again! I check my voice mail, and one is from Olga, a wonderful lady from the Red Hat Society. We had a tea for them a few months ago and a friendship has developed. (The Red Hats told us our tea was better than the Ritz Carlton's. Not too bad!) Another message is from someone who wants to be a working girl. I return her call and ask her to e-mail me recent photos. She has a soft, sweet voice and sounds enthusiastic. Hope she looks good. There are calls from vendors, photographers, and a Vegas radio DJ RSVPing for the party.

3:50 p.m. One of the ladies comes to my office in a panic. Her child has gotten in trouble and the school is threatening expulsion. She wants to leave, but is worried she'll be charged a fine for leaving before her scheduled departure date. She is in tears. People do not realize how difficult the ladies' jobs really are, being away from their family for two to three weeks at a time. I tell her to go home and take care of her child. I will waive the fine. She is so grateful that a smile emerges through her tears.

4:00 p.m. As I walk through the hall of the Ranch, I hear the page, "Ladies, dinner is now served in the dining room." I brace myself for the onslaught, as ladies from their rooms, the computer room, the workout room, the bar, and all over make a beeline for the dining room. The ladies have their dinner from 4:00 'til 5:30 because we tend to be busier at night than in the day.

4:10 p.m. I walk through the bar and see many familiar faces. Mack, a middle-aged regular who often comes with his wife, has stopped in for a beer and some dinner. Dusty, fiftyish, is also here. He comes most evenings for dinner and every Sunday morning to watch NASCAR. And there's Lenny, in his early forties, single. Haven't seen him lately. Mack makes his routine announcement: "Laraine, you have an appointment in Bungalow 3. Laraine to Bungalow 3, please." Mack, you gotta love him. He's been trying to get me in Bungalow 3 for three years now!

4:30 p.m. Back to my office. I place the order for eighty-five tables, six hundred chairs for the courtyard, and seven huge tents. This party gets bigger every year. More things off my to-do list.

5:30 p.m. Grab a burger and fries in the dining room.

5:40 p.m. I get paged that I have a call, my boss, so I grab my plate and head to my office.

6:05 p.m.   My daughter, Jennifer, calls. She wants me to babysit my granddaughter, Gianna, tonight. She's two and what a love! "Call your dad because I don't know what time I'll be home." Pretty much the standard answer these days.

6:10 p.m.   My husband calls to "thank" me for deferring Jennifer's call to him. Looks like he's babysitting tonight. I've been working sixteen-hour days, every day, for the past two months. I'm lucky he's so understanding. He calls me at work to introduce himself, to say, "I haven't seen you lately, how are you? Everything okay?" The bar calls; they need change. I'll be right there.

6:15 p.m.   I answer an e-mail from Tom at Mensa about their national convention in a few days at the Paris Hotel & Casino where I'll be speaking. Tom's e-mail states, *I booked you in the biggest convention space available. Looks like there is going to be quite a turnout for your speech. We're expecting approximately two thousand to attend.* I can't wait. My topic is legal vs. illegal prostitution. I'm not going to prepare a speech, but will ad lib. I think it's better that way. No one really wants to hear a canned speech, do they?

8:00 p.m.   All caught up on e-mail, for now. I answer all e-mails each day. The last thing I want is to come in and there are four hundred of them waiting for me! Another walk around the property to say good night, but no. Another lady wants to see me.

8:05 p.m.   I go back to my office. Seems she is concerned about another lady who is booking in to the Ranch next week. At times, not all the ladies get along. Imagine that! I explain that I expect each of them to conduct themselves in a professional and civil manner. They don't have to like one another, but they do have to get along while at the Ranch. I go on to say that I have always known her to be professional, so it shouldn't be difficult for her to continue in that fashion. She agrees. Another problem solved, for now.

8:20 p.m. Let's try this again. Another walk around the property to say good night. Some of the ladies are shooting pool in the bar, others are in the computer room in the back of the house. "Good night, ladies. I'll be on my cell for the next hour and then at home if you need me."

8:30 p.m. I almost make it to my car. Security catches me to say I have a call. It's one of the owners again. He wants to know what I'm still doing at the Ranch. "Didn't you have an early morning meeting at the Cabaret today? You should go home." My response, "I'm trying to!" We talk briefly about the "temperature" at the Ranch, exchange a few pleasantries. The closing statement is, "Drive carefully."

9:05 p.m. Quick, start the car and go. I feel like I'm driving a getaway car! As I drive down Homestead Road, I reflect on the day. I have twenty-five beautiful ladies in my care. I worry about them as I do my own children. I hope they get their rest tonight. I hope they don't miss their children, family, and pets too much. I hope everything is fine in their lives. They really are a great bunch.

10:00 p.m. I pull into my driveway. I realize I have the luxury of going home to my husband every night (even if he is sleeping when I get there!) and seeing my dogs. It's true, everything goes full circle. I leave with a smile. I come home with a smile.

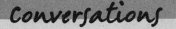

10:20 p.m. Trying to explain the theory of evolution to a four-year-old is a tough one, but I give it another whirl. It's hard to talk seriously to someone wearing SpongeBob underwear and arranging stuffed babies (all named Frank) on his bed. Theo is listening, though, and fills in the gaps as I forget them. I realize something has been lost in the translation because he asks, "When I get to be as old as you, will I be a monkey?"

Charly Haversat, 42, Freeport, Maine; owner, Funky Designs

10:50 a.m. In the store, I bump into Ethan. We fill each other in on what's new. I say, "Did you know we bought a house?" He says, "No, where?" So I start blathering on about what a great house it is. How it's a 1920s cottage with all the cool original moldings and lead-paned windows, not to mention a porch. A very small yard, but hey, we don't need much. I catch myself babbling and force myself to stop before he thinks I'm some sort of cult leader for home ownership. He doesn't want to hear all this. I'm like one of those annoying new parents who can't stop talking about their baby's first shit.

Laura Stout LaTour, 32, Somerset, Massachusetts;
publicist, Baker Books

7:55 p.m. Sitting outside while Martin cuts the grass. Ronica calls. My poor baby. She starts crying. She says she's tired. I tell her that her journey is just beginning. I remind her that she told me she knew what she was doing when she got pregnant again. I try to get her to see that this baby is not La Shawn, and she should have waited before getting pregnant again. I ask her if she is saving money. She says no. I tell her, even if she came here after she had the baby, she would need money to get her own place. All of my children's lives I've talked to them, especially Ronica, because I didn't want them to make the same mistakes I made. And I be damn if she ain't repeating the pattern. I tell her that she can't give up and shouldn't give in.

Monica Spears-Lombard, 39, Marshall, Texas; school
secretary

6:45 p.m. Consider making Hamburger Helper. Realize meat still frozen. Send instant message (IM) to my friend Mike asking how to defrost. *Should I remove it from the container? Should I watch it cook in the microwave? Oh, I should turn it over?* I put up an "away" message, *If you smell something burning, please check up on me in apartment 3.*

After seven minutes defrosting, I spread the meat apart. Notice it's not bright red in the center. Get paranoid and IM Mike again. He decides it's better to be safe than sorry and suggests dumping it. I put up another "away" message, *I'm not made to be a housewife.* Not wanting to waste food, I call home. I know if Dad answers, the meat would be okay;

if Mom answers, the meat would be poisonous. Dad answers. So I continue cooking.

Linda Szeto, 22, Lake Zurich, Illinois; grad student

4:00 p.m. I notice Miss Sassafras (thirteen-year-old miniature dachshund) is a little quiet. She's lying in her crate. I get down to her level and tell her that I washed her house so that it would be fresh like a little girl's room. I say, "If you need to go-go in the middle of the night, you can come shake, shake, shake by my bed and we can go out. That way, we can keep your kennel smelling clean." She looks at me and wiggles her little doxie nose. Oh, did she just say, "I like the way it smelled before it was washed." Dang it! I wish I was more sure of my communication skills.

Jan Dugan, 57, North Woodstock, New Hampshire; dog trainer

On June 29, 2004 . . .

29% of day diarists talked on the phone while driving.

31% talked to their mothers . . . 81% enjoyed the conversation.

15% said something they regretted.

〰〰〰

NASA Astronaut

Cady Coleman, 43, Houston, Texas

She's got a PhD in polymer science and engineering, serves as a colonel in the United States Air Force, has orbited the Earth 256 times, and has traveled at twenty-five times the speed of sound . . . yet she remains remarkably down-to-earth. Mom to a stepson, twenty, and four-year-old Jamey, she says, "Hurtling into space on the shuttle Columbia *was only a precursor to the velocity of motherhood." She and her husband, a glass-blower, have a commuter marriage. She lives in Houston; he's in Massachusetts. They've made it work for fourteen years, ever since they met after she called a wrong number. ("He was so funny that I called him back.") She chalks up the relationship to destiny. Long before she knew him, her husband was well known for making futuristic glass planets. "People tease us because he makes planets and I'd like to go to them, but how can you turn your back on*

what is clearly fate, just because it doesn't meet any logi-
cal standards of practicality?" In Houston, her long days
and nights tend to blur together, thanks to juggling full-
time work and motherhood, performing occasionally with
her Celtic band, and planning the logistics of frequent
family air travel. The couple try to find each other some-
where on the planet every two weeks. "It's tough having
your best friend living two thousand miles away, but it's
the only way we can make this unique family work."

0447 "Mommy, Mommy, I'm scared and I can't find my diaper . . ." Ohhh, I was hoping that the day would not start so early. First there is the realization that I'll have a small boy in my bed for a few minutes until I remember to wake up and take him back to his own. Then, quickly comes the follow-on realization that the bed he left proba-bly needs changing before he can go back to it.

0820 Johnson Space Flight Center. Timing is more criti-cal some days than others. Luckily today's 8 a.m. start time is fairly flexible. After our interrupted night, day-care drop-off took about twice as long as usual.

I slide into the simulator with moments to spare before the run. The simulator is our version of the International Space Station here on the ground. It is like standing in the middle of a very modern mobile home, except that there are video screens, experiments, and computers not only on the walls, but on the ceilings and floors as well. Today I am observing John and Sergei, the crew of Expedition 11, as they spend the morning pretending it's just another day aboard the space station. Being here brings back the magic of floating in space. I've flown twice on the space shuttle and can't wait to go again. It was amazing to fly through that tunnel that connects the cabin of the shuttle to the laboratory and suddenly arrive either facing the floor—or much stranger—facing one of the sides or the ceiling. I guess that your head is expecting "down" to be the floor, so it's always funny to end up somewhere else!

I am a Crew Support Astronaut for this expedition—someone who will act as the crew members' representative on the ground and help take care of their families while they are aboard the space station. I'm also in charge of making sure the crew's words and wishes get expressed as they intended. For example, an astronaut in space might say, "Would you mind if we did our workout periods early if we saw that the schedule was free?" That statement could easily be repeated as, "The crew members demand to schedule their own exercise time." Classic telephone tag kinds of things.

This is the first time that John, Sergei, and I have been together. They have been assigned to this space station mission for more than a year, but I am a new addition to their team, so I need to start building a relationship of trust and getting to know them. Does the commander lead in a military-type fashion? Do they feed us data as they go along? Will they tell us how they really feel, or do I need to encourage the ground team to coax it out of them? After the guys settle in to their simulated space station day, I run out to Ellington with the intention of making it back by noon for the end of the simulation and their debriefing.

0917 En route to Ellington Field (the airfield for the Johnson Space Center). The invention of the cell phone has saved my life. Well, it at least allows me to stay in touch with the outside world despite my wild schedule. I call my sister on my way. I chose to have Jamey a little later in life, giving my younger sister time to have two girls and experience everything first. She's my rock when it comes to advice about motherhood. I ask her if she thinks I am the worst mother in the world for not going on the zoo field trip tomorrow, when all the other parents who love their children are sure to be there. She convinces me that there will, indeed, be another chance to go to the zoo. As I pull into the parking lot, we end our discussion on the pros and cons of the various potty-training methods—you can never get too much advice!

0930 Ellington Field. This next stop is a tough one. After the loss of the space shuttle *Columbia*, neither life nor the schedule is simple at NASA. All of us understand that space flight can never be 100 percent risk-free. We travel at twenty-five times the speed of sound, hundreds of miles above the Earth's surface in a vacuum, dependent on the fragile ship that carries us. Hundreds of people, on a daily basis, work to make this inherently risky business as safe as humanly possible. The loss of our friends makes us even more committed to this mission.

Because I was a polymer chemist in my former life, I was given the task of helping to develop a way to repair damage to the heat-resistant tiles on the belly of the shuttle. I'm part of a team of experts: thermal engineers who think about how hot the shuttle will get when tiles are broken; space walk experts who are designing tools to apply the polymer "glue" that we have cooked up; and materials experts who actually design the glue. This is a daunting project, technically challenging and emotionally draining. I am studying a set of space shuttle tiles that have been intentionally damaged to imitate the worst case that we might encounter during a mission—damage many times more severe than is really likely. The tiles look like shingles with a black coating. The damage is immediately visible where the snowy white tile is exposed beneath. Some gouges are long

nasa astronaut **85**

and shallow and wouldn't even need fixing, but others are deep and span several tiles.

The repair method that we are evaluating is very much like frosting a cake, with all of the same skills that go along with it. I actually brought unfrosted cake to one of our meetings once and made everyone damage their cake and then repair it with stucco-colored icing. I did it to be funny, but with the serious intent of showing the intricacies involved in successfully squirting polymer goo in a hole to create an effective repair.

Now I need to go back to my office and tell my friends and colleagues whether we're on track to a good solution they should bet their lives on. I wish I could tell everyone that space shuttle tile repair will be easy, but the zero gravity influences on the repair are hard to predict, and technically it may be hard to prove that our frosting will stick in the microgravity of space. We'll continue to pursue our frostinglike goo, along with some other methods as well.

Seeing the damaged tiles makes me miss my friends. I'm still just so sad that they are not here with us. But they gave their lives to live their dream of exploring the universe, and there is no question in my mind that they would want us to continue what they started.

1600 Johnson Space Center. We've categorized all the tiles as to whether our repair method could fix them. Then it is back to the sim for the debriefing with Sergei and John. Apparently, they had some pretty tricky emergencies during their day in space—simulated of course! Were they calm? Did they make mistakes? How do they take criticism? Do they seem ready to live on the space station for six months? Are they having fun? By the end of the session I'm pretty pleased to have been assigned a fairly even-keeled crew to support—no ego problems to deal with on this crew.

1713 En route to day care. I call the center to assure them I'll be my usual "exactly-on-time." Where would we be without these people who take care of our kids? As I walk into the center, Jamey runs up. "I give you a kiss and a hug, Mommy."

1747 Home. My world revolves around the usual meetings, meetings, meetings, taking care of my ISS crew, worrying about whether I bought plane tickets in time to snag the lowest fares, trying to find time to call my mom. . . . It is all important, but not as real as the need for kissing a new boo-boo or explaining why the garbage men only come on Tuesday and Friday. Jamey is such a great little guy, so cute and smart. Soon I'll be sneaking copies of *Scientific American* out of the mailbox before he can find them so that I can read up on the latest technology developments before he can ask me about them!

"We get to have some special time together," I explain to him, "and then you and I are meeting Miss Kenya at the music place. You get to hear Mommy play music, and then Miss Kenya will take you back home for night-night." (Miss Kenya is Jamey's teacher and my favorite babysitter. It's so great I don't have to introduce yet another adult to trust in Jamey's already complicated life.)

"But I want to play music, too," Jamey says with a smile. We play hide-and-seek instead, as I sneak in a look for my music notes while searching for a small boy hiding in plain sight.

1900 We're in the car, eating nutritious (ha!) peanut butter sandwiches on the way to the restaurant-bar to meet my Celtic band. I think about the trip just a week away that Jamey and I will make to drop him at his dad's house in Massachusetts. In my head, I start planning the logistics of getting a four-year-old and his mom packed and to the airport in time.

"Mommy, Mommy, why do we go back and forth and back and forth?"

"Do you mean in the car today?"

"No, to Daddy's house and Mommy's house."

Eeek. I was planning to have an answer by the time he was five, so I'm not quite ready. "Well, Daddy has to live at Daddy's house, because he makes beautiful glass, and do you think he could make that beautiful glass in Houston?" No, Jamey shakes his head wisely. No studio in Houston. "And do you think that Mommy could work at mission control in Massachusetts?" No, no mission control in Massachusetts. "That's why we go back and forth and back and forth, because we are a family and we have to go back and forth to be together." He nods acceptance and returns to flying his toy helicopter in the air above his car seat.

1930   At the restaurant. Playing flute with my friends Chris, Della, and Annette (though Della couldn't make it tonight) is one of my selfish pleasures, a curious blending of my intellectual self—being smart enough to figure out what to play—and my other, inside, self that sometimes has music that is just waiting to come out. Sometimes when I'm playing, I let the outside world interfere. I look out and see someone that I know and feel self-conscious, wondering what they think. But sometimes it all just comes together, depending on the combination of people on the stage and in the audience (or sometimes lack of one) and a half of a glass of really good beer!

We haven't played together in at least six months, making this more of a public rehearsal than a polished performance, but tonight is perfect, to the point that Della, our magical cello player, doesn't even have to be present for me to play as if she was here. I can hear her in my head as we start into some of Chris's lyrical Canadian folk songs, and the whole world goes away. The first rehearsal back always goes well, just because I'm so thrilled that I can actually still play. None of us plans to quit our day jobs though.

2220 Telephone call to my husband, Josh. Sometimes we check in several times a day, but the end-of-day call is special. Tonight, I try to understand how it was to make platters and vases and attack the endless pile of paperwork that plagues every small business. Somehow, with just a few sentences, Josh understands that my day was crazed as usual, sadder than in a long time, that Jamey had a good day at school and wished that Mommy played faster songs, and that I was really glad I took the time to play music for a little while.

2245 In bed. I fish out the to-do list I keep and sigh. I'd like to be able to report that all the boxes are checked. There's the robotic arm training that has been on the list for months—maybe tomorrow. I was hoping to spend some time at the gym, or at least a good twenty-minute session on the VersaClimber that beckons at the edge of the kitchen and serves as both jungle gym and clothes dryer, but I didn't. There are just so many boxes that can be checked, and at a certain point you have to agree to make peace with the day and try again tomorrow.

2345 I am awakened by Jamey, who woke up with a nightmare. My day ends as I doze off, rocking him back to sleep.

Miscellaneous Moments

AM Radio

12:30 a.m. I listen to late-night talk shows, especially Art Bell's *Coast to Coast.* My grown children don't understand. Alien abductions, crop circles, out-of-body/astral travel, near-death experiences! Mother . . . puh-leeze!

Marilyn Cook, 59, Peoria, Illinois; salesperson

Fingers and Toes

1:40 a.m. Despite my tiredness, I can't resist the urge to sit here with Simon in the rocking chair, staring at his little baby beauty. I just can't wrap my mind around the fact that he is so perfect. How many parts are there to the human body? How many different things that could potentially turn out wrong? But they didn't. He's got ten long fingers and ten stubby toes and the world's longest baby eyelashes. And he has the world's best baby smell. He smells like Apple Jacks.

Martha Kimes, 33, Scottsdale, Arizona; assistant
general counsel, Make-A-Wish Foundation of America

Range of Motion

5:00–8:00 a.m.   At this time of the morning I am wheezing, and breathing is difficult. I do forty minutes of physical therapy and twenty minutes of inhalation therapy using a nebulizer. After this, I brush my teeth, take a sink bath, and get myself dressed. Thanks to my power wheelchair I am able to provide myself with a lot of self-care and can get from my bed to the bathroom. I make my own bed, which is not an easy task, but it provides good range-of-motion therapy.

Gertrude Krein, 75, Eureka, South Dakota; resident,
Avera Eureka Health Care Center

Angel

11:30 a.m.   I've got the flu. I try to read and almost pass out. I give in to a guilty pleasure and pop in a videotape of *Angel*. I lie on the couch and watch as a vampire with a soul and his trusty mates help to save the world. Episode after episode. I am embarrassed that I love these shows. All of my academic training tells me that you can study pop culture, but not truly like it.

Barbara K. Ige, 38, Santa Monica, California;
diversity director, UCLA

Olympic Trials

11:20 p.m.   I got in my house after working overtime. I wanted to make chicken fajitas. Slammed a beer right away. No one is home but me, dammit. I can't believe my judo career is really over. I am fatter for every day I am not working out, but I can't. I am in a cast and not going to the Olympics. It's over. Okay. Move on. You can eat and heal up. I say to myself, I've done well in my judo career. Oh well. Finish dinner.

Grace Jividen, 40, Littleton, Colorado; industrial
specialist and member of the U.S. Judo Team, 1981–2004

Kristin Banta-Bland, 31, Los Angeles, California

She was never one of those girls who dreamed about getting married. It didn't jibe with her contrary nature—"If they said black, I said white." Plus, her parents each divorced more than once, and she had her own troubles with dysfunctional dating. "Everything was pure drama and adrenaline rush." But then the right guy came along. "He made me feel beautiful." More important, he stayed, even when she was recuperating from spinal surgery. "Not pretty, but this man did not leave me." They married three years later. She used to be a child model and actress (following in her mother's footsteps), with a handful of guest roles on network TV and a recurring role on a popular soap. "A miserable experience. The script was terrible and my hair was huge." After a few indie films, she quit acting at twenty-one. "I was only getting offered the cheerleader, the girlfriend, or the victim, which upped the pres-

*sure of having to look perfect." Still, it was hard to quit.
"I was repped by a major agency, and I'd worked so hard
to graduate to working actor." She became a music supervisor for films, then started her own events planning business. Now she mostly does weddings. "To have the honor
of being part of the day when two people say, 'I pick you
to be my companion for life,' this is why I do what I do."*

12:10 a.m. I'm about to finish my wine while I contem-
plate the idea of another glassful. Every day I tell myself
that today is the day that I stick to my diet—no sugar, no
alcohol! As usual, I change my mind. Nothing seems to
soothe the stress of remodeling one's home as much as a
piece of birthday cake and/or a glass of wine.

I am writing detailed lists for the paint crew and contractors who are due here in the morning. They might as
well move in with us, as it feels like they live here already.
The other day I was awakened by the arrival of my period,
and when I made a dash to the bathroom I ran smack into
the electrician in my hallway. I ducked under his ladder
into the bathroom, shamelessly stopping along the way to
retrieve feminine products from the closet in full view of
the crew. What can you do?

We were told the first phase of the remodeling of our
1938 Art Deco duplex would be completed in five days.
Well, it is week six and I now sit in a plastic-draped office,
peering through a giant hole in the wall at our inappropri-
ately placed toilet, in the company of our 1920s oven,
smack in the middle of what was once the living room. In
the midst of this endless project, my biggest challenge
seems to be finding the balance between remaining kind
and being authoritative. But I have to start cracking the whip
around here before my husband has a nervous breakdown

and I start smoking again or become an alcoholic. Now if I can just let go of my obsession with having everyone still like me . . .

12:31 a.m. My husband just got home from seeing some band. He works for a record company. The important thing is that he just exited our wine closet with an exciting-looking French Cabernet. Maybe I'll have a touch more. For now, we are going to try to forget that our house looks like Beirut and watch *The Cooler*, which we just got in from Netflix.

2:01 a.m. Well, neither of us made it through the movie, as much as we love William H. Macy. We both fell asleep on the couch before waking up to the same ten bars of the movie soundtrack on repeat. We drag ourselves to bed, but not before pulling back the plastic, dry-wall-coated tarp.

7:45 a.m. I hit snooze three times on our radio alarm clock until I was finally assaulted by some guy rapping about "backing that thing up." This, combined with the threat of impending lateness, finally forced me out of our warm feather bed. Every day I seem to think that I can be out of the house in fewer minutes, resulting in my chronic lateness. I always get up with a promise that I can have a nap later if I need it, even though deep down I know that it is unlikely I will have time, and anyway I cannot handle the guilt.

I wish we had some food in the house. Everything became furry and green from weeks without electricity.

8:30 a.m. Ninety miles per hour down the freeway, late and stressed out as usual. My Pilates session technically starts now. At least I got things on track with the painters, plumbers, and electricians before leaving. Now that I am on surface streets, it's all about a high-speed game of "duck the left-turners," to avoid getting stuck indefinitely behind some road-nuisance and thus miss what remains of my private session to work out my once-flat, now-not-so-much abs.

I multitask through morning rush hour, drinking apple juice, returning the calls of only those who are not yet in to pick up, and jotting notes in my Day Runner.

Stopped at a light on Wilshire Boulevard, I look up at my old friend Chris who looms over me on a billboard for her new film. I think about how pretty and small she appears even on such a large space. We met on a soap opera audition fifteen years ago, but Chris somehow avoided the humiliation of soap work and having to take oneself seriously while a director instructs you to appear even more shocked at the vision of your long-lost twin waking up from a coma with a perfectly hot-rollered head of sprayed blond curls. Needless to say, I am no longer in the acting business.

8:45 a.m. I get my quarters out and prepare to make my usual mad dash to meet my trainer. Here's the thing: I cannot responsibly park in the lot for $6 versus paying 75 cents for a meter, even though the lot is much closer and will chop a full four minutes off my stressful run/walk to my trainer's building. Like every morning, I will not be terribly disappointed if there are no meters available, *forcing* me to park in the lot. I got a parking space—one that is out of order—a real luxury.

After forty-five minutes of Pilates, during which we discussed the genius of Michael Moore, I dragged myself to the Precore machine for my usual hour and fifteen minutes of aerobic activity. After ten minutes I had to quit because I was coughing so much, perhaps because I've been breathing in so much drywall. I really wanted to go for it today, too, especially considering the free time I have on the meter! I must say though, recently I've been relatively body-image shame-free, so I might just get away with a short workout, psychologically unharmed. This is unusual, considering I've gained a considerable amount of weight since quitting smoking five months ago.

It helps that my precious husband is always so conscientious about telling me I'm beautiful, whether I have just opened my eyes in the morning or whether I am in my party-best for a night out. He knows that I encounter feelings of inadequacy with regard to my body. Feelings of self-loathing have been present most of my life, sometimes so crippling that I don't want to leave the house. Lately, I only have occasional bouts of these self-defeating feelings.

10:00 a.m. I walked to Starbucks for a percent latte and a piece of low-fat coffee cake. I wonder how much fat this bad boy started with to justify the low-fat title crowned on this new version. You never know what to expect in Starbucks, although it's a seemingly benign yuppie haven. Like the girl in front of me in line, who screamed when she was informed that they were out of vanilla flavoring. She literally screamed. With all the existing drama in this world, is it really necessary to scream over a shortage of vanilla flavoring?

I am off now to go on my home-shopping scavenger hunt for tiles (fourth attempt at picking up the same damn tile), double-stick tape, rust remover, a pedestal sink, a ceiling fan, a new outside light, and something called a one-inch copper regulator (plumbing related), plus a prescription, office supplies, and some brass nipples.

I stop at a rental open house to see what a two-bedroom goes for in midtown. Fortunately, I am beginning to feel confident that we will be able to get a good price for our newly renovated downstairs unit when we finish all this madness. The guy who showed me the unit was deformed from the waist down. I don't know if he saw me look or not. I hope not, as I dread to think I made him feel self-conscious.

Back in the car. A band that my husband wanted to sign but who went with another record label in the eleventh hour, just came on the radio. Because of this, I want to hate this song, but I must admit it's damn catchy. Bastards. I hate it when someone else gets credit for something my husband discovered.

10:30 a.m. I'm waiting for my prescription in the pharmacy—birth control pills and something which promises to reduce this dreadful cough. I'm sitting next to two Russian women who appear to be mother and daughter. The daughter is plain, in her forties, and the mother, maybe seventies, looks like she was quite saucy in her youth. She is wearing bright red lipstick and keeps hacking phlegm. I cannot stop myself from giving her looks of subtle disgust.

I am quietly rocking out to Wilson Phillips' "Hold On" as it blares through the overhead speakers. How cheesy. If someone notices my enthusiasm for this song, I might possibly feel a bit pathetic, but not terribly so. I've become rather unapologetic since turning thirty.

At the pharmacy, I bought my usual "True Blonde" as my roots are crying out for attention. I've also nicked a new eye cream that is going to make me look younger and more radiant. Hahaha. We're all being taken for a ride by the media. When are we going to learn how to just be okay with the extra roll around our waists, our laugh lines, and our graying hair? My hips are two times as round as they were last year, but then again so is my ample rack, which isn't all bad, right?

Driving to Home Depot. I'm rocking out to the new

Beastie Boys record. What am I, eighteen? I think this eye cream is working already, hahaha!

11:30 a.m. After Home Depot, I dropped another sum at Staples on office supplies, only half of which I really needed. I have a strange tic—the greater the financial pressure, the more I seem to spend like a rock star. I'm going to give my husband a heart attack. He is the most generous man in the universe, and I never want to make him feel as though I take him for granted. Fortunately, I just booked two weddings, which will give me a bit of breathing room. (While this week is dedicated to home repairs, normally I'd be marking up vendor contracts with red pen, running around town doing site walk-throughs, tracking down sterling silver seashells for favors, trying to find out how to work the stepmother into the ceremony without pissing off the mom, and answering calls about long tables vs. rounds; chair covers vs. chivaris; filet mignon vs. sea bass . . .) My goal is to take on only one event per month in order to protect my sanity. Life is too short to agree to work with the bridezillas of this world just to get that pair of Manolo's I've not yet purchased.

When shopping, I always intend to just get one or two items, thus I never pick up a basket. But one or two items always translates to seven or eight. At both Home Depot and Staples, people had to catch my falling items as I stumbled towards the checkout. Why do I never learn? It's like when I say I'll be somewhere at 7:00, which I know means 7:15, so why don't I just say that??! Probably because, if I say 7:15, then I won't show up until 7:30.

1:15 p.m. I just arrived at Mom's office to go to lunch. She works at a talent agency but is in the process of crossing over into real estate full-time. I put on some lipstick.

Having once been represented by this agency, I never want to look like that once-attractive actress now on the fast track to Dowdy City. I pull myself together as best I can, considering I have to work with my tight gym pants and track shoes.

Nothing can perk up my day like my beautiful mom. Over lunch we enthusiastically plotted out my own personal game of Monopoly and how we will assure that my future children are guaranteed the option of private school based on our real estate investments. Not that I am presently trying to get pregnant—I have enough on my plate this week. Mom is just the person to reassure me with a good old-fashioned financial planning discussion.

3:30 p.m. This afternoon, I basically stalked the tile company until they produced the green travertine kitchen tiles they promised me three weeks ago. Now I fancy some sugar, so I drive out of the way to get a Milk Tea Bobat—this sweet, creamy tea with big tapioca-like balls at the bottom. Freakish really, but strangely addictive.

6:30 p.m. Home finally, after navigating through rush hour traffic while reading the *People* magazine I never fully indulged in due to a shortened treadmill session this morning. I know, I must sound like a road menace, but when you are stopped every twenty feet for long intervals, magazine flipping doesn't seem so inappropriate. I wondered, as I entered my third freeway of the journey home, when are hovercrafts going to go on the market to save me from this insanity? Having spent over three hours in the car today, I cannot imagine what I would do with all that free time.

Dinner with my friends is at 7:00 and it will take me twenty-five minutes to get there, so I leave at 6:47 (the math only seems to add up correctly in *my* head). As if I am drowning in time, I first compulsively check e-mails, do a bit of straightening, and change clothes. I have concealed my all-day-in-the-hot-car-without-a-shower look well, I think, sporting my cherries-print halter, Candies-styled heels, Seven jeans, gold hoop earrings, hair in a ponytail, lips stained with rose water, my red Kate Spade handbag, red cardigan, and a splash of Marc Jacobs perfume.

I dash out the door, bottle of wine in hand to accommodate for a lacking liquor license at our chosen spot for "Tapas Tuesday," stopping briefly to steal a quick sip of my husband's dirty martini and French kiss him good-bye.

By the time I arrive at Cobras & Matadors (pleased with my mere ten minutes of appropriate lateness), the always-on-time and perfectly chic Jessie is waiting with her own bottle of red. We immediately crack it open to toast her recent engagement. I cheer her beautiful new hand acquisition, perfectly paired with what look to be a new pair of Frankie B pants and a James Pierce tee.

She indulges me as I proceed with a diatribe about Carl the plumber, who I joked might shank me in the night since we fired him for making our pipes even worse than before he started. Jessie and I had just decided to proceed with the first round of tapas when S (short for Sarah) arrived, sweeping my own late arrival under the carpet for a change. We toast her new editorial manager position, and I notice how truly proud and excited I feel for her achievement.

Over two bottles of wine and a sinister number of dishes, we caught up since last month's dinner. At this point in my life, I truly value "my girls," whereas there was a time when I only had male friends. This particular circle of "Betties" I have known for about nine years. We all hugged good-bye as S and I waited for the valet to fetch our cars for a criminal price and admired Jessie's street-parking success.

this day in the life 100

10:30 p.m.   I just got home and jump on my husband's lap for a kiss. He is watching our beloved Jon Stewart on *The Daily Show*. After sending a couple e-mails and straightening my office, I am thrilled to be finally stepping into my white pajama bottoms (which I would live in if I could), a white tank, and some flip-flops. This is my uniform for instant relaxation. Then I sink into the couch for the second attempt at *The Cooler*. There are few things that I love more than curling up with my husband to watch a movie.

11:45 p.m.   I loved it when William H. Macy said to Maria Bello, who was sadly examining her bruised reflection in the mirror, "I'm the only mirror you're ever gonna need." This reminds me so much of my husband's efforts to make sure I feel pretty at all times. I think about my extraordinary partnership with him, my delicious family, and wonderful friends and wonder what else there is in life beyond that richness. We try so hard to buy, acquire, perfect, but it will never match this moment here on the faded green couch with my husband's arms wrapped around me in my white pajama bottoms.

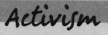

10:45 a.m. After looking at about twenty cards, I found one that imagined all kinds of possibilities for a baby girl, including marriage, or maybe not marriage. Then the gift. I found a wonderful Gund bear in overalls that taught four different kinds of skills (I can't help myself; I'm a teacher). A completely non-sex-identified toy. Last time I was in this store I argued with the saleslady to get her to put a pink ribbon in the bow she made for my gift to a boy baby. This time the salesman asked if I wanted blue for a boy and I said I don't identify children with colors. Okay, so it's a very small victory.

> *Lois Palken Rudnick, 60, Sharon, Massachusetts;*
> *English professor*

11:30 a.m. John is upset that I've put a bumper sticker on the parish van. "The church is not supposed to politic," he says. I guess he's right and I certainly believe that the *official* church should stay away from this "no Communion for abortion supporters" debate, but I don't think I'll remove the bumper sticker until he tells me to.

> *Maryanne O'Neill, 68, Los Angeles, California; Sister*
> *and parish social worker*

3:05 p.m. I am sitting outside at Starbucks reading my book when I hear it—the unmistakable sound of someone getting ready to . . . ugh! light up a cigarette. I get up and must have shot her a look because she assures me that she'll be blowing the smoke in the other direction (at someone else?). No, thanks. I move to the furthest possible table and then throw out the ashtray that is on it. I'm sure this is unlawful, but it's the most I can do in silent protest.

Robin Kall, 41, East Greenwich, Rhode Island; radio talk show host

7:15 a.m. Get dressed and put on my "I'm a child NOT a choice" pin that I'm too self-conscious to wear to my job at the newspaper. Our employee handbook is pretty detailed about some of the rules about political affiliations. No one has said anything about my "Choose Life" car tag, though. Usually I wear my Precious Feet pin, which is more subtle but sometimes prompts questions. I tell them that it's the exact size and shape of a baby's feet ten weeks after conception.

Jenny Taylor, 34, Jacksonville, Alabama; news assistant

1:30 a.m. Why is it that I'm always itching to go out on Monday nights lately? Like every Monday I feel like I just HAVE to go down and check out the seedy little bars or else I'll just DIE. Right, well. I feel like Monday nights are such underrated party nights, especially considering that it's summer. I mean, Monday night in summertime should be at least as exciting as Wednesday night, which apparently is the new Thursday. Or something. So yeah, I'm trying to start a campaign among my friends to instate Monday as a preferable party night to Wednesday. So far it's only worked once. Le sigh.

Lee Conderacci, 21, Baltimore, Maryland; Princeton graduate, 2004

activism **103**

6:30 a.m.   Up to post letters to all the people on our holiday card list, but it's not holiday cards I'm sending. I am copying the handout on the mandatory military service bills that are currently in Congress and sending one to everyone we know. I also enclose one in every household bill. I can't bear to think of some kid I love being sent into war without choice or more peaceful options of service. I stamp each letter, say a prayer (and I haven't prayed in years so you know this is important to me), and put it in my bag to mail.

Anna Viadero, 45, Montague, Massachusetts; editor of
a senior newspaper

7:30 p.m.   Ran on treadmill to relieve stress and watched *The Daily Show*. I have the biggest crush on Jon Stewart. Suddenly want to be VERY politically active.

Annie Wood, 24, Port Richey, Florida; technical writer

"Bubby"

Nadine Goldman, 65, Baltimore, Maryland

The ultimate Jewish grandma, her nine grandkids can do no wrong. "They love you and you love them and it doesn't matter what terrible things they do, you still think they're terrific." She emulates her own loving grandmother, who lived around the corner when she was a child. "I used to run away to her house." A caregiver. A softie. Married forty-five years, with three grown children. She tries not to be the interfering mother or mother-in-law. "Sometimes it's hard to bite my tongue." For twelve years she worked as a nurse, then as an office manager at her husband's magnet company. Always part-time. "I wanted to be home when the children were home." Now their son runs the business, but she still goes in twice a week. She's the kind of person who has trouble saying no. Doesn't like conflict. Worries about everything. Busy! Copresident of a cancer foundation. The volunteer you ask when you want something done. *She knits, needlepoints, paints, plays golf. Home has been the Baltimore suburbs virtually all of her life. As a schoolgirl, she was the teacher's pet.* "Good grades. Neat handwriting. I was the one who made the posters. You can just picture it, the little girl with the pigtails, that was me. It's still me," *she adds,* "without the pigtails."

6:00 a.m. Woke to the alarm after having been up at 3:40 a.m. and 5:30 a.m. It's so early, but today is my golf league. Why can't I just sleep until the alarm wakes me? I guess I worry about being late, but I'm always early. I'm so tired.

6:10 a.m. Stepped on the scale. Down a half pound. One day up, one day down. Seems like I should be able to eat what I like and not gain, like I did when I was young. It doesn't work that way at sixty-five.

6:20 a.m. Dressing. Bob is still snoozing. I put on navy golf shorts and a fun shirt with lady golfers all over it. It matches my white visor. Sometimes I feel that looking well put together improves my game, but it usually doesn't work.

6:30 a.m. I'm sitting at the mirror doing my makeup, thinking about the wrinkles on my face and my hair that's beginning to gray. I'm not upset. These are signs of having lived awhile. I'm reminded of my grandmother who had curly, gray hair and such soft, wrinkly skin that I loved to touch.

6:35 a.m. Woke Bob. He'd be upset to miss breakfast with me. Bob is a bit compulsive. He loves to set the table

this day in the life 106

the night before and takes pride in preparing breakfast for me. Since he retired twelve years ago, he likes to help with the daily chores like shopping and emptying the dishwasher. He teases that his middle name is "Errands and Duties."

6:42 a.m. Phoned the pharmacy and left a message that I hadn't received my prescription. That's unusual for them to err.

6:45 a.m. Had breakfast with Bob. He always prepares grapefruit juice, Raisin Bran Crunch, and coffee. After forty-five years of marriage, it never ceases to amaze me that he's always such a happy person, even so early in the day. It takes me a while to wake up. Our conversations used to be about children, school, etc. Now it's about my ninety-two-year-old mother, adult day care, her memory, our memory, physical complaints, etc.

7:00 a.m. Listened to the morning news on the radio. It's upsetting to hear about the terrorists. What kind of life will our grandchildren have to look forward to?

7:20 a.m. Driving to the golf course. I usually take Leda, Barbara, and Linda, but I'm driving by myself, which is nice once in a while. It gives me a chance to think about what I have to do today. I can begin planning for the board meeting of the Mildred Mindell Cancer Foundation. I have to make a list of the fund-raising projects that Carol and I discussed. I can plan an agenda. It will be my first responsibility as copresident. Hope there is a good turnout for the meeting. Summer is not usually a great time to get a group together because of vacations, but we'll do what we can.

It's a beautiful day for golf. Not too hot. And the cicadas

are gone. No more dodging them while I'm trying to drive the ball.

7:24 a.m. Passed by Slade Mansion, where Mom lives. It's so nice to know that she's being taken care of so well. Today, she goes to day care by bus so I won't be visiting. But she'll see her brother at day care since he's there, too. Too bad she won't remember, but at least he will. I try not to be sad about her Alzheimer's because she lives in the moment, and for that moment, she's really happy. She still plays piano very well, but doesn't remember that she played. I'm glad that I have recorded her at the piano for the grandchildren, because otherwise they won't remember.

7:31 a.m. I just dropped my cell phone between the seats. It's really hard to reach. I can't look now because I'm driving. It's too bad because I was going to call Phyllis, my sister who lives in a nearby suburb. That'll have to wait.

7:50 a.m. I'm at the golf course waiting to hear my tee-off time. There are about thirty women here, all chatty. I wonder who I'll be paired with. I like most of the women in the league, but there is one who I'd like not to be paired with. She makes me nervous because she corrects my playing, and I feel I have to be perfect when I play with her. I don't need a reason to play poorly. Today's contest is for the longest drive. I guess that leaves me out.

8:40 a.m. We're waiting to tee off. I'm so glad to be riding with my friend Marcia. It'll be such a relaxing day. I really like playing with her because we don't compete with each other. But I still have first-hole jitters. No matter how often I play, I get nervous driving the first ball of the day.

9:10 a.m. Pretty good drive on the first tee. I can relax now that that's over.

12:15 p.m. Had lunch that Bob made me. Two hard-cooked eggs and some grape tomatoes. He's so good to me. I eat on the cart between shots.

2:05 p.m. I've finished eighteen holes. Golf is a game that tells you a lot about people. Some women are so competitive. Others just play their own game without being concerned about winning. For the most part, the women in our league are honest about their scores, but I've played with women who must win, even if it means altering their scores. It's sad! And dishonest. Can't imagine doing that. I think everyone gets frustrated at one time or another, but that's golf. Even Tiger Woods has his frustrations. My game today was not great, but better than it has been. I'm really tired.

2:10 p.m. Called my sister Phyllis at work at Sinai Hospital. She wasn't there. Tried her at home and left a message. She went to Ocean City over the weekend, but I thought she would be back by now. Her friends are vacationing there and she may have stayed, but I don't remember her saying that. I'm a little concerned, but as Bob says, I always need something to worry about. Today's worry is my "baby" sister.

2:18 p.m. Driving home to pick up Bob so that we can go to visit our daughter, Wendy, her three boys, and their friends visiting from Omaha.

2:25 p.m. Bob's driving because we're going on the highway. I don't drive on the highways because of a phobia I developed in my late twenties. Someday I'd like to overcome that fear, but for now he can drive. We stopped to get some candy and gum for our grandsons and their friend Sophie. I know they'll be excited.

3:05 p.m. Arrived at Wendy's. My grandson Max, who's five, was at the computer, but stopped after he finished his game because his mom said that he couldn't play computer games while we visited. Reed, who's seven, showed me his sore arm that two boys from basketball camp fell on.

3:15 p.m. My daughter's friend and the rest of the group came home from car pool. My grandson Davis and Sophie had been at computer camp. They've been good friends since they were two, in Omaha. It's so nice to see them together now, at age nine. Wendy and Andrew moved to Omaha because of a great job opportunity shortly after they were married, but moved back to Maryland five years and three grandchildren later. It's wonderful to have them so near. We visited and chatted for a while.

3:50 p.m. Max whispered to his mom, "When are Bubby and Pop Pop leaving?" He wanted us to leave so he could go back to his baseball game. I thought it was funny. It's amazing how everything that grandchildren do is wonderful. They are really so special. It's certainly much easier to enjoy the grandchildren than our own children. We didn't have as much time then.

3:59 p.m. I picked up my phone messages from home. My sister is in Ocean City. One worry resolved. I guess I forgot that she might possibly stay. Forgetting seems to be becoming more frequent. I try not to worry about it. I also had a message from the pharmacy that the reason they didn't fill my prescription was that it was filled only two weeks ago. I didn't remember that. I must look in the medicine cabinet when I get home.

4:00 p.m. Bob is driving us home. We have to get ready for our dinner with friends tonight. We talk about the grandchildren and the funny and clever things they say and do. It's amazing how they never forget anything. I guess it's youth. Both Bob and I have concerns about our memory lapses.

This morning before I awoke, Bob boiled two eggs for my lunch. He then went into the den to watch TV until they were done but forgot about the eggs for about an hour. When he smelled something burning, he returned to the kitchen to find a dry pot and egg remnants all over the kitchen. He was really upset, even when telling me of the episode.

4:38 p.m. The pharmacist was right. I do have the medication. It's both a relief and a concern.

4:40 p.m. I'm going into the shower to get ready for dinner with the Newmans. Bob met Oscar Newman at a golf outing, then the wives met, and we've been friends ever since. We're picking them up at 6:15. We haven't seen Oscar and Eunice for a long time, since they spend their winters in Florida.

5:35 p.m. Made a few last-minute phone calls, and Wendy called. It seems that Reed's sore arm was not just sore, it was fractured. Fortunately, it's not severe and should heal quickly, but he can't go back to basketball camp. I guess that's the sort of thing you can expect from a seven-year-old boy.

6:06 p.m. We're leaving to pick up the Newmans. It's an informal evening and we're eating in the pub at the Johns Hopkins Club. Eunice really loves their Maryland fried chicken, and Tuesday is the fried chicken buffet. Oh well, what's a couple of pounds? It really is good.

6:15 p.m. The Newmans really look good. When I asked about their recent trip to Canada, they said that they would have enjoyed it if we had gone with them, but weren't very happy with the trip alone. We usually do travel together, but we weren't particularly interested in going to Canada, since we've been there many times.

6:35 p.m. Seated at the restaurant. The buffet is wonderful. In addition to the great chicken, they have lots of sides. I'm having a hard time restricting my intake.

Dinner conversation with the Newmans is diverse. We can discuss politics with the Newmans because we agree. We just can't understand why everyone doesn't feel the same as we do. They wanted to know if we plan to visit them in Florida this winter, as we usually do, but Bob and I have decided to take a vacation in the Southwest this year. They were disappointed but understood.

7:40 p.m. Ordered dessert—one chocolate sundae and four spoons. We just wanted a taste. After dinner, we sat around for a long time. It's amazing what four people can find to discuss when they haven't seen each other in a while. We catch up on the comings and goings of our children and grandchildren. We all have kids who make us proud.

9:34 p.m. We're home from dinner. Can't wait to get comfortable. I put on my pajamas and soft slippers.

9:40 p.m. I begin packing for a two-day getaway with Bob. We're going to Atlantic City for golf and gambling. I love to travel but really don't like to pack. I have always had the full responsibility of packing for everyone for vacations. Bob says he wouldn't take anything, so I guess in order for me not to be embarrassed, I pack his clothes.

Sounds like blackmail to me. But we're only going for two nights so I won't need much. Our golf clubs are already in the car.

10:25 p.m. Checked my e-mail. One was from my sister. She's at home, which is good. Responded to a few others from friends from nursing school and a few cousins who are in Florida, North Carolina, and West Virginia. It's so easy to keep in touch by e-mail.

10:35 p.m. I wrote a few checks and tied up a couple of loose ends that needed to be taken care of before our trip. Bob's asleep. He needs his rest so that he can do the driving.

10:50 p.m. Performed my evening rituals. I took my medications, brushed my teeth, and flossed, and removed my makeup. It's time to get into bed.

11:00 p.m. I watched the news in bed. Bob can sleep through anything, so the TV doesn't wake him. I don't know why I bother. It's always upsetting to hear about Iraq, local murders, accidents, etc. I guess I have a need to be informed, but I sure don't like the information.

11:20 p.m. Davis, my nine-year-old grandson, loaned me a book that he thought I'd enjoy reading: *The Westing Game* by Ellen Raskin. He probably finished it in a day, but it's taking me much longer, even though it's good. I'll read until I fall asleep. It's been a great day.

The Power of Prayer

9:30 p.m.   Oh my goodness! The phone has been jumping off the hook with a series of telephone blessings. First,
Chris called with a prayer for my French research tool exam
I WILL PASS tomorrow! Second, my new buddy from the
French class called and we shared insights for over an hour
on how members of the class have grown over the past
weeks. No one in the class may ever know how we brought
down the house praising God for what He is about to do
tomorrow! Third, Justin (my son) called to confirm our
postexam celebration lunch for tomorrow and to let me
know he is praying for me. I had to run around my little
dorm room dancing and praising God! I'm all studied up,
loved up, prayed up, and packed up! There's nothing like
shaking your shimmy for Jesus!

Denise Campbell, 48, Arroyo Grande, California;
associate vice president, California Polytechnic

9:30 p.m.   The courtyard close. I must get off first floor
back to the dorm. Before I go to bed, I get down on my
knees. Thank God for another day clean. Also I pray for
my family, everybody here at the Center for the Homeless,
for addicts still out there, the child that have no say-so.

Thank him for running my life today, how much I love him. And thank him for blessing me with a wonderful mother who I love so much and I miss.

Cynthia Vaughn, 40, South Bend, Indiana

10:00 a.m.   Kids still asleep. Now the worrying is settling in. Always happens if I am not busy and thinking about a hundred other things. Worry about my health mostly. Worry about my children if something were to happen to me. Actually, worry about my children MOSTLY. Always afraid to go to the doctor about anything. For some reason doctor visits equate with a death sentence or poking and prodding and tests and tests and tests. So I worry and worry some more. Time to pray. Pray for guidance. Pray for help. Pray for less stress. Do some deep breathing. This is helping. Relax and breathe. Relax and breathe. I think I'll take a bath.

Ann Pruett Tahir, 43, Allen, Texas; muralist

7:32 p.m.   I truly enjoy prayer group. I had a special gift for one of the ladies in the group; however, she didn't come this evening. I was debating whether I should bring it to her since she lived around the corner, but I also wanted to get home because I was looking forward to having ice cream with my brother and his wife. As if to answer my question, who comes walking in a little late? Sometimes I find the little things God does more amazing than the greatest miracles.

Deborah Ayars, 50, Vineland, New Jersey; engineer

On June 29, 2004 . . .

53% of day diarists prayed.

〜〜〜

the power of prayer   115

Baghdad Beth

Beth Garland, 42, Sierra Vista, Arizona

Nineteen years in the army. Married seventeen years ago on the Fourth of July. Two kids, ages nine and five. Army life meant relocating every couple years, but never to a combat zone, until Iraq. "There was no question of trying to get out of it. If I didn't go, someone else would." She's assigned to Saddam's Republican Presidential Palace. "It's part B-list palace, part trailer."

A master sergeant and senior noncommissioned officer, she actually hates conflict. "A lot of people in the army expect you to yell all the time, but I talk to my soldiers like they're human." A people pleaser: "But I'm getting better at expressing anger; kind of pissy, actually. Maybe it's Baghdad. I'm getting rockets launched at me almost daily, why should I fear a mere colonel?" An introvert. A die-hard Pat Benatar fan. She's a thesis short of completing her master's in clinical psychology. An alcoholic, sober eight months. "I drank to be more outgoing, but as the years went on I got more and more depressed." She goes to AA meetings at the palace, jokingly nicknamed the Sands of Recovery. "My worst days here are better than my best days before I got sober." She can't wait to go home to her husband and kids and leave "the sun from hell." Any lessons from Iraq? "I don't believe in everything our government does, but I do know we live in the best country in the world."

0826 I am groggy from too little sleep. Lately, I just can't slow my mind down until 1:00 or 2:00 in the morning. Maybe it's the constant coffee infusions—the black coffee that's replaced my nightly ration of beer since January. Maybe Freud was right and I've got an oral fixation, stuck in this stage of development because my mother didn't love me enough. It's as good an excuse as any for the mess I became.

Maybe it's the stress keeping me awake. The fear is always there. I just don't like to admit it. Last night, they said we could go home early, about 8:00 (lucky me) because the Intel folks expected "at least" seventy rockets, and mortars, and bombs (Oh my!). Not sure what good sending us "home" was supposed to do. You can't hide from a bomb. Definitely not from seventy of them, especially when your shelter is half a trailer, wrapped in one-sixteenth of an inch of sheet metal. I'm a sitting duck, trying to hide in a tin can in the desert.

Here in the "Green Zone," the headquarters of the coalition forces, we are supposed to be in the safest place in Iraq. Right. Concrete barriers, tight security, and lots of soldiers and civilians with guns and tanks fortify the area. Too bad they can't fortify the sky or the area outside in the Red

Zone to keep the enemy from launching rockets at us, because the number one and two targets, Ambassador Bremer (the administrator of the Coalition Provisional Authority, until yesterday) and General Kimmitt, work here.

Just as I was falling asleep, around 2:00, I heard them start. Only four. I counted. It seemed important to see if they'd really hit the magic number of seventy. After a few minutes of silence, I drifted back to sleep. The things I have gotten used to amaze me. Before you know it, I'll be like the ones who just stand there, talking on the cell phone. Will somebody lose it and scream at me the way I scream at them? The bad guys learn so much by what we say on the phones during attacks.

1019 I can't concentrate. People keep asking me for stuff. I just don't have the energy to help. I've finished learning to install and configure a printer on the network. There's something about fixing a problem that makes me feel good. I seldom get to see things through from start to finish. The big things in life never seem to get fixed. I've got my soldiers and Iraqi workers (mine get $12/day) preparing computers for issue and painting numbers on the doors of our new compound. I'm sure one of them is not happy. He worked until 11:00 last night and seems to think he deserves today off.

Smoking on the balcony. (Yeah, I know, it's bad. I can only give up one bad habit at a time. I'll be just about perfect on my deathbed.) The heat radiates from the concrete and marble on Saddam's veranda. Wonder if he'd laugh to see that it's now half filled with a plywood office (office-in-a-box). Goes with the trailers all over the palace grounds. The other half is full of broken-down office furniture, sand-caked, one-armed leather rolling chairs, and—that symbol of living large in America—the plastic patio table and chair set, $29.95 at Wal-Mart.

Marines sit around smoking Cuban cigars and flipping ashes into overflowing ashtrays. The Iraqi cleaning boys laugh, occasionally spitting on the old bastard's tile floors the coalition pays them $5 a day to clean. Every day, they risk being murdered by their fellow Muslims for working with us for $5. Now that no one will shoot them for not doing a good job, they seem to play at cleaning. These are my boys. I love them, but if they were soldiers they wouldn't think of doing such a half-ass job.

1249 I've been sent home by my Navy lieutenant to sleep. He's worried cuz I look like crap. Guess I look like I feel; now there's a surprise. It's supposed to be a day off for me, anyway. They try to give us at least a partial day once a week, a luxury for a soldier in a war. Drops the workweek down from ninety-six to eighty-plus hours. I came in to work because I thought there might be more moves, since State Department has just taken over from the Coalition Provisional Authority. All the really important people from Washington are here and need everything immediately. Yesterday, we turned the country over to the Iraqis. Just made me happy to be part of that. What a great day! I hope the colonel's picture of me in Bremer's office is better than mine! I looked like a geek!

1720 My short nap stretched to three-and-a-half hours on and off. Could be because of the six calls I got on the cell phone, one from the guy who made me go home. "Are you sleeping?" he asks. Somebody needs a key. Now.

1733 Trying to decide whether to go to the palace to eat. It's so hot. Don't know if it's worth it for the food they serve. There are so many things I want to do, but everything I consider doing doesn't seem worthy of wasting my precious time (still quoting Pat Benatar after all these years).

baghdad beth   119

1840   I just finished straightening up my room. Didn't take long; I have about six-by-six feet of living space, all but a small walkway taken up by the bed, wall, and footlockers. I don't bother with the dusting and floors. With all the sand here and the hot breeze, everything will be covered again within the hour. Still, I can't complain. It's cleaner and much cooler and private than the hundred-man tent I was in, or the top of a tank.

And thank God for those out there, trying to catch a few Zs on their Hummers. When it's 110 degrees for me, it's 130 for them in their flak jackets and helmets, with every manner of gear strapped to them. Getting shot at all the time. I'd never make it. I feel guilty for my luxuries, like I'm somehow less of a soldier. Sure I have inconveniences and the frequent barrage of mortars and rockets. Sometimes it's hard not to cry, thinking about cheating death because I had just moved fifteen feet to the left when a four-inch piece of lead shrapnel hit the ground. That's when I really started to want to go home.

Mostly I try to appear strong. It's my job and I hate looking weak. I see others do the same. The day the rocket hit the palace, we joked that at least they missed the pool. There'd be an ass whupping if the pool was wiped out. It's so cool under the palms—the site of nightly parties, booze, music, dancing, laughing, guns, tons of testosterone, two hundred guys and twenty women, endless flirtation and drunken shenanigans.

I remember the pool party we had shortly after I got here. Everybody was whooping it up except me. The colonel was introducing new people and saying good-bye to others. Then gunfire started up right outside the gate. He stopped talking for a moment and we all stood still. More gunfire. The colonel continued, saying, "We'll have to hurry." More shots. After the speech, the party started up again in earnest until it started raining. Then people ran like hell for cover. I was dumbfounded. Bullets get a couple of seconds of silent tension, but rain can clear out a crowd. Now I'm like that, too. I can ignore an explosion, but a door slamming will cause me to jump out of my chair.

1909 A shot just rang out. I feel a little rush in my gut, waiting for what will happen next. It's just some moron clearing his weapon into the sandbags before entering the palace grounds. Sounds like a 9 mm pistol. You're supposed to remove the magazine that holds the bullets, check for rounds in the chamber, and then fire into the sandbags to be sure your weapon is empty. Only certain people can have loaded guns in the embassy area. Evidently, this person forgot to remove the magazine. Gotta be a guy. Women are usually overly cautious with weapons. He will now have his gun taken and get escorted by armed Marines to the officer in charge of security. His boss will have to retrieve the pistol for him, and he will become the laughing stock of his office. This happened to one of my guys. We now call him Deputy Barney Fife.

1915 There's a boom in the distance, rocket or mortar. I am sitting next to a blast wall built from sandbags. Do I stay here? Do I go into the trailer and lie on the floor? Six minutes pass. I am about to miss dinner. Gotta hurry. The helicopters are flying now, heading out to check for damage and look for the culprit. Hopefully, the next one I hear won't be the medevac, going to pick up the wounded and dead. The hospital is overflowing with our soldiers and Iraqi men, women, and children.

1925 I get called into work on my way to dinner. I almost hit my bike into the wall trying to get the damn cell phone out of my pocket. Tomorrow is an Iraqi holiday to celebrate getting their country back. The embassy has decided to close. This is rare indeed. Must be all the new folks coming in to the State Department, not used to the twelve- to twenty-hour days. I need to make a schedule for my guys. We will all work a short period to make sure someone is here from the government side to cover emergencies.

1950 The scheduling took a few minutes; it's the software that takes so long. All the new stuff we have—smaller, better, faster—and more inconvenient than ever to do something simple. I stop to look at the pictures of my kids taped to the wall. In one, Matthew, the five-year-old, is dancing. He has lopped off one side of his bangs for the third or fourth time this year. Matthew lost his first tooth last week or the week before. I have no concept of time here. Can't keep the days straight.

To me, every day is Monday. It's the third Monday this week. My three months here have seemed like a year. I'm lucky. Only three months to go. If I make it. Did I actually admit that fear? I'll make it. I think God has sent me here for a reason, and I doubt it's to die. Maybe it's to finish getting well, to get more appreciative of all the good things I have at home, or to help others do the same. I have kids who need me. I will miss Matthew's first day of kindergarten, like I missed him swallowing that first lost tooth. On the phone he said, "Mommy, it fell all the way down my neck." I hope the tooth fairy remembered to come, since I wasn't there to remind him.

I missed my nine-year-old daughter, Lauren, making student of the week. And I have to live with the guilt of the kids being left with a sitter while my husband, Steve, went away on business. Lauren had a world-class meltdown, convincing the sitter, former lover of children, that she never wanted any of her own. Poor Steve. I think I have less stress amid the explosions than he does raising our kids alone.

I touch their pictures and get ready to leave. They are so beautiful. I won't be thinking that after I've been home awhile, except when they are sleeping or during some rare quiet moment. Instead of two-dimensional, quiet, smiling children—my babies—I get screaming, fighting, biting, bouncing-off-the-walls little monsters who demand more of my attention than my current sixteen-hour workday and 9,700 complaining customers. Sometimes, they just need more than I can give.

2010 I am late for my AA meeting. I'm going, anyway. Don't know if I'd still be doing so well without these meetings to straighten me out and make me laugh. It's Gordon's last meeting. I have to say good-bye. Well, at least he won't be kissing me on the neck and ear anymore. His little way of saying hello. He's really quite harmless, I think!

2100 The meeting is over. Gordon told his story, a tradition at a last meeting in a particular location. We all have so much in common—that void we try to fill with alcohol, only to find it's never enough. Multiple obsessions and addictions, not just to substances, but also related to perfectionism and fear. So many fears. They're at the root.

2110 I tell Lucy, my AA sponsor, about my day. She introduces me to the social worker at the Combat Stress Control Clinic. I joke that I have a long history with social workers. I've been to counseling on and off since '96, dealing with the depression that's plagued me all my life. Despite the counseling, my primary means of coping was beer, lots of it. Miller Lite, to be exact. Though, after the first one, who cares.

baghdad beth 123

I'm thankful to God, to the army doctor who sent me to AA against my will, and to all my counselors for finally convincing me that alcohol was more of a problem than solution. Without medicating myself with beers all day, I'm actually not depressed. I have moments of happiness, a real turnaround for me. I don't think I could make it here if I was still drinking. I'd have done my job, but inside I would've been hating myself and everything around me. Instead, my soldiers wonder how I take a seeming disaster and turn it into a joke. I guess I know a thing or two about disaster.

2215 I am finally eating chow. Tacos that taste like dog food, rubbery roast beef, greasy hash brown patties, and cold, mushy vegetables (at least the fork will cut through something). I've taken three bites and I'm already on my second plastic fork. I yearn for the "sporks" that used to come in our field rations. Once, when we ran out of the plastic ones, we got some actual metal ones. They were the size of shrimp forks. They had to post signs to keep us from throwing them away. We just weren't used to real utensils.

Yesterday, while removing computers from the British envoy's office, I found a complete set of silverware, heavy, expensive stuff. I really had to check myself to resist "acquiring" it. In army speak, "acquire" is not quite stealing, but you may have to break a rule or do some serious trading or sucking up to get it. I reluctantly left the silver behind. I'd just have to wash the stuff between meals, which I'm too lazy to do. (No hot water in the palace, anyway.)

I have just acquired two small packages of cereal and the lovely chalky-tasting long-shelf-life milk to go with it for morning. More hoarding. Who knows if we'll have cereal tomorrow? I do the same with toilet paper, paper towels, printer cartridges, trash bags, hand soap, office supplies, bottled water, you name it. As the senior sergeant, it's part of my job to make sure we have supplies. This place is making me crazy. If the bombs don't get me, the supply situation or the messy bathroom in the office will. The other seventy-nine people occupying our offices and using the same toilet don't seem to concern themselves with minor details, like ensuring we can wash our hands and wipe our behinds. No wonder dysentery (also known as "Saddam's revenge") runs rampant here. Oh, they make me sooo mad.

I probably do need to work out more, but maybe I get so angry over the silly stuff because I can control those situations. The other day, when a rocket hit by my trailer camp shaking the palace, all we could do was hit the deck and hope for the best. I just can't let anybody see me lose my cool or show weakness when something like that happens. I'm not supposed to be afraid, I'm supposed to kick butt and take names.

2355 All's quiet, unless you count the sound of the helicopters flying overhead. They're pretty much a constant at night, a part of the white noise that will eventually lull me to sleep. Tomorrow, *enshalla,* or God willing, I'll wake up to my alarm and not more bombs over Baghdad. Then I'll laugh and bitch my way through the ninety-fourth Monday in a row.

The Cost of War

1400 It is quiet around here. The last time it was this quiet a semi truck full of TNT exploded by the Mosul police station, injuring several and killing some of our military police from Post. It is hard on all of us. We held a memorial service today for our fallen comrades. It was their last mission to the police station downtown; the Iraqis were going to be taking over control. When the mortars hit, it makes you afraid to go outside, to go or do anything. All the mortars have been hitting close to the hospital. I thought there was a law against firing on hospitals? I am truly beginning to think that the only good Iraqi is a dead one. I hate feeling this way, but when they are continually trying to kill you, it just happens. I pray that my heart will be softened and that when all is said and done I will be able to forgive them. It is hard when an Iraqi patient comes in and we have to treat him with the same care and respect that we show our own.

Miriam Scott, 28, Elk Ridge, Utah; sergeant in charge
of the hospital dental clinic, U.S. Army (serving in Iraq)

Miscellaneous Moments

Personal Shopper

9:45 a.m. The mall opens at ten, so I thought I could get in fast to return the summer jacket I bought. I thought the saleslady and I were the only two souls in the department store, but as I turned to walk out, I saw a lady waving me to come over. She looked familiar, but turned out to be a stranger. She held out a pair of blue plaid slacks and asked me to help her find a blouse to go with them. Okay, I thought. She was sincere so I helped her. Then she said, "I brought in a bag of my slacks; they all need blouses." Twenty minutes later I had gotten her settled with blouses for all her slacks. She thanked me and then assured me that, when she goes to church, she wears a dress. That had not occurred to me, but I told her that she looked well dressed and I was sure was always properly attired. She thanked me again, and I rushed out to my car.

Louise G. Fradkin, 76, Levittown, Pennsylvania

Tradition

3:00 p.m. I am starving! Thank God for moms who pack lunches for their darling daughters. Mum is helping me get back in shape by preparing healthy lunches. Some folks wonder that I still live with my parents, but I could not imagine us living in the same town and not living together. After all, Indian daughters live with their parents until they are married or dead, and since I am neither, I get to be with them.

Sajida Shroff, 34, Atlanta, Georgia; education director

Athens

1:00 p.m.   I head with a teammate to the mall. We drive out the entrance of the Olympic Training Center and I see the sign that counts down the days until the Olympics. I will be competing in Athens in forty-seven days! Sometimes I just wish it would hurry up and get here; then other times I feel I am not ready and I want more time.

Tara Nott-Cunningham, 32, Mt. Pleasant, Michigan; Olympic weightlifter

Ethan "Hank" Hunt

Mid-morning   Went grocery shopping but, more importantly, I dropped off film that has been sitting on my countertop since late February. I even opened the box, Ethan's box, to get one cartridge out. Perhaps it seems melodramatic to deliberately drop off film of my dead baby on this particular day, but this way I can perhaps see his name in print. Ethan "Hank" Hunt. He won't be just the baby I lost, unnamed and unmentioned. People, especially customers at the library, ask me if I have any children. I have said no but flinched at the denial. And I have said yes, but the answers to the inevitable follow-up questions fluster the asker. What can anyone say?

LeAnne P. Hunt, 30, Pflugerville, Texas; library clerk

Nursing Home Resident

Marie Colwill, 87, Sioux Falls, South Dakota

She moved to Good Samaritan a year ago, after a back operation left her in a wheelchair. Married sixty-five years; widowed for five. Four adult children spread across the country. When her kids started school, she started cleaning houses. Retired at age seventy-five. Her own home of sixty years is up for sale. "I ask the senior transit driver if he can sometimes go by my place. At least I get to see it." She likes for her morning caretakers to dress her as soon as she's up. Get ready for the day. Most weeks, somebody—from her church or a neighbor—comes by to visit. "I like it when people are spicy and react with me." She loves reading, word searches, and game shows. "I'm interested in enough things; I just wish there was something else I could do." A happy person. "The Lord gave me an uplifted feeling about life. Every once in a while I have the thought,

*You're so alone, but never mind, make the most of it. The
Lord is my Savior, so keep on going."*

First I want to tell you I'm in this good nursing home, but
I can't walk.

6:00 a.m.   My caretaker dresses me for the day. Thinking of what I am going to do.

6:15 a.m.   Thank God for a new day. Also, ask him to
forgive my sins and to give me a clean heart.

6:30 a.m.   Ask my caretaker to take me to the beauty
shop. I am upset that two others beat me there. Listen to
some news and some gossip (not mean gossip).

8:00 a.m.   They take me to the exercise room to do my
exercise. I sit on this thing and hang on to the bars with my
hands. My feet are pumping when I move my hands so I
feel like it keeps my whole body moving. I do that for fifteen minutes a day, five times a week.

9:00 a.m.   Go back to my room to wait for some ladies
to come to have a Bible study. We meet every Tuesday. We
tell of good things, take prayer requests. We sing and then
study a chapter in the Bible. We've even prayed that the
next family who moves into my house might be Christian
and enjoy the place like I did all them sixty years. It was a
good study. They left at 10:30.

10:45 a.m.   Clean up and go to lunch. We sit at a table
and chit-chat before the food is brought to us. There are
three of us at my table. Some meals almost go by without
talking. The other day I was thinking, What table would I
like to sit at? There are two tables that seem to be talking

all the time. I could move if I wanted to, but it might not be the right thing to do. Maybe I'm supposed to be here.

Noon   I'm brought back to my room for an hour nap.

1:00 p.m.   Get up and read my mail. Also read a book, *Forever Ruined for the Ordinary* by Joy Dawson. I love reading biographies and Christian books.

2:00 p.m.   Watched TV.

3:00 p.m.   Went to dining room to listen to some music. Then try to guess the title of the song. I like doing this. I sing within myself a lot, but I wish I would sing more out loud.

4:00 p.m.   Watch some more TV, like *Who Wants to Be a Millionaire*. Some of the questions, I can answer them. I do fairly good. I don't know why I watch that *Jeopardy*. I always watch just the last five minutes of *Family Feud* to see if they win the $20,000.

5:00 p.m.   Get ready for evening meal. Good meal. It's such a variety of food here. I like best the pork spareribs. I do like the chicken, and I do like the thighs, and when they have a pie. Sunday is always a day for pie.

6:30 p.m.   Went to activities room to play bingo. I won a quarter and had lots of fun. One time I won three and was elated!

7:45 p.m.   Come back to my room to watch more TV and sit around 'til bedtime, which is 10 p.m. Reminisce about the day and plan for tomorrow. If something good happens, I say to myself, I've got to tell this to Eddie (he died five years ago).

Husbands

8:40 a.m. Dog walk. Bill interrupts walk reverie with dictatorial: "Heads up. Dog ahead. Shorten your leash." I am thoroughly annoyed. I don't need him to point out a pip-squeak dog. And then our dog, Alex, went ballistic, howling and barking and nearly ripping off my arm to get at the pip-squeak dog, which, incidentally, was littler even than little Alex. The other dog and its owner were unflappable. They strolled off grinning at my discomfiture. I hate when William is right.

> *Lynn Ruehlmann, 56, Norfolk, Virginia; professional storyteller*

9:15–10:30 a.m. We are here in Portugal because of the European Cup and my husband Jay is the number-one aficionado. He is such a fan that he brought soccer uniforms for all of the possible teams he likes that could end up competing. This way he can wear the right uniform during the game. That's right ladies, step off, he's with me.

> *Paulina Goldman, 30, South Brunswick, New Jersey; advocate, Latina nonprofit*

10:20 p.m.   I told my husband that I consumed moldy banana nut cake, and he was more upset that he didn't get to sample the cake before it went moldy.

Jackie Joice, 36, Long Beach, California; substitute teacher

5:20 a.m.   My husband rolls over and kisses me and partially lies on me. Instead of thinking, "I'm so lucky," I think, "This is hot and sticky." But I don't say anything because I know I am lucky. It's just a matter of remembering this at the right time.

Tamara S. Morgan, 46, East Randolph, Vermont; research associate

Morning   I'm in the kitchen where my husband, Mike, gives me a hug and kiss. He is not a coffee drinker but has brewed a pot of decaf for me. Bless him! In our earlier married years, this little act of thoughtfulness would never have occurred to him. After forty-two years, he performs these little touches that are so dear without being asked. He says he didn't help in the kitchen in our early married years because he wanted our daughters to acquire home-making skills. Is that a lame excuse?

Ann Moore, 69, Evergreen, Colorado; inventor of the Snugli

9:30 a.m.   My husband wakes and we talk about the day. He has been much kinder lately because he knows I am considering leaving. What he does not know is that I have already rented a storage unit and have started moving. I dislike leading a double life. Deceit makes me feel ugly inside. My husband thinks that if I do move, it won't be until August or September . . . my family is ready to help me move this week.

Diane Elizabeth Price-Powers, 51, Waterford, Vermont; copy center associate

Afternoon We drive along the shoreline of Lake Huron. My husband, Sonny, is a master of observation and detail. When we pass a green Porta-Potty—ever present in Michigan during summer roadwork—he says to my amazement, "I've used that outhouse before." I think, Who else do I know who might say something like that?

   Ann M. Green, 57, Brooklyn, Michigan; English
   professor

6:00 p.m. We get home and the kids try on their new clothes. They look great. Then my husband tries on a new suit he bought by *himself!* We were all a little bit scared when he told us this, but he looks like a movie star!

   Cecilia Angell, Verona, New Jersey; professional opera
   singer

8:15 a.m. My husband is up. I'm so glad I married this guy. I still don't know who he is, but after twenty-eight years together that doesn't seem to be a critical success factor.

   Susan Bowers, 55, Santa Cruz, California;
   costumer/artist

On June 29, 2004 . . .

42% of day diarists spent quality time with their partners.

88% did not have sex.

11% fought with their partners . . . 65% of those who fought made up.

~~~~~~

Foreign Correspondent

Ayla Jean Yackley, 32, Istanbul, Turkey

She moved to Istanbul in 2000, a reporter for Reuters News Agency. Half Turkish on her mom's side, she already knew the language. At first, she covered "softer, gentler" stories (camel-wrestling), but then came September 11, the war in neighboring Iraq, suicide bombings, anti-U.S. street protests. "Turkey's one of the best places to be a reporter. Sometimes it's emotionally difficult, but I have to say it's exciting."

From a small town outside Chicago, her parents opened up her world. At age three, she took her first trip, solo, to visit her grandparents in Turkey. At nine, she spent a year with relatives in Germany. Now she gets back to the States about once a year. Single, she chalks it up to kismet and the job. "Work really is the most important thing in my life. It defines me right now." Despite her heritage, she feels more like a tourist than a Turk.

Loves the excitement of Istanbul and the mix of people;
hates the machismo. "I get into fights daily with cab driv-
ers because they're not being respectful to me. I'm trying
to fight an age-old tradition in a ten-minute cab drive."
Social. Optimistic. Ambitious. She's at a crossroads. "Part
of me dreams of buying a flat with a Bosphorus view, or
maybe I'll go back to the U.S. or move to a crazy, new
place. I need another five-year plan."

Midnight Turkey's largest city, Istanbul, is hosting a
two-day NATO summit attended by more than forty world
leaders, including President Bush. His visit coincides with
the top world news story: The U.S. administration handed
over power to the Iraqis two days before scheduled in a
low-profile ceremony held in a basement.

12:30 a.m. In Istanbul, the news continued late into the
evening. I'd spent most of my day in the air-conditioned
bowels of the NATO convention hall, waiting to interview
the Romanian prime minister, far away from the street
protests in which hundreds of leftists decried U.S. policy in
the Middle East. Dozens were hurt in clashes between protesters and police. I leave the bureau past midnight after
writing about an explosion at the Turkish Defense Min-
istry in the capital.

A series of bomb blasts have rattled Turkey in the days
before the summit. In the deadliest attack, a left-wing
bomber killed herself and three others on a bus last week.
Chaos is knocking at the door. Most of the ire is directed
at Bush. For many, he represents an arrogant, belligerent
side of America, and people here are increasingly loath to
discern between Americans and the policies of their gov-

ernment. What is good about my country has been over-shadowed by those perceptions, and I think it will take generations to undo the damage.

Security is unprecedented. Police have sealed off a vast section of the city, the so-called NATO Valley, where Bush, other leaders, and thousands of alliance delegates and journalists are gathering. A lot of people I know have fled Istanbul for the beach. Good for them. This roiling city of fifteen million people has ground to a halt, while my cab zips through dark, empty streets.

1:30 a.m. It was my umpteenth day in a row at work and I am tired. But it always takes me a couple of hours to wind down after leaving the office. I putter about, trying to do something about the disaster zone that is my flat. Something in the fridge stinks—chaos also looms at home. Kismet, my white cat, squeals when I open a can of cat food. It is good to come home to her warm body, but I am painfully aware of the cliché about unmarried women in their thirties with cats. The Turks have an expression, "She was left behind at home."

Not fair. I am a long way from my hometown in Illinois. It's a strange life, but it's often exhilarating. Being a reporter helps satiate my endless curiosity, but I also count the opportunity costs. I miss my family and sense I have fallen off the radar screens of many old friends. They're getting married and working on the next generation. I always thought I would have a gaggle of kids, but I haven't even met a contender for a husband yet. So, I've resigned myself to spinsterdom, just so that I won't be disappointed when I really am old and alone. I'm such a Capricorn.

The call to prayer begins, so I know it's past 3 a.m. Mosques in Turkey, no matter how old, are invariably outfitted with loudspeakers. One by one they launch into the *azan* until it is a cacophony of prayer. It's loud, but I've always liked the rhythm of the call and fall asleep before it's over.

I wake up past 10 a.m. I am still tired and linger in the shower. I feed Kismet again and wonder if she should be on a diet. I put on a skirt and a cute top in case I need to head back to NATO Valley. I skip breakfast, as usual, and walk outside into a sunny day. I live in an older part of Istanbul, with crumbling Art Nouveau buildings, old churches, and cobblestone streets. I feel good about being here. I need to head back to the bureau for the late shift.

10:40 a.m. I turn the corner and see dozens of police in riot gear blocking the top of the street. Anti-NATO demonstrators have descended upon a square in my normally cheerful neighborhood. I phone the bureau to let my colleague know it is simmering here, and then all hell breaks loose.

Members of labor unions, the Turkish Communist Party, and other political groups are chanting the classic "Yankee, go home" and "Get out, imperialist America." Around fifteen young men carrying orange flags emblazoned with some obscure affiliation on long wooden poles march up to the square. They are jumpy, ready for battle. The orange flags turn toward the police line and suddenly begin bashing the cops' shields with the flagpoles-cum-weapons. The police set off more tear gas and tackle protesters trying to move into the side streets.

The air is noxious. The gas clusters in the narrow streets that characterize this district. Despite covering many protests in Turkey, it's my first time inhaling tear gas. Spit and snot stream from my mouth and nose. I watch three cops pin down a guy who is not resisting arrest and spray Mace into his mouth. Police academies in this country seem to have skipped the chapter on "how to restrain your suspect." Turkish police pull hair and bite and kick their detainees in the stomach. It's like a bad bar fight.

I chase after two officers carting off an angry young woman and ask her what she is protesting. "This is about the struggle of the world's people," she shouts. She tells me she's from Austria before the cops yell at me to back off.

I am pressed up against a small nook in a wall and call the bureau to begin filing material to my colleague. I am carrying my reporter's notebook, and three press accreditation cards dangle from my neck. I am wearing a smart skirt, for crying out loud. I am clearly not part of the Maoist brigade. But a cop picks me out and, from an inch away, sprays Mace into my face.

Pepper spray stings immediately, but it takes a few minutes to pack its full punch. My face and chest are on fire, I cannot breathe. Someone I can't see gives me water and I gag. The noon sun scalds my face. I stagger up the street and see a pharmacy. The owner has shuttered her shop during the demonstration, but she and her daughters arc inside eating sandwiches. They usher me in and are frantic to help. I beg for ice while the pharmacist mixes eye drops, and one of the girls applies ointment to my face. The burning won't stop. I'm pacing and crying and worrying I have ruined their lunch. The girl giggles and says, "You look really scary," and urges me to look in the mirror. My face is swollen and purple. The pharmacist puts the medicine and an ice pack in a bag and won't take my money. She strokes my hair and orders me straight home to bed.

2:00 p.m.   I make my way back to the square and spot a friend. He offers me a cigarette I cannot smoke, then says he hears the police are using a spray that makes your skin peel off. Great, all I need is more skin problems. Even police assault won't curb my vanity. I inspect myself again. That cute top is streaked red with dried pepper spray. My friend gets a call: A bomb has exploded on a Turkish Airlines plane. I need to go to the office to help handle the mayhem. The protests are a mere sideshow to the summit.

Three cleaners are hurt when a package bomb left on board the plane detonates. No deaths. I watch TV as Bush urges Muslim countries to fight terror and emulate Turkey, a secular democracy. The backdrop of his speech is a Baroque mosque on the Bosphorus waterway and one of Istanbul's modern suspension bridges that links the city's Asian and European sides. My eyes keep watering and the skin beneath my fingernails burns. A Turkish news channel filmed the rogue Macing me, and it's repeated a few times for posterity.

7:00 p.m. The Turkey bureau chief, our editor from London, and other Reuters correspondents plan a fish dinner out on the Bosphorus to celebrate the end of the NATO nightmare. I handle a few more stories and arrive at the restaurant after 10 p.m. and am high-fived by the crew. They get a kick out of my street-fighting tale: "You should have seen the other guy," and so on. I leave the restaurant to meet a journalist friend in town for the summit, and our one drink turns into six.

He has covered a few wars and, though I've never been on a front line, we talk about violence when it becomes a part of life. I am inured to it. I've seen the rag-doll torsos and missing faces of suicide bombers, gotten sick from the ammonia of fertilizer bombs, talked to victims maimed or blinded in an attack, felt my desk shake and known instinctively it was a bomb. I am no longer shocked by an attack. Instead, I am constantly irrationally preparing for one. I scrutinize the security when I enter a public building. I case out exit points or protective doorways when I walk down small streets. I don't tell people I'm American. Buses unnerve me. When I cross the bridge to Asia, I think, They could take the bridge out; this would be a good target.

Turkey isn't in the middle of a war. Neither is Spain nor Bali nor Morocco. But the trouble in this region has infected other parts of the world. It's a bit childish, but I think of it as a monster that has been released from its cage and won't return quietly. I am afraid the guys who say they are protecting us are the ones who have actually created the monster, that their actions plunge us further into peril.

I get home in the wee hours and collapse into bed. I don't like that I take bloody street protests or suicide bombings in stride. They are outrageous, and it's inhumane to be so cynical. Stray cats outside my window are fighting. Chaos on my street. Then I wonder if I have anything clean to wear to work tomorrow. Don't forget to pay the electricity bill again. You're almost out of toilet paper, I tell myself before drifting off.

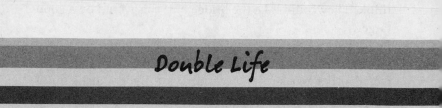

Double Life

7:00 a.m. A quick look into their open bedroom door—I see them still sleeping side by side. My mother, eighty-nine, with her broken wrist casted to the elbow; my dad, eighty-eight, sleeping on his back. Even in sleep he seems less powerful than before his heart attack and that broken shoulder of three months ago.

I put on my paint-encrusted dungarees and work boots, heavy and broken in ("too manly," my mother once said with a curled lip). My mind flashes on my home life a few hours away in Provincetown and my professional life in San Diego. Deadlines and phone calls and e-mail. I'm up to number five on my mental to-do list for the university when I tell myself out loud, "Stop. Not now. Later. Now is for this and this only." Saying this out loud is a trick I have taught myself—quiet one life while I live the other.

7:30–11:00 a.m. Scraped an entire side of the house. Mid-morning, Dad waves to me from a bedroom window. I think he'll insist on coming out to help. He never does. Oh, how the mighty have fallen. I taste dust, flecks of paint. Use my kerchief as a sweatband and goggle cleaner.

11:15 a.m.–12:15 p.m. Debbie (home health aide) arrives in red pickup truck. She is sweet. We will probably never see her again. Different one will come every day. Jesus. I show her Mom's stuff. She talks nonstop, flat affect, about her husband's cancer. My mother likes this. She feels better when discussing the misery of others. Too bad Debbie can't come every day. She brings great tragedy. A healing bonus. I shower.

12:15–1:00 p.m. Dad has made grits, toast, and one egg for the three of us. Mother says, "Shame on you," for having only one egg in the house. I say, "I'll go to the store," and the tension diffuses. We sit outside in the speckled shade, Mom trailing her fifty-foot oxygen cord. I say, "Let's make the Day's Plan." They are hard of hearing (okay, nearly deaf) and the conversation is loopy and annoying to them both. But we agree. A trip to town for Mum and me, and Poppa will stay home and ponder a railing installation for the front step. I watch him use his foldout wooden ruler, stoop shouldered, and I am flooded with how much I love him and identify with him.

1:00–about 2:00 p.m. I take the thirty-eight-pound wheelchair (yes, I weighed it once) outside, but first sneak a minute to make my bed. Sloppy, but it'll do.

I walk Mom on the sandy driveway. Oxygen tank on wheelchair seat, she pushes the chair with her one working hand. Oxygen up to 4 for exercise. I hold her waistband in the back, in case I need to keep her from falling. I am part gymnastics spotter and part service dog. I picture myself sporting a vest that reads, "Working." We walk with no stumbles. Success. She sits, laboring for breaths, while I push her down the bumpy driveway.

2:00 p.m. I read her *Cape Cod Ghost Stories*. She loves this. I do dramatic stuff, wind sounds, horse hooves clacking on the road. Then I use the flimsy excuse of wanting online research about a telephone bell ringer enhancer to call my partner, Suze, in Provincetown. My personal life gets thirty seconds of airtime. Suze's voice makes me feel whole. We hate being apart. I hear our dogs bark in the background. Back to the ghost stories.

2:30 p.m. Prepare to go into town. Fill two oxygen tanks (in case one malfunctions). Dad gives road directions. I could drive this blindfolded, but I listen patiently. Drive eight miles into town: video store (rent *Cast Away* for them for tonight); groceries (including a dozen "shameful" eggs); and hardware store. Mom rests, head back, eyes closed. "The sun feels good."

4:00 p.m. (Or 1:00 in California.) Now I can do some university work. Maybe while Mom naps? Tree Guy is not due until after 5:00. Get Mom's sneakers off, tuck her under the lightweight blanket. Kiss her forehead. Years of steroid use have made her skin tissue thin. I look at my own olive skin, tan and taut, and get a lump in my throat.

Shit. Tree Guy is an hour early—smiling, gap-toothed Sebastian. There goes Mom's nap. She wants to be part of this. I help her dress (third time today) and seat her outside in a folding lawn chair. I decide to throw out the chair beside her because she could get cut on its sharp edges. Must do this on the sly as Dad might see it as wasteful. Could trigger a Great Depression lecture.

My dad's deafness and Sebastian's working English make for a convoluted but friendly exchange. I decide I'll be here the day Sebastian comes to do the cutting. I picture a razed yard and wood chips everywhere if I don't. You're not a savior, I reprimand myself. You can't be here all the time. Time! Call the office and see if the graduate student pay scale was sent in on time.

this day in the life 144

5:00 p.m.   I asked Dad, fifty-two-year maven of running his own country hardware store, to teach me how to cut window glass. So on the picnic table he shows me. "Keep the sheetrock underneath brushed smooth and clean," he intones, and I lean in to see how his fingers hold the cutter. He watches while I practice. I listen for the correct "crunch" as the cutting wheel bites the glass. I see him become Hardware Man again, a scholar of home fixing. Mom even comes over to watch. They applaud when I make a few crisp cuts and snap off the glass cleanly. I decide right then that every time I am here I will ask my dad to teach me a skill. We decide next time it will be how to replace leaky sink washers. This plan tickles us both.

6:15 p.m.   Put Mom to bed. She says it's just for a nap, but I know that's it for the day. Put her slinged arm on pillow, check oxygen tube for—What am I checking for? It's never had a leak or come disconnected. I stoop and pat her silky gray hair and say I love you.

"Today was wonderful," she says. Wonderful? This is a rare compliment and I feel heady.

Outside, I put the ladder away from today's scraping, load their laundry into my car, show Dad how I mended my windshield crack with Superglue. "Good job," he says. "No need for a new one," and he claps me on the back. He thanks me for everything I did today. "You don't have to come so often," he says. "I know you have your own life."

I tell him I wanted to be here (and today, I did). We hug good-bye. Twice. I don't want to leave, but I have to leave.

Susan E. Cayleff, 50, Provincetown, Massachusetts and San Diego, California; professor and chair, Department of Women's Studies, San Diego State University

Eternal Optimist
Working Two Jobs

Paige Balter, 28, Portland, Oregon

She'd tried college before—even had an academic scholarship—but was miserable, flunking out. "I had no idea what I was interested in." Five years working at a coffee shop taught her a trade. "It was cool. I discovered I loved customer service." But it also convinced her she needed a degree. Now she's a full-time fine arts student while working as a barista and computer support technician. Retro. She loves to sew hippie dresses. Wears her hair down to her waist. Her favorite movie is Jesus Christ Superstar. *When she was five, her parents divorced. She and her mom and little brother moved every year. A shy kid, a worrier. "Books were my friends." At twelve, she decided to live with her dad and stepmom. "I wanted so badly to stay in one place." Her philosophy now—she's where she should be; God's got a plan; things will always work out. Married going on two years. "We* got really blessed. We wanted to be healthier, make good decisions, and we saw we could do that together." They put their TV in the closet. "There's so much more time in the day!" A hugger. A Pollyanna. "I'm always playing the Glad Game, where you find something to be glad about, even if the world's falling apart."

5:30 a.m. Alarm goes off. Radio, Air America. Randi Rhodes is ranting. She makes me laugh sometimes. I hit snooze.

5:39 a.m. Alarm again. I have to reach over my husband, Daniel, to get to the radio. It wakes him up. We spoon. I love this time of day. He whispers, "You're so loved. In a minute someone else is going to come in here and tell you he loves you." He is referring to our sixteen-pound tabby cat, Pooka.

5:48 a.m. Radio/alarm again. Cat shows up. He likes to lie so that half of him is on Daniel and half is on me. I usually get his back half. Everything around me is so warm and soft right now. I loathe the idea of getting up.

5:57 a.m. Alarm again. I sit up, dislodge cat in process.

5:59 a.m. Walk naked to bathroom. Look in mirror. I always feel my body looks best early in the morning without clothes on. If we had a digital thermometer I'd take my basal temperature to chart ovulation.

6:05 a.m. Back in bedroom staring at basket of clean clothes. I really should have laid out an outfit last night! Find a pair of underwear full of holes. You mean I still

eternal optimist working two jobs **147**

haven't thrown these out yet?! Well, I can't now. I'm running late.

6:10 a.m.   Find cute tank top and skirt, unearth yesterday's bra, find sandals. Dress!

6:12 a.m.   Snuggle with "Baboo" (Daniel), kiss, love up. He smells so good! His left hand is on top of the covers and I click my wedding ring against his. It's our solidarity gesture. He's sort of awake, so I give him a quick rundown of my day, where I'll be and when. His degenerative disc disease keeps him in constant back pain and unable to work.

6:15 a.m.   Feed cat, gather purse and keys, out the door. I love the cool morning air and quiet. The sunflowers filling the flower bed by the door say hello. Some of them are taller than my 5'10" self.

6:16 a.m.   I see that Daniel set out the garbage and recycling bins after his walk the night before. "Good man! What a good man!" I say. Neighbor woman across the street drives away. I wonder where.

6:17 a.m.   I need coffee. I'll stop at Starbucks on my way to the freeway, though that may seem weird since I'm going to my job at a coffee shop!

6:18 a.m.   I see a woman walking a papillon, a little French dog. I think of my mom. She has one named Maddy. I miss Mom. She's living in Minnesota, far from us here in Portland.

6:19 a.m.   There are two women in surgical hospital outfits in Starbucks. I have more and more interest in women around me and what they do. I get my usual twelve-ounce Double Americano with cream and a ginger lemon scone. Pretty unhealthy, but dang, I love them! It's the only caffeine I allow myself, since I heard a few months ago that caffeine affects a woman's ability to conceive. I want to have a baby so much, even though I still have a year left of school. But I'm already twenty-eight and Daniel's forty-five. I don't want to wait any longer.

6:20 a.m. Boy, that first sip of coffee is good! I think being a coffee shop customer first thing in the morning sets me up to have empathy for my customers the rest of the day.

6:22 a.m. Low fuel light in car comes on. I feel the same old helplessness. I just spent $1.65 on coffee; I could have bought gas with that. Well, I guess you could say I bought gas for me! I would like to paint this morning light. It's gorgeous!

6:24 a.m. Relatively smooth freeway merge. Never thought I'd be a freeway commuter, listening to the traffic report on the radio. Traffic slows, I'll be late. Damn!

6:28 a.m. I love this bridge! I always feel like I could fly right off it over the Willamette River. The sign for the exit I take says "Ocean Beaches," but I have to take the 12th Avenue ramp. Sometimes I think, What if I just stayed on the freeway? My heart squeezes up. I can't remember the last time I felt able to be spontaneous, the last time I didn't feel just a little bit trapped. So much depends on me.

6:29 a.m. Good parking spot near work. I'll plug the meter at 8:00.

eternal optimist working two jobs **149**

6:30 a.m.   Unlock coffee shop door, turn off alarm. Brew coffee, count out till, open store. Automatic pilot takes over at work.

8:15 a.m.   Boss, Jenny, comes in. She is really nice, cheerful, and always up front about how she thinks the employees are doing. I like not having to guess about that.

9:00 a.m.   Lila comes in. It's her last day! She's worked here for three years. In between customers, I tell Jenny and Lila a story from last night. Daniel and I went grocery shopping. We couldn't find the canned vegetable aisle because the store hides it among the paper product aisles. I bitched to Daniel about this. He said, "First-world complaint." It made me laugh and think. Same for Jenny and Lila.

9:15 a.m.   I make Lila a "Today is my last day!" sign to wear so she doesn't have to tell everyone.

9:30 a.m.   Break time. I toast a blueberry bagel, grab an orange cream yogurt, get the paper. The headline says, "Supreme Court rejects detention tactics." YAY! That was such a grief. My faith in humanity and, more so, America, feels somewhat restored.

9:45 a.m.   Break over. It's so rushed! No time to eat the yogurt. Hard on me, on my mind, stomach, body, posture, to have to hurry like that.

11:20 a.m.   My turn to sweep around the outside tables. What is up with people throwing their cigarette butts on the ground?! It's like people just dropping their used Kleenex! It's so GROSS. I will NEVER understand why that is socially acceptable.

11:55 a.m. Jenny shows me a new copy of the schedule for next month. She is hoping I can work more hours. Oh boy. I want to; it just means making changes in the schedule at my other job.

Noon Count out tips. $22.28, that's $11.14 each. Give Lila her half; hug her good-bye.

12:05 p.m. Grab yogurt, tips, new schedule, head for car. Oops, I forgot to take the garbage out again. Dang! Figuring the budget in my head on the way to the car. It's so tight! We want to go to the Rainbow Gathering this year in Northeast California. Twenty thousand hippies camping in the woods for a week. This will be my first time! It will cost a lot for gas, and we leave in two days. I'm just hoping we'll have enough money for the trip!

12:08 p.m. I have to poo. There's NO TIME. I have to stop and get gas before I get on the freeway. I have to get home, then back downtown to start other job at 1:00. Stress!

12:20 p.m. At gas station. I can just afford $7 gas. Sigh. I give the guy a 50-cent tip. I wish I could do more. Ever since that summer Daniel pumped gas, I've always tried to remember to tip the station attendant. Low fuel light is off for the moment. Yay!

12:25 p.m. On freeway to home. One place, where the overpass meets the ground, there's a homeless camp. They have a full-sized mattress. The bed is ALWAYS neatly made, with a gray coverlet, pillows, and a pink stuffed animal on the pillows. Almost surreal. I think about the people who live there. I wonder how I could help them.

12:30 p.m.   Freeway musings: I met a girl named Rainbow at the coffee shop this morning. Maybe we could name our baby Rainbow if we have one. Hey, what if we conceived at the Rainbow Gathering! That would be perfect!

12:37 p.m.   Car has this weird squeak. That sucks. How can we still be so poor? I'm working almost forty hours per week! A few blocks from home. There's Daniel! I pick him up. He was on a walk to get coffee.

12:45 p.m.   Home! Poo. Yay. Call second job, tell them I'll be there around 1:15.

12:50 p.m.   Get back in car. Daniel is driving me back downtown. He needs the car tonight for his writing group facilitator training.

12:52 p.m.   Daniel just compared me to Rain Man. Smile.

12:55 p.m.   Take hair out of ponytail. That feels better. My armpits smell good.

12:56 p.m.   Tell Daniel about Rainbow, my baby-naming idea. He says, "If you go through the experience of pregnancy and shit a baby out, you can name it anything you want." I love him.

12:57 p.m.   He asked me to braid his hair when we get parked downtown. I can only find sparkly pink rubber bands to hold them, though. We laugh at that.

12:58 p.m.   I'd picked up a bottle of insect repellent when looking for rubber bands. Got some on my fingers. It smells good. I put some behind my ears. Interesting mix with the coffee smells.

1:00 p.m.   We talk on the drive about whether sexual molestation at a young age could lead to interest in sex at a young age.

1:05 p.m.   We park. I braid his hair. It looks good! We hug, kiss, pray God's protection over each other. As he drives away, I meow at him and flash the sign language shorthand for "I love you." Another ritual.

1:15 p.m.   Going into work is hard. I'm hungry. Wish I'd had time for lunch. Take elevator to 8th floor.

1:20 p.m.   Check e-mail. My boss, Diego, wants me to look at quotes for new computers. All three of us student workers need new computers. It's funny, we're the computer desktop support team and we've got the crappiest machines! Cobbler's children.

1:50 p.m.   Wow! Computers are expensive!!!

2:10 p.m.   E-mail from Nick, the server guy. He wants to have a meeting July first. I'll be gone! I write back.

2:20 p.m.   Reply from Nick: "I'm not worried about you." That's cool. It's okay for me to miss the meeting.

2:30 p.m.   Trying to install a program. It's not working. This problem is going to take up the rest of my day, I just know it.

3:00 p.m.   Work on budget Excel sheet I created for myself. Boy, money is tight!

3:44 p.m.   Go on break with Lena, young student worker. Decide to get slice of pizza and salad. Not cheap, but will probably be my dinner. Lena gets me a fork. That's so nice.

3:56 p.m.   Waiting to get on elevator. A bunch of large people get out, one by one. It starts to seem funny, like the clowns packed into a tiny car at the circus.

4:00 p.m.   Back at desk, eating, still can't get program to install.

5:15 p.m.   Time to go home! I'm one of the last people out of the office, as usual.

5:20 p.m.   In elevator. Woman going out says to woman coming in, "Nice haircut!" Woman who has come into elevator says, "Really? Oh, I don't know yet. I just ran out at lunch and did it." The doors close. She looks at us (me and an older janitor guy) and laughs. She says, "I was in a mood. It has nothing to do with turning forty."

5:25 p.m.   Walking downtown in the sun. I'm glad I don't have to drive. I feel urges to go buy a book, a magazine, a caramel vanilla Drumstick ice cream cone for that wonderful last bite of chocolate at the tip of the cone.

5:30 p.m.   I pass a big jar of sun tea. It's a symbol of summer, of having time to brew sun tea, like I did when I lived in Eugene. I pass the under-garage of a motel. It's full of new motel furniture. Mom bought us motel furniture for our bedroom once. It lasted forever.

5:35 p.m.   I'm going into a bookstore, "just to look."

5:45 p.m. Got the newest *US* magazine. Another indulgence!

5:50 p.m. I go to 7-Eleven for a Slurpee. I get a mixture of cherry, piña colada, and blue raspberry. Hey! Red, white, and blue, how patriotic!

6:10 p.m. At the post office. I check my box. Daniel sent me postcards!!! One that says, "I love you I love you I love you I can't say it enough or loud enough." There's a drawing of him and our cat. It works. I feel so loved, and lucky to be loved by someone who is good at telling me so. Second postcard is *really* special. I had made a zine called *Sunflower*. I didn't have enough money to make many copies. The PO box address was on the few I made. I gave one to Daniel. He said he'd get back to me with feedback. This is how he did that! He wrote a postcard to *Sunflower*, as if he were a random reader. So creative! It inspires me to scrounge up the necessary cash to print more. What a WONDERFUL man!

6:35 p.m. Had to run a block to catch the bus. Get a seat, toss my long hair back off my shoulder. Woman behind me says, "Whoa!" I quickly pull it back, embarrassed. She says she hasn't seen that much hair in a long time. The joke is her hair is iron gray, boy-short. I laugh to let her know that I got the joke. She says she used to have hair to her waist in the seventies. Her hair is still quite thick, and I imagine the lovely fall of it on a young woman back then.

I feel a pang, the way I often do, when I think of the seventies. I see photographs of the time period, and everyone always looks so much more attractive to me. I love the naturalness, the long hair on women and men. On this bus there are twelve women and six men, and I am the only one here with hair long enough to cover my earlobes. Sometimes I feel so out of place. Out of time, really.

6:37 p.m.   We go over a bridge, over the lovely but sick Willamette River. I see the double-decker Fremont Bridge up the river and try to draw it. The flags are at half-mast; I'm not sure why.

6:40 p.m.   Past Legacy Emanuel Hospital, where I was born.

6:50 p.m.   Get off bus, take a long, leisurely walk home, reading *US* magazine. For a while I'm lost in the world of the stars.

7:15 p.m.   Home! Cat comes into the bathroom to rub against my legs. It's hot in here! Check mail. Yay! I got the check for doing the in-painting in a house that was being remodeled.

7:20 p.m.   Looking in mirror at hair. Blond streaks are growing out. Should I restreak it? If so, tonight's the night.

7:22 p.m.   Phone call. Answering machine picks up. We screen calls. I still have creditors lurking. But it's Daniel's brother! He and his wife want us to come to their place for a barbeque Fourth of July. I'm so touched! We've wanted to visit, but this is the first actual invite in a while! I pick up, let him know we'll be at the Rainbow Gathering, but we'd love to come later in July. I hardly ever talk to Daniel's brother. Cool!

7:25 p.m.   I need to pack for our trip! I must take drawing and watercolor stuff. Tomorrow evening we leave! I can't wait. This will be a memory that we will make and, dang, it's about time I made a few more of those.

7:30 p.m.   I need to start packing. I'm just sitting here.

7:50 p.m.   Landlord just dropped off SASE envelopes for rent. That's nice!

8:15 p.m.   Done reading magazine. Start cleaning and packing, maybe?

8:20 p.m.   Decide to restreak hair with bleaching kit in the bathroom cupboard.

8:50 p.m.   Okay, I put the new blond streaks in my hair. I think it has something to do with my husband's love of blondes and my fantasy of being a tan, towheaded hippie girl. We talked about this the other night, after I'd sunburned my back again. Part of me did it on purpose because I once saw a young hippie girl with her back all tanned and it meant that she didn't live in such a way that required shirts and bras and being inside. I was jealous. So on my day off I sewed myself a backless shirt and lay in the sun. It was cheating, I know. My back got burned and that's fair because I was trying to shortcut the process. What I want is not a tanned, bare back. What I want is the lifestyle that would naturally lead to having what I saw on that hippie girl.

9:00 p.m.   Time to wash the goop out of my hair and see what I did. Smile.

9:20 p.m.   Done with shower, dressed, thinking about what to pack. Procrastination? What's that? Hard to tell about hair yet.

9:40 p.m.   Trying to pick up the house. I am drowning in paper. I have two big sacks full, and NOWHERE to put them. The closet is already full, and we can't really get into it with all of the clothes piled up in front of it! Where did all of those clothes come from? Do we wear them?

9:50 p.m.   Go out to play with the cat in the front yard. He's so fast! I will miss him a lot when we're out of town.

10:10 p.m.   Daniel's home!

10:25 p.m.   I listen as he reads stuff he wrote, shows me drawings. We talk about my day, his class, the idea of habit and how to break it.

10:40 p.m.   Pray to God about going to the Gathering. God says, "Go ahead, just remember to check in. Remember who you are." God really is like a good parent.

11:30 p.m.   Water sunflowers with Daniel. We wonder why they all stubbornly face east, instead of moving with the sun. Daniel says he likes the bachelor buttons I planted among the sunflowers. I was hoping he would.

11:50 p.m.   Fold clothes that need to be put away. Think about getting ready for bed. I love my little family. This was a *good day*.

Dad

6:30 p.m. I sit down on the couch with a glass of wine and read my father's autopsy report. My husband, Michael, is grilling burgers on the porch. What I really wanted was the investigative report, but there are a few interesting facts in the autopsy report. I learn that he was 5'7" and weighed 164 pounds. Michael tells me that when we got married he, too, at 5'7", weighed about the same. I learn that my dad had slight emphysema and bronchial something or other. He used to say he smoked to clear out his bronchial tubes. I guess he wasn't kidding, but since this predates the Surgeon General's report, maybe he thought he really was doing them some good. His liver wasn't all that healthy either. No surprise there. Slight atherosclerosis. Had his appendix out. He'd eaten meat and vegetables for dinner, got shit-faced drunk, and then purposely overdosed on barbiturates. He was fifty-three and so will I be in two weeks.

Judi Forman, 52, Etna, New Hampshire; research associate

Earplugs

9:10 p.m.   I can't believe I told a friend last week that I didn't mind living with my family. That damn TV all the way down the hall in the living room is so loud I cannot sleep. Getting out a pair of earplugs I got on a flight recently.

Stephanie Abraham, 28, Temple City, California; substitute teacher

Air Show

2200   The shift is over. We saw only three patients tonight. SPC Williamson and I are outside waiting for a ride. It is a spooky feeling standing here on the dark, abandoned flight line in the middle of a country at war. I remember that the DNVT phone was hooked up yesterday and I run back to the EMT area to call and make sure someone has left to pick the two of us up. For entertainment while we wait, we watch the Apache pilots doing some practice maneuvers on the end of the airstrip. They have all of the lights out, and you hear the helicopter as it hovers before you see it. There is a glow stick in the window to let you know how close they are.

Deborah Bryant, 45, Lexington, Kentucky; emergency department nurse, U.S. Army Reserves (serving in Iraq)

Cursive

4:30 p.m.   At the post office I mail a check to Cingular, a check to a student who did a couple of hours work for me, and a check to my ex-boyfriend, who recently sent me my pasta maker, which I had for some reason left at his house in Seattle. The check is to cover the cost of the mailing, with a note asking him if he had found my laptop plug-in device. I imagine my ex getting this letter and worrying that it is going to be me telling him all about his faults and then finding, to his relief, it is only a check and a quick note about my computer device. Then I imagine him looking at my note and thinking how bad my handwriting is. (He used to tell me I had terrible handwriting.) I almost rewrite the note or add a P.S. to say, "Sorry about the bad handwriting," but then I think, What the hell am I thinking! and shove it in the mail.

Jennifer Scott, 43, Middletown, Connecticut; physical anthropologist

Happy Rays

6:00 p.m.   Back to the Gazing Ball. Attaching small square mirror tiles and irregular pieces of colored stained glass onto an old bowling ball. It is gradually growing more beautiful and rewarding, as I did it all myself. Can't wait to see it sending out happy rays among my flowers. I wish I could send out happy rays to all the world and help every one live in peace.

Maysel Galiga, 81, Country Club Hills, Illinois

Thirty-two Years at the
General Motors Plant

Peggy B. Potts, 52, Douglasville, Georgia

Her title is welding equipment maintenance repairperson, which means she tracks the inventory, maintains the parts, and heads to the factory floor when something goes wrong. On an overtime week, she works 4 a.m. to 4 p.m. Cheerful. Orderly. Born-again Christian. She can tell a good story. Here's one: Her first year of college, she came home pregnant. No one said a word about it, but when the baby arrived, her mama took over. "My mama wanted another baby. She said the Lord sent her one through me. I said, 'What?!'" When her son was about six years old, she left home to move closer to her job, but her mama wouldn't let her take the boy—not until she got married. Now she's been married twenty-six years . . . and that's another story. Their first night out, they went to a club. "You know how guys want to rub your butt when you dance? He tried that and I pushed him back—

'You don't know me.' " *But they kept company, nothing serious, until one visit to her folks.* "My mama said, 'You know, Larry's talking to your dad about you getting married?' I said, 'Getting married?!' But Mama was already planning the wedding." *She calls her husband* "a likable person. Ever since I corrected him that first time, he's been a gentleman." *How would Larry describe her? She laughs,* "We ain't going to ask him."

1:15 a.m.   It is so hot, I'm about to burn up (heat flash). Forty-five minutes and the alarm will be going off. GO BACK TO SLEEP. Larry, please stop snoring.

2:00 a.m.   Alarm goes off, hit the snooze.

2:09 a.m.   Alarm goes off again, get up and prepare for work. Thanking God for this day and safe transportation to and from work.

3:10 a.m.   Leave house, put my daily confessions tape in.

3:50 a.m.   Arrive at work. Met a coworker in the parking lot. Some people are so negative, never have anything good to say. It's too early for this.

5:00 a.m.   On computer. Last Sunday, I captured robot problems while changing CPU and SMB batteries. There are 239 robots, with one battery per robot controller and one battery per mechanical unit. It's awkward because you have to work on your knees to change the CPU battery, and the SMB batteries are fastened to the base of the robot with four screws that are difficult to get off because weld slag builds up on the screw heads. I completed about thirty robots. Now the spreadsheet needs to be updated. My supervisor will want to know, how many did I complete? Like I can finish this project in one day. If he wants it done any faster, he's going to have to assign more people to this project. Must e-mail list of names for planned maintenance training document. Can't find list. What did I do with it? I don't want to go and have to ask those guys if I have their names spelled correctly again. Oh, thank God, here it is. A mind is a terrible thing to waste.

7:00 a.m.   My supervisor is out sick; I hope he gets better. But what can I say, sounds like a good day for me.

7:30 a.m.   Eat breakfast—two oranges. Why did I think I could keep this food journal? Eight months and I still can't get the hang of it. Maybe there's some magic about this little pink book. If I look at it long enough, maybe it will satisfy my appetite. What else can I eat?

7:45 a.m.   Larry calls to see how my day is so far.

8:30 a.m.   Working with spare parts inventory, getting correct vendor part numbers and prices. Arranging parts on storage shelves in these pretty new blue storage bins. The bins with part names and part numbers look great. "Peggy, you're doing such a good job." "Why, thank you, Peggy, I appreciate that."

10:20 a.m.   What the heck, I think I'll take my morning break and lunch break now. Eat my salad; remember to check it off in the food journal. I hope I don't get too hungry before dinner. May have to eat two protein bars for the snack today. Read the Bible chapters assigned for today. I'm reading the Bible in a year schedule.

11:30 a.m.   General supervisor calls—get hand tools and go to floor for the rest of the day. It's hot and humid down there. And these big waves (heat flashes) I'm having don't help out any.

1:30 p.m.   Machine breaks down. "Got to go get help," I say. I know my coworker heard me, as loud as I talk, but he ignores me. That is so rude. Men and their deaf-ear switch. Why do I always let that bother me? Do the best I can. What is wrong with this machine? I don't have any more suggestions. My coworker and I have exhausted all our knowledge. "We're not getting anywhere; I'm going to get some help." I think it's a man thing to not be able to say "I don't know." I got help. Thank God, we're back up and running again.

2:20 p.m.   Still answering breakdowns. Machines, please run!!! Less than an hour left for production to run. I'm hot, sweaty, and nasty. Fans blowing hot air. My hair is all over my head. This is the life of a maintenance worker in a non-air-conditioned factory.

3:24 p.m.   Production finally ends. GOOD-BYE. Getting machines ready for second shift.

3:55 p.m.   Just finished, but I'll be here past 4. Got to wash up, change shoes, and uniform.

4:30 p.m.   Clock out and head home. Traffic is pretty good.

5:45 p.m.   Arrive home, change, and head back out to Healthy Inspirations, my health club. I really need the one-on-one counseling, the main reason I joined. But I dread it.

I'm fifty-two years old and tired. The pounds just don't come off like they used to. HELP!!!

6:00 p.m. Arrive at health club. Why is she in here? I doubt if she weighs 120 pounds. Please don't ask me for that food journal. Forty-five minutes on circuit training. It's time to weigh in. Praise God, lost 3.8 pounds. What's up? She didn't ask for the journal. Guess she's tired of my lame excuses.

7:00 p.m. Leave health club and start home. I should stop at Bruster's ice cream parlor and reward myself. Nah, go on home.

7:15 p.m. Arrive home, turn on TV, eat a small dinner, check mail, listen to messages, and get ready for bed.

8:30 p.m. Larry comes home. Discuss the day's events. Prepare our lunches for tomorrow. Watch some TV together. I'm nodding. I don't have a clue what this picture is about.

10:00 p.m. Larry and I kneel at the foot of the bed and thank God for all His blessings. Kiss and say good night.

Higher Education

12:50 p.m.   I see Daniel and Vesta standing in wait for me after class. Dammit. I knew they'd trap me. I remember what it was like though, feeling any kind of a kinship with a teacher. It's not that I don't want to help them. It's just that I have so much to do today, and even though a six-foot tranny and her five-foot German boyfriend have an awful lot to say that will hold a person's attention, I'm not up for it.

Today they want to talk about how their four absences and nine tardies shouldn't count against their grade because they've had unavoidable circumstances—they had to move again and had trouble getting their mattress. Vesta actually raises her voice, asking, "How many homeless students have you had?"

I say, "Several."

She says, "How many of them are homeless *and* drug addicts?" Is this supposed to convince me? What I'd like to say is being an addict qualifies you for drug treatment, NA, serious therapy, and methadone. It does NOT qualify you for excused absences. I explain the course policy.

They both start yelling. I don't know who to listen to.

They point at my face to punctuate their case, and I suddenly realize I'm in a bungalow on the edge of campus, alone with two screaming people, at least one of whom is a drug addict.

I grab my bag and head for the door. They follow me and continue screaming, seemingly unaware that I've brought them outdoors. A few people walk by, which is embarrassing, but also comforting. When Daniel yells, "You say all these positive things in class but you don't practice them," and Vesta shouts at the same time, "You're party to those who are working toward transsexual genocide." I say, "Well, now this is downright abusive and I'm leaving." They scream some stuff after me, but I try not to hear.

Cindi Harrison, 34, San Francisco, California; instructor, City College of San Francisco

On June 29, 2004 . . .

50% of day diarists took prescription drugs.

59% did not get enough sleep.

〰〰〰

Co-owner, VirginBush Safaris

Cindi Crain, 35, Nairobi, Kenya

When she was twenty-two, she quit a job in direct marketing and traveled around the world solo for eighteen months. "I was bored to tears at work. I had to shake things up." Her adventure not only fed her wanderlust, but inspired a love of writing. She earned a master's in journalism, then worked for years as a travel editor in New York City. In 2001, she visited her best friend living in Kenya, a fellow adventurer named Lisa Rolls. "Everything changed after that trip. Lisa and I ran around like children in the bush; it was like playing in a sandbox. I knew Kenya had to be a part of my life." Together, they started VirginBush Safaris, offering clients customized safaris and a spiritual experience. A dream job. "The bush is such a fundamental place. You feel connected to the people around you, and connected to the bigger picture." Settled? "Kenya feels like home, more and more as time ticks along." An introvert with wild tendencies. Single. Loyal. Despite all her journeys, she's just now making peace with good-byes. "It used to be devastating. I was convinced my relationships were suffering because I was always leaving, but I'm realizing I give so much when I'm with people I care about that it's okay when I go. I'll be back." How would she describe herself? "Never around . . . I'm everywhere and nowhere."

9:00 a.m. I sit propped up against a bunch of beige and chocolate pillows, looking between masses of palms and bougainvillea at the Indian Ocean. Breakers offshore provide nonstop white noise here on the east coast of Zanzibar. My best friend of twenty years, Lisa, sits about ten feet away on a pretty Indian-style daybed with a sparkly beige fabric flowing overhead.

Yesterday, I was unbelievably ill with what we think was dehydration, which I get a lot now. I'm rather stupid that way. Living here on the equator, I do drink water, but obviously not enough. I spent yesterday practically unconscious, except when I had my head in the toilet. We were worried it was malaria at one point; we prayed not because our big safari season is about to commence. (Recovering from malaria is at minimum a few-week process, unless you're Lisa or her mom, who have both blown through their malarias as if they were merely allergic sneezes.) Last night, I went straight to bed after supper and woke around 8:00 this morning feeling strangely well and starving.

This morning Lisa and I are at a beautiful six-room hotel called the Palms. We were given a three-day freebie since we've been sending so many clients here. The service and food are exquisite, the beach white as sugar, the ocean a greeny turquoise. It's heaven. We live a great life.

Ironically—or maybe not—I had an emotional ("nervous") breakdown about six months ago and had to go back to America to get my head screwed on straight again. But the breakdown had nothing to do with where I live or how I live; it had to do with how I love, and especially how I love myself. I feel even more grounded in life now having gotten the direction I needed, even if I do find my relationships with people confusing at times. I am much more detached from others now; those who show up in my life want to be there. And those are really the only ones I'm interested in. I have never felt more sure of how I am living my life and that I am living to my fullest. Perhaps it's because I have a partner and best friend who shares this conviction.

I had breakfast of toast, coffee, and peanut butter. During breakfast a big gale knocked everything over on the table, but it was cool to watch the weather over the ocean. I've always had a thing for beaches and the sea, even though I grew up near Chicago. And the weather here changes every five minutes.

10:00 a.m. I am reading Don Miguel Ruiz's *The Mastery of Love* because I'm frustrated that I'm peeved I haven't heard from a certain guy in the States for about a week now. (Where is my detachment?!) This is someone I've been developing a close friendship with, I thought. Now he's suddenly stopped being in touch and I'm blaming myself. (I have a big penchant for getting hooked on men who don't treat me with equal attention; this was the reason I had to get help when I had the breakdown.)

Ruiz teaches us not to assume or take things personally. However, today I am both assuming why my friend—and he is only a friend at this point—isn't in touch. And I am taking this lack of contact from him personally. So I'm looking to Ruiz for inspiration to pull me out of this silly place. I worry that I think about men too much. And yet they're hardly a part of my life at all. I haven't been in a relationship in almost two years and have never been married. I've had a tumultuous love life from which I've learned a lot. I do not assume it will all "work out," that I will marry, etc. There is no such thing as life "working out." It is not a fixed destination.

For instance, I have never applied the term "worked out" to my relationship with Lisa. It just is, and it is a constant flow of support and love and synergy from which I draw so much. We always describe our relationship as a marriage, and I've never had a romantic relationship that ever came close to this friendship in terms of understanding, inspiration, support, and fun. We are talking about each of us having a baby next year; to basically make our own kind of family together. She is thirty-seven and has a beau. I am not planning on waiting to see if I find someone to marry before having a baby by forty. I want to be a mom, and I am reasoning that I may someday have both (the husband and the baby), but they are probably not going to happen simultaneously for me. And so, as scary as the prospect is, I am psyching myself up to go to a sperm bank sometime in the next months to learn about the process.

We really hope Lisa's beau of five years will want to father hers, and we've been talking about what we'd do if he didn't. We love him to bits and he'd be a great dad. He's just younger than us and isn't sure if he's ready. Are you ever ready?

11:00 a.m. Lisa and I are both lounging on the veranda of our villa. The staff does a lot of sweeping here at the Palms. One of them just handed me two sheets of some meetings notes that a colleague of ours had typed for us a few days ago. Unbeknownst to me, they had blown away in all this wind, and the pages were soaked from one of the five-minute downpours we've been getting. Now one page is missing amid the dense foliage here. Oh well. Our colleague can print us another copy back in Nairobi.

The notes have to do with our business, VirginBush Safaris. We have been in talks with an über-investor from Britain who approached us to possibly develop the ultimate safari lodge in Kenya. It's the big-time; he's a big player. We're floored. We have been kicking around ideas, and Lis especially has been picking everyone's brain, peppering our safari guide friends and others about what could work or where there might be unforeseen problems. Doing business in East Africa is a tricky business indeed. It takes immense patience and instinct. Money alone buys very little here. That was one of the first lessons I learned when I moved here three years ago from New York.

11:30 a.m.   I just put on some tunes on my iPod, a mix I made for walking on the beach at 5 p.m. in Watamu, which I do every day when I'm staying at my house there. Currently playing is *Private Lounge.* Next up is one of my favorite holiday albums, *Cape Town Beach Sessions.* I love Cape Town. Was there twice last year.

Just realized how grateful I am to not be throwing up today.

It's a happy day. Sun is blazing, great tune playing. Best friend here, making fun of me now for playing with our new $800 digital camera, which we bought several months ago and only now are figuring out how to use. It will be kick-ass for our website and for giving pix to magazines. We've had a lot of press to date—two American chicks give up the urban jungle for the African one, blah blah blah, which has been great. But no more stories are on the horizon. We'll have to be like Madonna and keep reinventing ourselves, or at least finding that next PR spin.

Noon Lying at our *banda* down on the beach, a gorgeous berry-colored mattress covered with pillows, under a thatch roof. I, of course, sit in the blazing sun, as taking sun is as important to me as taking water. (Lis is the exact opposite, taking refuge from the sun as much as possible.) I am back to reading Ruiz and do find the words of inspiration I am seeking: "Love has no expectations . . ." It's my job to remind myself that I am complete and that my friend, living halfway across the world, is in his own situation that I should not wish to control. Ruiz reminds me that I have all the love I could ever need, in the "magical kitchen" of my heart. Corny, but true.

I doze, read, take a few pictures, get browner. Lisa returns following her massage, asking about lunch, carting her computer, doing some e-mails. She sits in the shade. But wait, then she does take some sun on her lower half! Extraordinary! We are both gobsmacked again and again by the color of the water, so beckoning. So ethereal. And it's not even the best time of the year here. About a half hour later, we head up to the lunch/bar area.

1:00 p.m. Now we're plotting Zanzibar as the destination for us and our British mogul. We don't know the politics here, but the island seems at first glance to be underdeveloped, ripe for opportunity for a project like ours—to protect some land while putting in a sexy chill spot for twenty guests and ourselves. We talk aesthetics for the umpteenth time over Caesar salad and penne with some yummy cheesy eggplanty sauce. The Palms, we've decided, might very well have the best food in East Africa. Then the barracuda arrives, the first time either of us has tried this fish, and, with just a bit of lemon, it is divine.

During lunch, Lisa sees one of the Palms' owners whom she's met a few times in Nairobi. She beckons him to our table. It turns out he is originally from Vermont and came to East Africa by way of his wife, whom he met in New York but whose family is from, well, it seems Scandinavia, Kenya, and Croatia. (Now I am confused.)

We picked his brain a bit about Zanzibar, and he invited us for sundowners, which we will go to at 7 p.m. We are now stuck on the Croatia connection, as that's been Lisa's buzzword all year. She and her beau, Tor, have had the idea to invest in property there, and ever since, there have been little signs everywhere of the country. My own friend who has dropped off the scene is Croatian, for instance. We're all going to go there in November.

3:45 p.m. About to go walking on this empty, gorgeous beach. I was too sick yesterday when Lis walked it for three hours. We'll walk north today to what looks on the map to be a beautiful cape and bay.

I had anticipated a walk together, but we didn't keep the same pace and Lisa was soon way ahead. So I walked partway on my own, past two or three curiously deserted hotels, but otherwise along a glorious stretch of white, white beach. Along it were millions of shells, mostly pulverized. Cowries with purple in the middle, anemone, and many others. I popped off a few more shots with the camera, now knowing how to work it. Once I was passed by a white couple on a motorbike; twice I was given a sales pitch from local African "beach boys." ("Come into the village for some nice crabs, velly nice!" "Come into my shop; *hakuna matata* is free to look!")

About an hour into the walk I started to tire, feeling the effects of yesterday's illness. I sat and waited for Lisa on the return lap. On the walk back, we couldn't resist poking into one of the "ghost" hotels, this one called the Sultan's Palace with tall *makuti* (thatch) roofs. So we braved the row of stoned *askaris* (guards) who were not doing much of anything—just loitering and smoking *bangi* (local kind of pot)—and asked them if we could have a look. Being in the business we're in, we do this sort of thing a lot. They said, *"hakuna matata."*

We said, *"asanti"* (thanks). The room we went into was humongous, indeed fit for a sultan. The views over the ocean breakers were breathtaking, but it was all a bit kitsch, having that palace kind of feel. Shapes of minarets for doorways, for instance. We then went to see the "mess," as we call it here: the main hangout building. There we encountered a South African woman who was desperately setting the place up for the *wageni* (clients) who were arriving in two days.

She had a lot of work—and sweeping—ahead of her. It seemed that no one was helping her; very odd in this part of the world, where even staffs in modest homes number at least four. Why weren't the high *askaris* helping her? She gave us a tour. It was all too big for a place that only accommodates thirty guests at a time. Owned by Italians. They do the grand kitsch thing up and down the East African coast. You should see what they've done in Kenya. Sheesh. Horrid.

7:00 p.m. Back at the Palms. We did a half hour of yoga with Rodney Yee (our guru) on DVD. I realized how weak I was still, but it felt great to stretch. The *mozzies* (mosquitoes) were ferocious. Even with the *mozzie* net down around the bed, we still need to spray Doom (the equivalent of Raid) under it to kill those that lurk there, waiting for juicy girls like us to fall asleep so they can attack. We absolutely cannot afford to get malaria right now. People who live here don't take antimalarial antibiotics for prevention. We can't stay on antibiotics all the time, so we just know when we've got it and then it's easily treated. (But it's still a bitch to suffer, even if you catch it right away.)

this day in the life 176

I take a bath. Try to dry my hair and lose patience halfway through. (It's curly and takes forever.) Makeup. Black top and flowy pants. I'm tired as I always feel at the beach at this hour and am not motivated to socialize.

7:40 p.m. We're late for drinks at the Palms owners' house, next door. (We had changed the time to 7:30, but alas, we're still late as usual.) Paulina and Aaron are kindly waiting for us, bar laid out with bitings (snacks) and drinks. Sweet, ambitious, interesting young couple that built the Palms and the sister hotel next door, the Breezes, with their bare hands (okay, and about two hundred workers). They're in their late twenties and have done all this. Their story is inspiring.

Lis and I had dinner on our own. I had a rock lobster thermidor starter, which I didn't enjoy so much, and a yummy prawns main course, but still not much of an appetite. More talk about what we'd do with the British mogul's money, hotels, the market here. Makes one's head spin. How does one pick a direction and just go for it? I assume we will, but I'm still waiting for my gut to say, "This is it." Yet, we also joked earlier today that, Hey wait, we're going to have babies next year, so bugger the hotel idea. We don't want to do all that work, right? VirginBush Baby! We were joking, but there's an element of truth. Our business now is small and manageable and ours. Plenty of room to do a bit of safari and manage families. So what do I want, really?

Midnight passes with Lis and I watching *Something to Talk About,* which we dub a "heartwarming look at adultery across multi-generations and how to not be upset about it so that everyone can just get along and be happy." And we hope Julia Roberts got paid $20 million for donning that fluffy hairdo.

Great, Lis is now saying it looked like my hairdo in 1984. Gee, thanks (but she's right).

Essentials

10:00 p.m. Ponder. Our safari season starts in just ten days, and then I will be away on "back to backs" for nearly three months, showing urban professionals how to identify leopard tracks in the bush. Nairobi will be full of responsibilities and preparation, getting my bills paid and planning for all eventualities. Oh yes, and I must make out my wish list for those coming soon from my former life. Those bearing gifts. Things once commonplace, now jewels. Things a girl may never learn to part with—MAC Gleam lipstick, Lancôme Rénergie, Origins A Perfect World. Need to also add YSL undereye concealer and *How to Freeze Your Eggs for Dummies* to wish list . . .

> *Lisa Rolls, 37, Nairobi, Kenya; co-owner, VirginBush Safaris*

12:30 p.m.   I just got back from a two-hour meeting with our foundation's newest nonprofit grantee, along with my boss and one of the investing partners. The tough part for me is facilitating these business meetings where my boss is all about strategic goals and alternative revenue streams and puts every nonprofit person's teeth on edge with lingo and acronyms he can't seem to lose from his days at Intel, like SOs (Strategic Objectives) and ZBBs (Zero-Based Budgets). It just makes my eyes roll. Like he can't just say "goals" or "budget."

> *Susan Forrest, 38, Phoenix, Arizona; foundation*
> *associate director*

9:00 a.m.   Diaper change time. Wonder how many diapers I've changed in eleven years? (Four diapers per kid per day, average of three kids a day, five days a week, fifty-one weeks a year, times eleven years = 33,660!!! God, I've got to get out of this business. Help! I read a story to the kids.

> *Kathryn Ohlerking, 39, Aurora, Colorado; child care*
> *provider*

9:01 a.m.   Mrs. Sanders wants me to start passing her wood to the attic. We finished that task at 9:11. So I went into the house and began to do my housework, such as washing dishes, clothes, straightening beds, and ironing. It is noon and it's funny how I plan to do one thing, but Mrs. Sanders always comes in with more work, which expands my time.

Doris Stallings, 40, Cleveland, Mississippi; housekeeper

6:39 p.m.   My client just left. She loved my jewelry designs! She was reluctant at first as these new designs are definitely not trendy. I told her to go with her heart, to carry her own "torch." Thank God I have known her for a few years. I didn't care if I lost her as a client or lost the sale. I wanted to be true to me and to her. When I wrote up her invoice I said, "Know that we are blessed to have these material things; give back in some way." Wow! What is going on with me? My boundaries?

Katherine Azarmi, 32, Los Angeles, California;
owner/designer, Kaviar Jewelry

10:00 a.m.   A whirlwind of subversive activity this morning amidst distributing faxes, revising letters and legal documents, date-stamping and distributing mail, answering the phone, and forwarding e-mails. The script I'm reading— really good!—is up on my typing stand so I can read it without looking like I'm reading un-work-related stuff.

Jaye Austin Williams, 47, New York, New York; artist

On June 29, 2004 . . .

52% of day diarists worried about money.

67% of day diarists felt stressed out.

~~~~~~

"Parte de la diáspora cubana"

Virginia Cueto, 47, Miami, Florida

She works as a Spanish translator and editor of a magazine targeting Latino small business owners. "If I had my own magazine, I'd focus on the immigrant experience or women's lives here in the U.S., because there's nothing more relevant to me personally." She was born in Havana into a prominent family. Her great-grandfather was a key figure in the wars for independence. Homeschooled by her mother, "so we would not be indoctrinated by the Communist regime of Fidel Castro." When she was nine, her family came to America on one of the first Freedom Flights from Cuba. "Everything about the U.S. was wonderful. It was a great adventure." At eighteen, she married a fellow Cuban and promised her father she'd finish college. She did, but not until her own two children had started school. When people asked why she majored in English literature, she replied, "It doesn't matter what

I'm going to do with it. I love it!" Her first marriage turned out to be too confining. *"Every time I turned, he would draw another line in front of me."* In 1997, she helped a family friend from Cuba through the immigration process. *"He was kind of lost; I was just separated."* They married three years ago. She considers the U.S. home, but, *"Someday, I'd love to go back to Cuba and rebuild it. After all, I'm a lot younger than Fidel!"*

Midnight I am at the computer working on a translation with my husband. It's really *his* translation, but as usual, when either one of us gets a freelance assignment, we take turns. Although we are both bilingual, I am stronger translating into English, having grown up in the States. Ed is a more recent arrival, having won a visa in an immigration lottery in 1996. This job—an employee manual—is into Spanish, which is his forte.

I'm energized after a brief nap after dinner. So is Ed, even though he spent all weekend with a cold. I'm glad to see him upbeat. Aren't men horrible when they feel sick? It's good to work together. My daughter Irene, twenty-two, is still up, but that's not unusual. Her kitten meows outside her room and I hear her let her "child" in. She's on the phone (why am I not surprised?). I am so glad she's home and okay and happy. Dear Lord, thank you for my child.

12:45 a.m. I'm getting sleepy. Eduardo is still working. I go around the house and turn off the lights, check the doors, plump the pillows on the couch. I like my house neat.

I notice my prescription pills on the kitchen counter where I left them to remind myself I need to renew them. Okay, so I'm getting senile. But I'm coping. I call them in to pick up tomorrow.

1:15 a.m.   We tussle with some tricky wording. What's the best way to get the meaning of "long-term medical leave" across? As opposed to "regular" medical leave, or family leave, or personal leave? How many kinds of "leave" does this company allow, anyway? Only in the U.S. . . .

Irene comes in. "Mom, you need a new nightgown." (I like this one.) "Isn't your birthday coming up soon?" (In October.) "I'm getting you a new nightgown." (I like this one.) Okay, I tell her, but make sure it doesn't itch and make me hot. We tease about what size to get me. "Mom! Are you sure you don't need an extra X in there?" Ha-ha.

2:00 a.m.   Teeth, face, cell phone charging. Check, check, check. Dear Lord, thank you for my family; bless and protect my child Irene; bless and protect my child Emilio and his wife Heidi; let them grow closer to You. Bless and protect the children of the world, Lord, and lift the darkness from the world. I pray for my family members, going in order so I don't forget anyone—my mother, father, husband, sisters, brothers-in-law, nieces; my children's father, his new wife and child; my husband's sons, assorted friends . . . I drift into sleep.

6:48 a.m.   I feel my husband snuggle up. Did he just come to bed?

8:18 a.m.   Get up, get up, get up! I am not exactly disposed to listen to myself. Duty, however, calls.

8:30 a.m.   Breakfast. Orange juice, toast, margarine, and of course my pills. White for allergy, beige for thyroid, red is estrogen, and green for blood pressure. What a *vieja*. I open a jar of guava marmalade, even though I already have an open jar of peach preserves in the fridge. Yum.

"parte de la diáspora cubana"   **183**

8:50 a.m.   I put the dishes in the sink and notice a solitary spoon already there. Humph. Who ate what out of which container? I can't tell. I rinse and place all the items in the dishwasher. Gotta get moving.

9:00 a.m.   In the shower. Should have exercised but didn't (the story of my life). Well, the story of my life the last five or six years. But hey, I've been busy. I promise myself I'll get on that treadmill in the spare room SOON. Let's go, let's go, you're late as usual.

10:02 a.m.   Kiss hubby good-bye. Dash out the door. Irene still sleeping; I'll catch up with her later. Another scorching, steamy South Florida day. It seems some part of Miami is always under construction. By now morning rush hour is over and traffic is moving, another reason why I don't even try to leave the house any earlier. I zigzag my way around a couple of slowpokes in the left lane.

10:30 a.m.   Sign in. Good morning, good morning. All kinds of stuff piled up on my chair that was not there last night. I quickly sift through it. Today is newsletter day, so I check the news filter. For the last three years I've been working at a publishing company focused on Hispanics. Although a year ago I was promoted to editor of their newest magazine *(Hispanic Trends),* I still help out with the website, which I enjoy enormously.

I scan the news for Latino-related items. Kerry endorsed by the Hispanic Caucus; we've handed over the Iraq government to the Iraqis; yesterday was Gay Pride Day. Same-sex marriage the central theme. Instinctively, I repudiate the idea. I am not sure what I am reacting to. I know enough gay and lesbian couples, and I am unfazed by their actual relationships, so it is not that. But why this insistence on civil marriage? Why aren't civil unions enough? Or religious marriages enough? This seems one more challenge to the status quo, and it is not clear to me that it will be a good change.

Anyway, the issue is not Hispanic-themed so I move on. AHA! Marvel Comics is coming out with a Latina teen version of *Spider-Man,* who wears hip clothes from the barrio, not spandex. Good for her. I select that story for the Lifestyle section of the website.

I find a story from the *Albuquerque Journal* commenting on the cover story of *Hispanic Trends'* latest issue, on the changes under way at the U.S. Hispanic Chamber of Commerce. Good! My publisher will be pleased.

12:20 p.m. Practically done updating the website and putting together the newsletter. Five people have walked in my office for one thing or another. Good thing I'm a pack rat and keep even old articles in my computer for reference. Have to get back to a couple writers who have questions about their stories.

Joe, managing editor with *Trends'* sister publication, *Hispanic Magazine,* wants to have lunch. He's one of my favorite people in the office, but I have tons of errands to run. We compromise: he'll drive me to drop off a translation at a nearby law office and then we'll have lunch. We end up going to Subway where he can have his low-carb wrap and I can have my tuna sandwich. Yum.

We're both stressed out and on deadline, but we talk shop and politics, and that, plus the comfort food, puts us in a better mood. Since he's driving, we listen to Rush Limbaugh and have a good laugh. We're both pretty conservative, but Rush is outrageous. We wrap up lunch with a quick stop at the supermarket, where I pick up laundry detergent. I know there's something else I need, but I can't remember what it is.

"parte de la diáspora cubana" **185**

1:45 p.m. Back in the office. I'm worried about my art director. I haven't heard from her since last week. She's new and working freelance. What I'm really worried about is getting the next issue out on schedule. I hate falling behind and depending on someone else to get things done. If I could, I would just do everything myself. HA! As if I weren't practically doing so already!

4:20 p.m. Had an hour-long meeting with Conrad, my new (and also freelance) associate editor. What a relief to have him on board. Hopefully, he'll help me get up-to-date on all the writing, assigning, editing, brainstorming, calling, research, phoning, proofreading, meeting, drafting, budgeting, planning, dealing and wheeling that comes with the job. Not to mention actually coming up with a coherent vision for the magazine!

4:35 p.m. Phone call from Jorge, the proofreader. Nope, nothing for you just yet. Meet with marketing manager regarding a guide to colleges the company is publishing. It's not really my project, but I've seen the proofs and noticed a series of grammatical errors and want to point them out to her. Didn't an editor look at this? Apparently not. I'm itching to get my hands on this, but frankly have no time. Picky, picky, picky. But in my field that's an asset.

5:00 p.m. Give hubby a call and see how he's doing. Much better! Good. Haven't heard from Irene all day.

6:13 p.m. Progress! Heard from the art director. No matter, she's coming in tomorrow. Thank you, Lord.

Had a call from the director of the Hispanic Voter Project at Johns Hopkins. We discuss an article for my October issue; and he promises to help me clinch interviews with the candidates. E-mails back and forth with several political cartoonists, trying to pick an editorial cartoon for the August issue that will be thought-provoking but not offensive (especially to my publisher).

Have a couple of e-mails from my twin, Susan, in New Jersey. She's back home after settling in my niece in Delaware, where she will be starting her first job out of college. The kid will be making more money than me, with more vacation time and benefits, and she's not even twenty-two yet! But those are the benefits of being a Cornell grad. She did good! Make mental note to get back to Sue. Getting feedback about our last issue, so far so good.

7:12 p.m. Edited the story missing from our "Focus on Franchising" package scheduled for August. I want to finish the package today, but the list of franchises I want to include is in Excel format and it's a bear to edit. I decide to finish it up tomorrow. The cleaning crew is here; that means it's time to go home. Well, I crossed off two more things on my to-do list and made headway on a couple of others. Could be worse.

As I'm leaving, I notice a box unopened on top of the file cabinet. I figure I might as well see what it is. Wow! A Polaroid camera! And, of course, a press kit. Nice. That's one of the things I like about my job. The pay could be better, but it comes with nice little perks.

7:40 p.m. I call Eduardo to let him know I'm on the way home, then call Irene. She has a headache. Oh, great. Is she coming down with Ed's cold? I call my mother to catch up with the latest family news. She tells me my dad, who's flying down from New Jersey next week for a visit, got a bargain and has upgraded to first class and isn't that much better?

"*Sí, Mami.*"

"After all he's been through, *tu padre* shouldn't be flying standby. Your sister told me you were taking some days off while he's here."

"*Sí, Mami.*"

"He wants to go see Olga; he hasn't seen her in ages. And Geraldina. I think on one of those days when you're not off, Geraldina should pick him up and they can go see Olga together. They can have a nice lunch."

"*Sí, Mami.*"

"Your sister is taking off that Thursday and Friday. Are you taking off the same days?"

"No, *Mami. Mami,* I'm on the cell phone."

"Did I tell you I went to Rosa's talk on Saturday?"

"*Sí, Mami.*"

"*Ay, chica,* it was excellent. *Magnífico.* Rosa is so intelligent! And then we had dinner with—"

"*Mami,* I'm on the cell. I'll call you when I get home."

"No, no, I'm going to bed right after the *novela.* I'm exhausted today. How's Irene? And Emilito and Heidi? They never call me. I never hear from them."

"I know, *Mami,* they're so busy. *Mami,* I'm on the cell."

"Well, tell them I say hello and to call me. Do they know your father is coming down?"

"I think so."

"What do you mean you think so?"

"*Mami,* I AM ON THE CELL."

I feel guilty about cutting her off but can't afford to go over my minutes. I should tell her I love her more often. I don't know why I don't, but I think she knows it, anyway.

8:00 p.m. At Walgreens drive-through picking up prescriptions. I'm actually surprised I remembered.

8:10 p.m. Home! I get a nice hug from my husband.

More hugs, this time from my daughter. She has that glassy-eyed look people get when they have a fever. Two

Tylenols and two slices of buttered toast later and she has perked up. She tells me about a new TV program, *Nip/Tuck*. I'm glad she's all grossed out about it, and we discuss the absolute lack of necessity for this type of cosmetic surgery. She feels better now, and I'm struck by how pretty her hair and skin are. Does she know how beautiful she is? She's like a flower child from the sixties, rebellious and focused on her inner self.

She tells me she'll be going with her dad to Marco Island for the Fourth of July weekend. She's excited because her brother and sister-in-law, who live in Orlando, are meeting them there. I almost feel envious. It's tough to get together as a family, and I could use a long weekend away myself.

For a brief moment, I think about my ex-husband. Although we never talk, I know he is looking forward to this trip, to being with the kids. He was always more of a father than a partner. I am glad for him and a bit sorrowful I won't be there. But I have made my peace with my decision to divorce after twenty years of marriage and am happy with my new life.

9:00 p.m.   Start dinner. Irene has decided to go to a friend's house, so it's just us two. I'm craving pizza, but we shouldn't be spending. We settle on spaghetti. I mix in the leftover *picadillo* in the sauce. Ed likes the taste combination of the ground beef cooked Cuban style with the "American" spaghetti sauce. Plus it adds a little protein. Not that I am too concerned about that.

9:15 p.m.   Drat. Forgot I had garlic bread in the freezer. Decide to put it in the oven, anyway.

9:40 p.m.   Dinner is served! We eat in the family room and watch TV. Ed's got this idiotic Spanish-language show on, *el Mikimbin de Miami*. It's like a parody of a parody of a variety show. They are so bad—today they have this skit poking fun at the Cuban residents of an imaginary local condo, and their take on the U.S. electoral process.

I have to laugh. One of the residents is a cigar-chomping Santería priestess who can apparently work some potent magic. Even President Bush shows up to consult her, and she, of course, agrees to fix the election if he will change U.S.-Cuba policy to her liking. It's outlandish, but it works, playing off most *cubanos'* inflated sense of our own importance. But hey, we do have a great sense of humor!

10:00 p.m. Doing the dishes. Thank God, *el Mikimbin* is over and the news is on. I need a break. I change into my jammies and play a couple of rounds of Spider Solitaire on the computer, and check my home e-mail. The day is almost over, and I still have so many things to do. I let my mind go blank, hypnotized by the clicking and whirring of the computer as I play cards.

10:20 p.m. Ed, plugging away at the translation, asks me to take a look at a passage. The problem is the original in English is badly written. Ed's eyes are bloodshot, so I take over for a while.

11:59 p.m. Still working. The day has come and gone. Well, at least we weren't hit by a hurricane, and my a/c didn't conk out (like it did last summer). Thank you, Lord, for all your blessings.

Miscellaneous Moments

The Cost of Living

Noon Eating a Burger King lunch at the car inspection center for annual checkup and oil change. One other task that I didn't have to do when I was married. It's a small price to pay for personhood. Keeping fingers crossed on inspection. I do so enjoy sitting in the car repair office with *Sports Illustrated* to read.

Deborah Grotfeldt, 54, Houston, Texas; nonprofit executive director

Me and Raina

3-something p.m. Raina called a couple of hours ago when I had just made the first part in my hair. So I applied and talked, talked and applied. I actually was gonna wait to dye it, let it grow out and go back to black, but I like it better all one color. And, c'mon, a fierce orange 'fro is the perfect balance to my not-so-fierce self. Raina and I talked about everything. Tomorrow we're planning to go to the beach. I hope it's fun. I hate to sound wussy, but I want her to move down here so I can have a chill partner. Somebody to look at boys with and cut up T-shirts with and watch Style Network with.

Darlene Anita Scott, 29, Richmond, Virginia; adjunct assistant professor

Trying

11:17 a.m. Time to begin my OPK (ovulation predictor kit at $18 a pop), but here at work there's no paper coffee cups in the kitchen. What am I going to pee in? I head to the supply closet to decide between the little stack of 3M face masks and the plastic Staples containers full of binder clips. I pick the Staples container, empty the clips into my desk organizer, and march to the restroom. I've spent a year of perfecting the exact angle to hold the cup in order to catch all the urine. Two dark purple lines bleed through on my OPK, and I'm sad this cycle is a bust. Every month is critical for me. After a year of trying, I'm still not pregnant.

Jackie Walker, 40, Washington, D.C.; information coordinator, National Prison Project

Grandmother

My grandmother is reading in the living room, so I go join her. When she begins to talk I realize she is not in a great mood and her speech is a bit funny. After a while of listening to her talk about health problems, I just sit there thinking, How much longer do I have to sit here before I can get up? I love her and I know she is old and hurting, but I don't really have anything new to say about it all. She has said no one should live after ninety, and she is ninety-two. I feel for her and don't want her to be unhappy, but I don't want her to die either.

Kathleen Korosec Holmes, 38, Overland Park, Kansas; realtor

Dona Crowe, 65, Louisville, Kentucky

A Southern Baptist with a master's degree in religious education, she works in fiscal services at the University of Louisville and does the books for her church. Except for a brief period in her twenties, she's always lived at home with her mom. She was serious about a fellow in the army, but the feeling wasn't mutual so, "I guess I pulled in my little tentacles and stole away and never actually sought anyone else out." She loves flea markets and yard sales. Her house is overrun with boxes and bags—she collects anything with teddy bears on it, plus picture frames, music boxes, jewelry. "If I wore a pair of earrings every fifteen minutes, I'd still never get through them all." At work, she organized the Christmas Elf Exchange, even after the new VP tried to scotch it. "Only six people did it last year, but I'm not going to let the Grinch steal my Christmas." She's in the mind to retire. "I figure I'll have to practice living on what I'll get for social security—get up a budget, maybe give up newspapers and magazines. I can always read them at the library." What she'd really love to do is see the Seven Wonders of the World, "but I need to win the lottery or marry a millionaire. And I don't play the lottery enough."

6:00 a.m.   Got in bed last night about 11:00. Time now to get up and take medicine for blood pressure. Must have turned off the alarm in my sleep. Running late again. How soon can I retire and not have to worry about setting the alarm? Maybe in a year, IF the stock market improves!

Going on 6:50   Eat breakfast and get dressed. Thank heavens I work where I can dress casually in slacks and a top. The time is flying by. Hurry to put on my compression sleeve. Sometimes I wonder, Why me? Why breast cancer? But I have survived three years after the mastectomy. Lymphedema developed after surgery, thus the sleeve. It helps to keep the swelling down in the arm. I am thankful to God that I have survived when so many others have not. The sleeve is a constant reminder of God's blessings. Well, it's time to make a last potty call and leave.

7:00 a.m.   Headed for work and dreading every minute I have to spend there. We have a new vice president and things have changed so much. I used to enjoy leading the benefit orientation sessions for new employees and working with those planning on retiring. Now I do little customer service, and my job is shifting to working with figures and reports—all because I have some accounting experience. Yuck! At least I have a job.

7:30 a.m. Went straight to my cubicle and didn't see anyone. Computer on. Water glass filled. Need to clear out twenty-five pieces of junk e-mail. Where does it all come from? Work on sending COBRA notices to employees who have terminated but still want to continue their health insurance. This is part of my old responsibilities, but I still have to do it.

8:00 a.m. Starting to get calls regarding COBRA. Since there are about 175 graduating residents, I will probably average fifty phone calls from those with questions or who are worried about losing their coverage. I try to assure them they will not experience any lapse as long as they complete the application and return it promptly. Most of the residents calling now are pleasant, as they are just finishing up their residency. The calls will take on a different tone next month when they suddenly realize they haven't done anything about their health insurance.

10:00 a.m. Checked e-mail. Looks like another change coming. Now everyone in the building is going to be connected to one of two central printers. We'll no longer have printers on our desks. I think it's a time waster. You have to print and then walk to the printer and pick up the copy. Of course, you stop and chat with your friends in their cubicles as you head toward the printer. The central printer also prints out a cover sheet, thus it is not only a time waster, but a paper waster, too.

11:30 a.m. Still working on the COBRA notices.

12:30 p.m. Finally. Lunchtime has arrived. A chance to get out of my dungeon! Pardon me, my cubicle. What shall I have for lunch? Let's see, shall I go to McDonald's or

Burger King? It's good to get away from the building and enjoy a quiet hour. I can use the time to read, since I usually eat alone.

I'm going to stick to my diet and have the usual salad. Need to lose weight. I have gained about forty pounds since my mom passed away last October. I just don't feel like doing anything after I get home from work. This isn't a church night, so I should go through some more stuff Mom and I accumulated over the years.

Around Christmastime, we usually cleaned off the tops of the furniture and put the stuff in bags. Somehow, we never got the bags emptied after the holiday and, when the next Christmas came, we filled more bags with more stuff—papers, magazines, mail, Christmas cards, birthday cards (Mom's birthday was December 31). So there are plenty of bags to go through, and I have to be sure there isn't any money tucked away in some of the cards.

Well, I'll glance through the newspaper before returning to work.

1:30 p.m. At least I only have two and a half hours before heading home. Checking on payroll run. It's still not balanced. Hope it's balanced and confirmed by 4 p.m. We had a big problem last week and were late in finishing our part of the payroll process. Still sending COBRA notices for June terminations. Computer system sure is slow in responding to commands and processing. It drives me crazy, just staring at that spinning world icon. Good title for a soap opera, *As the World Turns*. That's what I always think when that icon just sits and spins, not moving quickly enough for me.

3:30 p.m. I find my friend in the cubicle behind me. She's going to court in the morning as she is suing her husband for divorce. He's not working, but asking if he can

this day in the life 196

live in the house while the divorce is pending. I hope she doesn't have to pay the house payment and utilities for him until the house is sold. Her attorney is sure her husband won't be given the house in court, but my feelings are you can't be sure of anything. Judges do their own thing.

It's hard on my friend, as she is literally living out of her car. Or she stays a few nights with one sister or brother and then a few nights with another, partly because she doesn't want her husband to find her. She knows I am concerned about her and that she is on my prayer list. That's why I stop by and give her a hug and a word of encouragement.

4:00 p.m. Finally, time to head for home. When I get there, I turn the hose on trickle to water my one lonely tomato plant. Looks like it has a bloom on it. Better remember to get the Miracle-Gro. Not much of a garden this year. Usually I put in about four tomato plants and two pepper plants. Now I only have this one plant from my friend from Sunday school. Hope I get that six pounds of tomatoes the ads promised.

Nothing much in the mail, mainly junk and bills. Still don't have the packet from the stock company to change the stock from Mom's name to mine. It's been almost eight months since I started trying to get the papers. This means another phone call tomorrow. Change clothes, punch on TV, shred the junk mail, put the bills in the to-do file. What's for supper? Mom used to have the meals ready when I came home from work.

5:00 p.m. Found some frozen, cooked hamburger in the freezer. Have a jar of sauce and some spaghetti. Cooked it up and enjoyed my meal. Watched the local news, washed the dishes, cleaned the stove. It's polka-dotted with sauce. Now, soak my compression sleeve and brush my teeth.

7:00 p.m.   Start getting things together for work tomorrow. Since it's Wednesday, I'll probably wear my favorite purple-striped pantsuit. It is the most comfortable one I have. I put a book in my bag for reading during lunch. Oops, almost forgot. I've got to get outside and turn off the water. Hope I haven't drowned my tomato plant.

7:05 p.m.   The plant is okay. Sure glad I put the hose on a trickle. They say you should water tomatoes deep. Well, this one was watered good and deep. Now I have to get the garbage together to go out.

7:30 p.m.   Phone call from a friend. She was my dancing teacher way back when, so I've known her for about sixty years. She and her husband have just returned from a trip out West. It's always good to hear from her, but the green-eyed monster in me always comes out after talking to her. She's been to so many wonderful places I can only dream of visiting. Dreams cost nothing, but trips do. Can't think about going anywhere right now as I need to get out of debt. Maybe I'll be able to do a little traveling after I retire. Need to get my bath.

7:45 p.m.   Another phone call, this one from a good friend from church. This is Bible School week and she is cooking the main dish for the workers tomorrow night. She isn't feeling well and has come down with a case of shingles on her forehead. Since she promised to bring the food, she wants me to pick it up after work and take it to church.

I worry about her. She is eighty-seven years old and just lost a son who had been in ill health for quite some time. I know she is still grieving, and I don't think her family members grasp the depth of her grief. They still expect her to clean, cook, and wash clothes. Maybe they will realize what they have lost when she is gone.

this day in the life   **198**

I miss my mom terribly. This is the first time I've lived alone with no one to take care of me, but I cherish all the good times we shared. She has always been my biggest supporter and encouraged me to do whatever I thought I could accomplish, like quitting work and going back to college. She was always there for the ups and downs. As she grew older and her health started to deteriorate, I couldn't leave her alone, so we just became best friends. Sometimes, I would go out with other friends, but she never minded.

Mom grew up during the Depression and saved everything. Unfortunately, I have her genes. There's a half-done afghan and a bicentennial quilt to piece somewhere in my closet. How long ago was our bicentennial?

8:00 p.m. Shower and start winding down for bed. Worked on the church's books to finish the June financial statement. I've been doing the books now about fifteen or twenty years. When the church treasurer resigned, there was no one who wanted to tackle the books so they asked me if I would do it for a small stipend. This small stipend is now about $55 a month. I'm glad to take care of the books and the money does put gas in my car.

11:00 p.m. Dozed off and missed the news. Oh well, tomorrow is another day. Lock up, get a glass of water, and to bed. Looking forward to a family gathering for July Fourth. I always look forward to our family gatherings, as I seldom see my youngest nephew and his family, or my brother and sister-in-law. That will be the bright spot in my week!

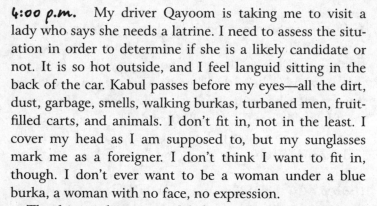

Latrine

4:00 p.m. My driver Qayoom is taking me to visit a lady who says she needs a latrine. I need to assess the situation in order to determine if she is a likely candidate or not. It is so hot outside, and I feel languid sitting in the back of the car. Kabul passes before my eyes—all the dirt, dust, garbage, smells, walking burkas, turbaned men, fruit-filled carts, and animals. I don't fit in, not in the least. I cover my head as I am supposed to, but my sunglasses mark me as a foreigner. I don't think I want to fit in, though. I don't ever want to be a woman under a blue burka, a woman with no face, no expression.

The driver is listening to Madonna *(La Isla Bonita)* and I just laughed out loud, which made him laugh. But he has no idea why I laughed. "The beautiful island" is just so NOT true here in Kabul, where there is barely enough water to keep everyone alive and where things are not too beautiful after twenty-three years of war and four years of drought. Ah, now the music is Afghan and I feel a shift in my feelings. This is the music that goes with the surroundings. It fits here and I feel comfortable with it. Madonna has no place in this country.

4:45 p.m. I have just finished my interview with the woman who requested a latrine. She is bringing me tea to thank me for coming to visit. Two gorgeous children are staring at me, wondering who I am. I ask their names, but they just giggle behind their hands, touching my shirt from time to time. Ah, tea is here . . .

5:35 p.m. I know there are plenty of people here with really bad latrines, because I see and smell them every day. But, when you don't have a latrine at all, that is really bad. I write on my assessment form, "Desperate need for latrine. Build immediately." I tell her that tomorrow she will receive her ID number. She thanks me as though I had personally donated the money. I so much want to hug her, but it would be shocking. Instead I say, *"Tabrik basha"* (congratulations) and shake hands. Moments like this make working in dust and flies totally worth it.

Tanya Abadia Weaver, 34, Kabul, Afghanistan;
humanitarian worker, Shelter for Life International

Melissa Summers, 30, Royal Oak, Michigan

Two cute kids, an executive husband, a house in the suburbs. "It's all I ever wanted, but I'm still filled with angst and conflicting emotions." She started her own website that reads like a dark comedy about the realities of at-home momness. "I hate when people complain about how hard it is, then instantly apologize—'but I really love my kids.' That's not even up for debate that you love them, so let's talk about the more complex issues." She met her hubby when she was twenty; married at twenty-four. Surprised—"very surprised"—to find herself pregnant eight months after the wedding and a few credits shy from a degree in English. Analyzes things to death. A perfectionist. Cynical. "I'm not walking around all sad, but I see the reality a lot of times, and my realities tend to be pessimistic. Humorously pessimistic." Born, raised, and still living in a bedroom community of the Motor City, but she drives a Japanese SUV. Part economical choice, part "I don't want to have the same minivan as everyone in my moms' club." She likes knitting, running, nurturing her relationship with her husband. "I call him my robotic husband. He's can-do, energetic, all the qualities I aspire to." When her youngest starts kindergarten, she'll finish college. And look for work. Her dream job? "To be a stay-at-home mom without the kids."

8:00 a.m. My morning started at 6:00 with my son, Max, coming to my door every thirty minutes to see if it was time to get up yet (it wasn't). I miss his crib in the morning. He used to sleep later, and he would entertain himself in bed until I'd showered and was ready to face the day. I put it off for as long as I felt I could (he is nearly three and a half, after all), but last week we put away the crib. When we put away the crib, we put away our sleepy little boy as well.

Also, we recently started potty training and there were a few trips to the bathroom between 6:00 and 8:00 this morning. He stayed dry all night long. This is a first and extremely exciting for me because I truly believed my son would never get the hang of the toilet. It seemed far beyond his grasp, but five days later (and two accident-free days) I think he has it.

This is the kind of triumph I live for in this stay-at-home-mother job. I suddenly feel like a potty expert. Like I could teach the world how to use the potty or maybe something else equally as complex, like how to create a sustainable world peace among all nations.

10:00 a.m. I spend the first twenty minutes I'm awake running around getting breakfast for the children and the cats and the fish. I have counted the number of requests from my children I have received in the last fifteen minutes:

Something else for breakfast (after they got what they asked for): 1 (denied)
Potty help (urgent): 2
Clarification about our plans for the day (a trip to the zoo—this plan hasn't changed since yesterday): 3
More juice: 3
Help getting puzzle out: 1
Help getting dolls out: 1
Need a napkin: 2 (foolish mother forgot a napkin!)
CAT IS ON THE COUNTER TRYING TO EAT FISH: 1
Can we watch a video: 1 (denied)

Number of requests from me:

Please don't tie shoelaces around the cat's neck: 1
Please stop fighting about nothing: 1

I try to remember that this is my actual job, but sometimes (almost all the time) the never-ending requests and needs overwhelm me. I'm a little disenchanted with my job currently. This has been an overriding theme of my stay-at-home life, but it seems to have reached a fever pitch in the last six months. I'm functioning in burnout mode a lot of the time. Now, at 10:30 in the morning, I am really having trouble facing ten more hours of work (seven and a half more until my husband, Logan, gets home). This is how I feel every morning at this time.

1:00 p.m.   We were supposed to meet up with women from my mothers' group at the zoo this morning. Of course we were late (as usual) so we missed them. I don't mind taking the kids to the zoo on my own. It's nice to go at our own pace and see the things my kids like. We can eat lunch when we want, and we don't have to hold up the group with potty breaks (very important in this infancy of potty proficiency).

I've found myself pulling away from the other mothers. I'm not sure why. Partly it's this low-level depression I walk around with all the time. Partly it's that a lot of the moms I know are planning on having more kids. More, like three or even four.

I look at them with their babies attached to their breasts and the toddlers in the double strollers and the bags full of supplies and I feel so thrilled to be released from that part of motherhood. It took every bit of my energy to do that part. But these women enjoy it. They have complaints, yes, but they enjoy it so very much they're having two or three more of these little people, and I just can't relate and it makes me feel a little inferior in the mothering realm because having more children sounds like a small death to me. I would love another child just as much, that's not the issue. It's the day-to-day work of raising them that drives me to the brink of my sanity.

We live three minutes from the zoo and have a membership. It's nice because if one's child has a monumental tantrum within five minutes of arrival, you can just leave and try again another day without having thrown away the $30 price of admission (plus parking). Not that this has *ever* happened to me. (Sure.)

We walked around the zoo, just the three of us, and it was nice to be out of the house and in the sunshine. I feel fortunate to get to do these things, while other moms I know are in the office when they'd rather be taking their kids on fun outings. The kids were good, got along, didn't whine too much. Max used a public restroom once in two hours and didn't have an accident. (Have I mentioned how excited I am about pee pee in the potty?)

I'm a little torn because I feel left out of my mothers'

group, but also I am in desperate need of some interaction with other women during the day. Today would have been a nice day to let my kids play and to let myself talk about more than poo poo and pee pee in the big boy potty. But if we had spent time with my mothers' group, I'm sure that topic would have come up since I bring it up to just about anyone who stands near me for more than one minute. It's probably the most exciting thing that's happened to me in six months. The last exciting thing was the discovery that the Magic Eraser from Mr. Clean was not an exaggeration at all. It really is *magic*.

2:00–3:00 p.m.   Nap time used to involve real naps. The children went to bed right after lunch and either fell asleep (Max) or played quietly in the bedroom (Madison). I used this time to eat my lunch in peace and to regroup emotionally. I also caught up with work, read, checked e-mail. Now that Madison has been in afternoon kindergarten, she feels she is too old for a nap. I have found that difficult to argue with, so nap time has become: please-for-the-love-of-god-keep-yourself-out-of-mommy's-hair-for-an-hour-or-two time.

Now Max also is finding himself opposed to the nap just like Madison. Today I have to walk him back to his room every fifteen or twenty minutes and set him up with a few books in bed, praying he falls asleep for a little while. It's possible, since we walked all over the zoo this morning. I drove him like a personal trainer, making him walk when he was tired; making up games at the zoo playground involving lots of running and jumping, just trying to wear him out.

It's 2:00 p.m. now, and this means I only have six hours left until I'm sort of off duty. I still have to get through the 4-to-6 p.m. festival of whiny, bored, hungry children. That late-afternoon time is difficult because both the kids and I are tired from the day, and we're all ready for a fresh set of ears, hands, brain . . .

When my husband walks in the door, we will all start talking at the poor man at once. I know that it would be nice for him to walk in and go to our room for thirty minutes to change clothes, use the bathroom, and unwind a little before coming to dinner. It's just that the kids and I are all sick of each other and here is fresh blood!

It's difficult because I REALLY want to talk to him. I want to tell him about what I've been doing all day. I want to make him laugh. I want him to make me laugh. I want to share a drink on the porch with him. I want to hear about what it's like to make actual money for a living, and I want to hear about the other adults he saw that day and how they had lunch in a restaurant and how he didn't have to help anyone on and off the potty thirty-four times. But we mostly have to wait to chat until after the kids are in bed because it's too hard to talk over their needs.

4:00 p.m. I don't really like to physically exert myself in any way. I'm mostly lazy in fact. But I am tired of not recognizing my body anymore, so I've been going to the gym. But if we're being honest here, the real reason I've had continued success with my gym routine is the simple fact that I hate with all my heart being with my kids by the end of the day. I rarely have sitters for financial reasons, but the gym has free child care, so I get thirty minutes to myself, not really doing anything I find pleasant, but at least it's worthwhile and it kills nearly an hour between nap and dinner time.

I also keep hoping the running will help snap me out of this low-level depression. I have been on depression medication before, but I'm not sure I want to be on it again. I worked hard to wean myself, so I keep running, hoping I'll find myself in a better place eventually. Motivation comes in the strangest forms.

5:30 p.m.   The kids are being unusually cooperative as I cook dinner. One of the problems with my late-day workout is the second shower and then the race to cook dinner. I feel overwhelmed by my dinner duties even without a workout, so it just adds another element of chaos. I find it amusing that I have several cookbooks I use over and over that are mainly geared to the working mother who finds herself sprinting at the end of the day to fit everything in, including dinner. I don't like to cook, so these cookbooks appeal to me. I want to do it fast, in thirty minutes preferably. Kind of like my workouts. They have to fit in a thirty-minute time slot because that's all I can force myself to tolerate.

   We're having a spicy peanut chicken tonight that Madison believes is the food of the devil. If Satan himself were coming to dinner, I would serve spicy peanut chicken because that's what he loves. Of course, there are about 427 items on Madison's do-not-eat-no-matter-what-anyone-says list. So while I'm making the chicken for Logan and me, I'm also making a chix nuggets (fake chicken) meal for the kids. Again. Making two dinners is something I had on my own personal "I'll Never" list. But here I am five years later making two dinners, and I hate every minute of it. The reason I started making dinners for my family each night was so we could enjoy each other's company and start a tradition to carry through the years. If we're all going to cry and whine through dinner, I'd rather eat a bowl of cold cereal at the kitchen counter every night.

7:00 p.m.   After dinner, Logan gives the kids their baths while I clean up the dishes. I enjoy this division of labor, not because I love doing dishes (I do not), but because I like the silence and my inability to do five things at once while I am washing them. "I would help, but my hands are all soapy. Sorry!"

It is hard to admit this, but when Logan got home tonight he vacuumed the living room and cleaned up the toys that I didn't get to after my visit to the gym. While he gave the kids a bath, he also folded the laundry. Most days, there's a long list of the things I meant to accomplish. Then suddenly my husband is home from work picking up the slack, and I don't know why it keeps happening.

Tonight Logan decided to mow the lawn at 7:30 so he wouldn't have to do that job over the upcoming three-day weekend. I can't imagine mowing the lawn at the end of my day. I don't know where my husband finds this energy, and I wish he didn't have it because it makes me feel like a horrible failure as a wife and in this job as a stay-at-home mother. This has been on my mind lately because it's almost time for me to reenter the workforce.

I think maybe I'll feel like I'm pulling my share if I'm working outside of the house. But the thought of going back to work fills me with an ugly mix of anxiety and self-doubt. I really don't know how I'll overcome my fears and insecurities and find the right job for me and for my family. I hate to think about it, but when my husband plays the part of Super Spouse like he did tonight, I think I have to get out of this house because I'm not doing enough.

9:30 p.m. Max's nap earlier today prolonged the bedtime routine. There is more talking and requests for things: water, a specific animal, trips to the bathroom, which is fine with me. I'm still on a potty honeymoon. We started at 8:30 and I think he's asleep now. I pray he's asleep. I try to get to bed at 11:00 each night, so this dawdling at bedtime eats into my freedom.

diary of a misfit housewife 209

9:45 p.m.   I was so tired most of the day and now here I am suddenly full of energy. This late-evening burst of energy often keeps me up past my bedtime and makes the mornings even more exhausting than usual. Logan and I are going to put in a DVD and enjoy this evening because tomorrow night he has a photo shoot for a catalog he's working on at work. He won't be home until 10:00 or so.

I'm planning for my day tomorrow, which should be a little less kid intense since Madison has a birthday party from noon to 3:00. We have to go shopping for the gift in the morning. This is dangerous because Target is kind of a personal addiction. In January, we decided to get a handle on our finances and it became clear after evaluating the data, I have a Target problem. Since then, I have avoided Target. Tomorrow I will struggle to avoid putting extra things in my shopping cart. Sounds easy enough, but it isn't easy for me.

I will need to come up with something to fill in the evening because my reinforcements (Logan) won't be showing up at the usual time. So my normal afternoon witching hours of 4:00 to 6:00 becomes more of a 4:00 to 8:00 run. What will I plan? I have no clue. But tomorrow, I'll dust and I'll clean the bathroom and I'm going to do my fair share, because—until I have a job—this is my job and I do need to do it better. Even if I do hate a lot of it.

Good Idea!

2:00 p.m. I'm at the carpet store choosing carpet for the living and dining room. It takes away time spent for other activities I consider more important. I'd rather be quilting. I think I will get sand-colored carpet; it's light and airy. The salesman is an idiot. He's complaining to ME about women not being able to make decisions. What an asshole! Although I know what I want, I think I will go through each sample at least three times.

Carolyn L. Mazloomi, 56, West Chester, Ohio; artist

Noon Peace Café. It is about to close its doors for good tomorrow unless there is an intervention by people like myself who will cover operating expenses for at least five months. In the meantime, we will give our individual input with ideas. I think the café is too narrow now, discriminates against about 99 percent of the town because it is strictly vegan, and even the "vegan" argue about such things as having mayonnaise in the refrigerator. It is ridiculous. I will suggest it be changed to the Peaceful Valley Center.

Dorothy M. Sheldon, 80, Ellensburg, Washington; minister

11:00 a.m.   As we're leaving, my friend Trish tells my thirty-nine-year-old bachelor brother-in-law that—as she'll never see him again—she must tell him that his 1980s-style, blue blocker sunglasses must go. They are out of fashion! Naturally, his response is to tell her that they have a lifetime guarantee, and whenever they break he just sends them back, along with $2 for shipping a new pair. She tells him she's heard that story before, but it's time to make the break.

Janet L. Misamore, 53, Moscow, Russia; homemaker

11:30 a.m.   Finally, LUNCH! The salad with grilled chicken (leftovers from last night) was good, but I really want some chocolate. Really. I'll admit it here since my husband (who is dieting with me) isn't reading this. Low-carbing sucks. It sucks rocks. I want some bread, pasta, rice, cereal, and sugar. Oh my God, I want some sugar. I want some chocolate coated in sugar covered with more chocolate and even more sugar.

Holly McDonald, 29, North Richland Hills, Texas;
training coordinator; MedTrials, Inc.

1:00 p.m.   Florence, Italy. Still at shoe factory. No one ordered the ruffle fringe for the fall shoes, which needs to ship next week. I will go to fringe maker tomorrow and refuse to leave until he promises to make them in one day. Will bring pastries and cash.

Holly Dunlap, 32, New York, New York; fashion
designer, Hollywould

12:56 p.m.   Still in my damn pj's. What will I do this afternoon? I have no freakin' idea. But I know one solution and that is to find a book on self-love and to fuckin' forget that yesterday's drama ever came into play and start my day over right now by taking a shower and looking at this negative energy wash away from me forever and forever.

Kathy Thompson, 36, Portland, Oregon; jewelry designer, U-nik Kreashuns

5:42 p.m.   Put more laundry in the dryer. In my next life I am not going to have laundry or taxes or bills. There also will be no religious nuts.

Shirley Knight, 67, Tarzana, California; actor/writer

On June 29, 2004 . . .

28% of day diarists stuck to their New Year's resolutions.

52% got together with friends.

Laurie Stewart, 55, New York, New York

A junkie-drop-out hippie in the sixties. Fast-forward forty years, now a clean and sober development secretary working nine-to-five for a paycheck and a pension. She's also getting her BA at Columbia, one class a semester. The middle-class lifestyle has its advantages: "Drinking and drugging is a very insecure life. When you come back you want things steady and safe." A musician and songwriter, she had a career of steady gigs in small venues until a drunk driver almost killed her. Over the past twenty years: two hip replacements, two amicable divorces, and an ongoing struggle for sobriety. She's inspired by Merle Haggard and his triumph over adversity. "Music saved my life. My guitar grounded me; it's a way of always knowing who I am." Ten years ago, she met her boyfriend, Ira, in a bar—two musicians living parallel lives. "He was a junkie in New York while I was a junkie in L.A."

They both got sober six years ago. His apartment is 210 blocks from hers, "practically cross country." Most weeks, they only see each other Saturday nights. "In many ways, I'm the same as when I was sixteen. I'm still in a romantic haze about my boyfriend. We can't get together on weeknights. I'm still in school . . ." Meanwhile, her biggest wish: "that Merle would record an original song of mine."

6:40 a.m. Wake up with the alarm. I check to see if I'm as fearful and anxious as I was last night. It appears I am. Like the eczema on my fingers, my anxiety pops up from time to time and needs no provocation. Is it really worth going to a therapist to find out why it's in me? That doesn't make it disappear.

As I pass a mirror, I think matter-of-factly, I hate my face. I do. It's so big and old. When did it get so wide and haggard? Just awful. When I was young I wanted to look like Jean Shrimpton or Catherine Deneuve. I had a moon face at the time. My mother told me my lack of cheekbones would make me look young when I was older, and it's true. I was carded 'til I was thirty, and people are surprised to hear I'm fifty-five. But not this morning. Not with this huge, fleshy face with drooping jowls and dried-out old skin. I hate my face.

8:30 a.m. On the subway, heading to work. Why am I so resentful of the other passengers? Odds are they are not here to annoy me, but are commuting to jobs they don't really like, just as I am. The rage and resentment inside me are overwhelming. From what I hear in meetings, rage and resentment are common among alcoholics. Do you think we rage against and resent sobriety? That's a joke. I know the rage and resentment came first, but somehow my two younger sisters don't feel this way. And my older sister is just nuts, born that way I believe.

11:47 a.m. My spirits have lifted considerably here at work, especially with my boss on a business trip to Florida. Talking to my coworkers pulls me out of myself. And talking about my upcoming hip replacement operation makes it more pedestrian and less threatening. Both Mary and Joy already knew, even before I told them, about the long-shot possibility I could end up with a paralyzed leg. Until my current surgeon told me this, I had never heard of this potential side effect, and I've had my hip replaced twice! You should always discuss medical procedures with girl-friends. Women are their own greatest health resource. That's probably why we live longer than men. We share knowledge, while men compete and die.

I keep reminding myself, this time we're not replacing the whole hip, just a part, so it won't be such a big deal. And the six weeks I get to stay home to recuperate after this upcoming operation will be a blessing. Nothing I like better than being home alone.

I think one of the major bonds between Ira and me is that he loves being home alone, too. We're happy when we're together, and we're happy when we're apart. I am so blessed to have finally found my perfect match. It just seems my whole life was spent getting to the St. Marks bar in the East Village in 1994, so I could meet Ira there. He's *that* perfect for me in every way. In the moments I believe in God, I believe he gave Ira and me to each other as a peace offering. I have to admit, my faith was sorely tested with the breakup of marriage number two to Wacek, the Polish violinist, in Branson, Missouri. There's a tale . . .

2:52 p.m. I went downstairs to get a check from a messenger and decided to go outside for a cigarette. I seldom smoke during the day, but I guess now that I've decided to quit during my six-week recuperation (since I will not be able to descend the five flights of stairs to the street to buy cigarettes), I feel I can just smoke away with an end in sight. The pathetic bargains we addicts make with ourselves! My attempts to quit now number in the double digits. The cigarette was good, very good. I am amazed anyone can quit this habit.

3:47 p.m. Leslee just stopped by and told me she's retiring in July. Oh, I can hardly wait to retire! But since I made a living as a freelance musician, I have very little saved up either in social security or IRA-type stuff and will have to wait 'til I'm sixty-five. Retirement! I love the sound of it. People who can't enjoy retirement are like people who keep working after they win the lottery. What's the matter with these drudges?! Why would you buy a lottery ticket if you're not going to quit your job when you win?

5:50 p.m. I bump into Ann, the head of research, and broach the subject of moving the file cabinets out of my office—correction, the room in which I work that clearly was a supply closet at one time and then outfitted with a long counter, but which has lost none of the charm of a supply closet. This has long been a pipe dream of mine. (Nothing like a day job in an office to screw with your priorities; imagine, moving file cabinets has become a pipe dream.)

For the several months Ann has been here, she and I have done no more than nod hello, so this is a chance for us to get to know each other. We are presenting, the way animals do when they meet. I notice her right eye is twitching and I wonder if I'm responsible. I'm a taller blonde to her petite Asian frame. Do I look threatening? Has she heard what a cranky-pants I am?

Bottom line: I know there's no room anywhere else for these files and that's why they're in my workspace, but I've gotten into this boring discussion and can't seem to get out, even though I keep looking at my watch and saying, "Oh, I've really got to go . . . I've got . . ." I let my voice trail off, hoping she'll think I've got a child in day care. I have no kids, but I know everybody here is responsive to working mothers nowadays, since almost all the women in my office are working mothers.

Ann starts talking about scanners for the contents of the files, and now I know for sure they'll never be moved. This is not the first office I've been in that pins its hopes on scanners, those wonderful marvels of engineering that will make paper obsolete. Clearly a scanner-believer, Ann has the gleam of a zealot in her eye, and she seems to have lost the original point of our conversation about moving the files.

Perhaps if I bring in some plants to put on top of the cabinets . . .

7:30 p.m. At home. I got a letter today from a woman I was best friends with in grammar school. Except for one time in the early seventies, I haven't seen Linda in over forty years. Turns out she's a commune-type hippie; she went all out. I was a junkie-drop-out hippie. Candice, another old friend, was a psychedelic–Laurel Canyon hippie. Both Candice and I came back to the middle class from whence we'd split, but I'm not sure from her letter that Linda ever returned from living "outside."

She handwrites—with spelling and grammar mistakes galore—about the past forty years. It seems she's lived on communes all across the country, fighting the war machine, etc. With the war ended over thirty years ago, I assume some other activities have occupied her time, but she never refers to a job. Her spelling and syntax would seem to indicate getting an education was not one of those other activities.

One thing all the hippies had in common was our opposition to the war, but beyond that our values and priorities were divided. Music was pretty much universally revered, but again, there were many splinter hippie groups with different loyalties and levels of engagement. Take the Grateful Dead and the Deadheads—please.

Candice and Linda and I were all hippies, but our lives were more different than similar. Commune hippies were too sunny and confident that love was the answer and that both material goods and individual alliances were destructive. I like monogamy and I like my things and I've never been moved to give either up. Anyway, I always felt commune hippies were smug. Give me the backstabbing, self-involved, narcissistic dope addict any day. Kidding.

In her letter, Linda describes the beauty of the countryside where she lives in Oregon, but since she never mentions working, in spite of her self-proclaimed communism, I'm thinking she has somehow become independently wealthy. How else could she be sitting in all those gorgeous meadows contemplating the river and her dogs, while vowing to force herself to pick up the paintbrush or charcoal again? Also, she tells me how sorry she is that I have to occupy my time with my demanding job. Me, too!

Linda also is under the misapprehension that: (1) I work for someone I haven't worked for in four years; (2) I have three kids; and (3) I was involved in a murder trial! Maybe she heard I was a witness in a murder trial because the drunk driver who hit me was killed in the accident, but that doesn't really make sense. Linda also brings me up-to-date on what's happened to several people who are

tuned in, turned on, dropped out... came back   **219**

complete strangers to me. Is she high or does she have brain damage? And why am I resentful? Am I going to answer this letter? I guess so, if for no other reason than I'm curious about her.

8:30 p.m. I play a few songs. I haven't played in weeks; partly the psoriasis on my fingertips, but mostly, without an upcoming gig, I've lost my inspiration and drive. That could be why the fear and anxiety have rushed in, to fill a hole. I miss performing so much. What a triumph it was to sell a song to the audience, to have some measure of control over their emotions. Now that I don't have gigs, my relationship with music is as strained as mine with God. What am I going to do about that? I think rather than "deal" with it, I'll just start playing again. It's great discipline, anyway, and discipline is always welcome in my life. Doesn't stay too long, but a welcome guest.

11:30 p.m. *Seinfeld* is over and *Everybody Loves Raymond* is coming on. I watch too much TV; even when it's awful it's always on. Do most single people turn it on when they get home from work? I sit on the couch and look at my Visa bill, a bit of a shocker. Crewneck sweaters on sale from Ann Taylor, pillows on sale from Anthropologie, pants on sale from The Gap and J. Crew online. If everything ends in 99 cents, how can my Visa be maxed out?

I really need more money. It's tough to be single with no income other than wages, pretty much living hand to mouth. When I made my living singing, I remember that concept of extra money from extra work. Now it's always the same, although expenses only rise. It's tough. All my friends got down payments for their first homes from their parents and in-laws. I missed that step (happy couple buying their first home) in both my marriages, along with the alimony step. If I'd been able to have children, of course, I would have had more money coming in from the ex, his parents, and my parents. Children are held for ransom. You can't tell a parent that, don't even try, but to single people it's laughably obvious.

If I lost my job now, I'd be on the street. I'm not lonely, ever, but I sure would like to be pooling my money with another wage earner. And no matter how I beg, plead, or threaten, my cat Lucky is not getting a job. He walks away when I bring up the subject.

11:45 p.m.   I can't believe the day is over. I'm supposed to be in bed around 11:00, but here I sit as if I don't have to get up early and jump back on the treadmill. Who do I think I am? I'm not a commune hippie with nothing but freedom and time to kill. I'm a subversive hippie, locked into and totally dependent on the system, and I really need to get some sleep. Guess who's gonna be cranky again tomorrow?

Culture Clash

7:00 p.m.   My husband Gagi's relatives live in a small, hot apartment. Being from Eastern Europe they seem to believe a "draft" is bad and will make everyone ill. So the a/c is set at something like 80 degrees. Gagi's parents and brother, Backo, are here. (Actually Backo is Gagi's cousin, though Gagi calls him his brother. It's a little confusing the way they refer to relatives in Yugoslavia.) Also here in the apartment are Backo's parents and his baby, Andre. But Backo's wife, Tanja, isn't. I guess she is at work or school.

7:40 p.m.   We all sit around the living room table and eat some meats, cheeses, and meat and cheese pie. I have a glass of ice water and my baby, Aleksandar, wants to drink some, so I let him. Backo says I shouldn't because it is too cold for a baby. It's that crazy cold aversion again. My reaction is, please, he drinks ice water all the time and has not been sick once in his life. (Sure that's just ten months, but still.) Backo's baby always seems to be coughing or have a cold, even though he is not exposed to the horrible things I expose my son to, like ice water!

7:50 p.m. It becomes clear that Tanja is actually in the apartment, but not feeling well. She is in the bedroom with the door closed. I find it unbelievably rude that she hasn't even said something like, Hi, sorry I'm not feeling well. Come on, it's not like the closed door is hermetically sealed to prevent us from catching whatever she has. We are here. We are already exposed. Which reminds me, it is also quite rude not to have informed us that she was sick when we are bringing a baby over. Whatever. This is not the first time she has behaved antisocially.

8:00 p.m. I try to feed Aleksandar, but there is too much going on and he is overtired. Gagi, Backo, and I go out to find some Serbian groceries at local stores. I'm very excited to find imported Fanta from Macedonia. It's the real thing, none of the corn-syrup-laden crap you get in the U.S.

8:45 p.m. Back at the apartment. Say good-bye to everyone except Tanja, of course, and head out. Aleksandar is way overtired and cranky now. Gagi's mom says maybe he has to poop. I say maybe he shouldn't be dragged to Queens when he should be winding down and going to bed.

Mary K. Blanusa, 32, Hillside, New Jersey; associate director, National Council on Economic Education

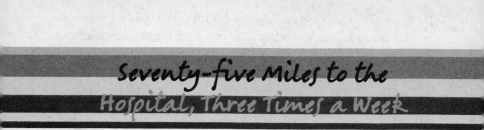

Doris J. Underwood, 66, Berryville, Arkansas

Five years ago, she suffered kidney failure. She's been on dialysis ever since. Mondays. Wednesdays. Fridays. Ailing, but still fighting. She used to be the one who cared for others, like her hairdresser who got a brain tumor. She took her in when the woman's own family wouldn't. "I'm willing to help anybody I can, especially older people." A small-town girl, she moved to Dallas after high school to work as a phone repair technician, eventually becoming the first woman the company recruited to climb the poles. "They called me a hellcat. I wouldn't let nothing stand in my way." A kidder. A bowler, two pins shy of a perfect game. An independent spirit. After thirty years at the phone company, she retired and bought 160 acres to raise cattle. "I'd never been on a tractor. The first time I brush-hogged and looked behind me, I saw how pretty I cut that grass. I just didn't want to stop." She used to have a high temper. "One time I couldn't get the mower started and kicked it. Broke my toe." Her temper's gone now. So are the cows and all but forty acres. She got past the bitter phase of her illness, her humor intact. "She can still laugh like a maniac," says a long-time friend. "Her laugh comes from the soul."

Note: Doris dictated her day diary to her friend, housemate, and caretaker Carolyn Suit, who recorded these entries throughout the day.

9:00 a.m. Wake up hungry, but nauseated. The thought of food is not appealing. Drink a can of protein supplement. My back burns from the ruptured discs. Rising is a trick. I'm dizzy from the low blood pressure.

Today is dialysis day, rescheduled from Monday. Without the blood-cleansing technique I will die. With dialysis, I suffer and ache. Carolyn and our dog, Cuddles, are still asleep. It's raining, gray, cloudy. Flip on the television, more Marines killed in Iraq. I am angry thinking of those young lives crushed over a piece of land and oil. Cats have been fed. Carolyn must have been up already.

10:00 a.m. Cuddles brings the ball to play. He is the joy of my life. He sticks close to me all the time and seems to know something isn't right. He is trained to get Carolyn if I fall or need help. I say to him, "Go get Ma-Ma." He is off like a bullet and won't return without her.

12:30 p.m. Showered and washed my hair. I had to sit down before I could finish my shower. I am frustrated; some days I'm just angry to have lost my independence, my abilities to function. Cuddles is sitting at the bathroom door. I tell him, "Go get Ma-Ma." Carolyn returns to help me dry my hair and get dressed. I have to lie down for twenty minutes before we leave for Fayetteville where the dialysis center is. The nausea is from stroke damage and hemodialysis.

2:30 p.m. I am exhausted from the seventy-five-mile drive. My mind is whirling, trying to escape the reality of what lies ahead for the next four-plus hours. The nurses smile. As the nurses hook me up to the dialysis machine, I look around this sterile room. I try to psych myself up, seeing those around me who are in wheelchairs, unable to move themselves away from the tubing and vacuum system that cleans the body wastes from their blood. My heart aches for those who have lost legs, feet, or other body parts due to acquiring diabetes from dialysis. I am so nauseated, tired from anemia, another side effect of renal failure. I realize they also have nausea, anemia, diarrhea, take twenty-five to thirty pills a day, obtain infections constantly because of a compromised auto-immune system, but at least my body is still intact. I do not yet need a wheelchair. With assistance, I can walk. They will deal with the same problems that I must, but so many will have to go by ambulance to nursing homes.

I am hooked up to the machine. The antiseptic smell is overpowering, somewhat like having your head stuck in a pail of alcohol. The dark bluish purple blood is swirling into the tubing from my neck, racing toward the condensed vacuum filters into a larger tube that will finish removing the waste material my body has collected in two days.

I am nervous, slightly agitated, my hands won't be still, partially from my stroke in January, partially from wanting to jerk out the tubes and run out of here. The warning

this day in the life   226

beeper is going off, alerting the nurse that my blood pressure is dropping too quickly. It is at 90/55.

3:00 p.m.   I drink a cup of chicken broth, my blood pressure stops dropping. The machine is turned off, adding more time to sitting in this awful chair. The nurse turns the vacuum back on. Beep! Beep! Beep! Off goes the machine. I cannot turn my head or move due to the tubes in my jugular artery closing off blood flow. The machine is extremely sensitive to arterial blood flow. My back is burning along my spine and between my shoulders. I probably am doing some emotional numbing now. Carolyn, who worked as a social worker, used to tell me I was the textbook example of "creative denial." She doesn't say that anymore, just tells me, "Having your head up your butt is not a bad place to be!"

4:00 p.m.   Beep! Beep! Beep! I would like to tear this machine apart with my hands or beat it with a hammer. My blood pressure is dropping again, down to 88/44. Nurse stops the machine. Calls Dr. Wu and the charge nurse. I am exhausted. Is this really worth the effort? Now two nurses are listening to my heart, pushing, probing, shaking lines, tubes, filters.

4:15 p.m.   Dr. Wu comes sailing in from his office and reads all the blood pressure checks that have been taken every five minutes for the last thirty minutes. Listens to my heartbeat, checks my pulse. He is attempting to smile, but his eyes project concern.

We have been through so much together, down a long, weary, treacherous road. He tells me the infection I have is activating again, and the stress of the hemodialysis is causing my blood pressure to drop too quickly. He orders only

1500 cc removed instead of 2000 cc. He smiles, hugs me, and says, "Too many more patients like you, I'll retire." I tell him that he is too young to retire and probably doesn't have time to cash all the insurance checks he receives.

5:30 p.m. The machine is pumping away, gurgling, swooshing, dark liver-looking blood gliding along. Extremely nauseated. Intense back pain, searing. If pain is the body's index to being alive, I guess that I am. My muscles are cramping, probably too much potassium is being removed.

I look around the room again. Renal failure causes one to see the world—the real world—through different eyes. In this room, there isn't any prejudice. There isn't age, gender, skin color, religious preference, intellect, height, weight, fashion, or any of the other societally imposed distinctions that separate us from the true human beings that we are.

What do my weary eyes see after a four-and-a-half-year struggle with staying one step ahead of death? There, in one chair, a young woman, barely eighteen, bright blue eyes old before their time, staring blankly into space. An older African American covered to his chin with a white sheet, sleeping as his purple-bluish blood surges into the tube and filters. A young Hispanic boy, perhaps twelve years old, plays with a computer game. He has youth. He still believes this disease is beatable. Perhaps he will receive a transplant and actually live a productive life.

6:30 p.m. I drink some ice water. Beep! Beep! Beep! Must have a nausea pill, beep or not! Nurse pushes buttons, listens to my heart again, as if listening makes it beat more regularly. Carolyn has been reading Bill Clinton's book, *My Life,* to me between beeps. I am a die-hard Democrat. My buddy, Karl, is a Republican's Republican. Wish he were here; we'd talk Clinton politics. Maybe get us both kicked out. At least I wouldn't hear the swish sound.

Carolyn keeps on reading. We are determined to finish the 900-plus pages during dialysis. The nurses stop by to hear some of it. I am covered up by my "angel blanket" my friend Maggie bought me for Christmas. I snuggle underneath it, knowing Karl and Maggie searched all over Nashville to find a comforter with an angel embroidered on it. I believe it's knowing so many people care about my health, all the little extras they do, that keeps me trying. I think of my friend Helen, who rarely misses a day without calling to check on me, even though she is dealing with her own personal loss.

6:45 p.m. Without my caregiver, my friend Carolyn, life would certainly be more difficult. People supporting me, encouraging me to keep on trying. My grandson, young, healthy, in the prime of his life, mid-twenties. He never misses a day to come in, say hello, bring me some type of "forbidden food." I've told him that I suspect the pretty young nurses here are a part of his reason for stopping by.

I wish my family could understand more about renal failure. They don't have any concept of going into the hospital, having surgery or acute care, and not getting well. My sisters want me in a larger hospital so I'll get well. I know I won't ever "get well."

7:00 p.m. This beep means I'm done. Another battle finished. Another day of dialysis marked off the calendar. We put on masks. The nurse turns off the machine. With gloved hands, she disconnects my two lifeline tubes. She checks my incision. It is infected, as is the exit site from where the peritoneal catheter once was. It is oozing yellowish, bloody liquid. She sterilizes both sites, places gauze on them and takes a sample to send off. We don't make eye contact, as each of us knows this is the infection that caused my PD catheter to be removed, and resulted in me being placed on hemodialysis.

9:00 p.m. For a while I am free from the nightmare of dialysis, blood, disease. I am home, in the peaceful, quiet Ozark Mountains. It is raining again. Looking out the window, I see a mother deer and her two spotted baby fawns stepping from the edge of the trees. Cuddles is snuggled next to me, giving his warm, wet licks, his kisses. Carolyn says good night and goes to finish the laundry from this morning.

Perhaps I endure all the intrusive, painful medical procedures three days a week to hold on, at least for a while longer, to the real world that I love. In my quiet moments, my reflective times, I am aware that I love and am loved by family and friends. I am at peace knowing so many care and want me to live. What more can we ask of life than that we would be missed if we were not here.

From the Other Side of the Dialysis Chair . . .

3:00 p.m. Dorie is having a miserable day with her machines that beep every time she moves. Her arms and legs go to sleep. I read Bill Clinton's *My Life* louder and faster to her. Maybe my quiet, pacifying voice will calm her. I get us some coffee. Who shows up but the dietician! Coffee is NOT on the hemodialysis diet. Laura gives Dorie zinc in an attempt to stimulate her appetite and increase her sense of taste. Laura gives me a NOT-so-happy look! Fortunately, Laura, a marvelous dietician, doesn't know about the can of tomatoes Dorie ate several bites of last night.

Carolyn Suit, 56, Berryville, Arkansas; social worker

Reality TV

10:00 p.m. On to the next cop show, *NYPD 24/7*. Here we are, three prosecutors watching a show following cops on their jobs—we really need to branch out. This is fun though. We all search for police officers or detectives with whom we have worked and recognize a few. It is strange to see people we know on television doing their job. In one segment, officers execute a search warrant. Interesting to see how it is done. We all know the steps the officers must take, but to see how what we draw up on a piece of paper is put into action is very enlightening. The potential danger is far more prevalent than I want to believe. It takes guts to do the work of a police officer. Work blending with television—too strange.

> *Barbara J. Hutter, 38, New York, New York;*
> *prosecutor*

Heaven on Earth

10:55 a.m. The dogs rush to the water to drink and wade. It's really a jungle here. Lush and moist, large ferns, towering trees, very heavily forested. Beautiful, eerie, mysterious, like God. I always think of God when I am in the forest, think that if he's anywhere, he's bound to be here—not heaven. Or, maybe this is heaven. Fine with me. I'd rather have it now than wait to die for it later. Ouch! Stung by a sweat bee.

Brenda K. White, 50, Somerset, Kentucky; writer

Feeling Her Age (Almost)

I'm getting ready for my granddaughter's wedding in Faribault, Minnesota, so I'm up early for the four-hour drive. My daughter and her husband are taking me. The day is sunny and there are beautiful flowers. This is my first outdoor wedding—so nice! I got a little stiff from sitting, so I said to my daughter, "I feel like I'm ninety years old today!" She said with a grin, "Mom, you're ninety-five!"

Margaret Murphy, 95, Sioux Falls, South Dakota; resident, Good Samaritan Center

Dr. Love

2:00–5:30 p.m.   My visit to the dentist. What a nightmare this turns out to be. I don't know what's worse, the fact that I have to pay $858 on the spot or that I spend three and a half hours in the chair being drilled, sanded, and shot full of novocaine. While the dentist—who sports a soul patch and feathered hair, keeps calling me "sweetie," and is much younger than I am—leans over me, filling my mouth with an impossible number of tools, I keep thinking of the movie *Marathon Man* as I always do in any dental situation.

The good news is that I don't need a root canal. Small mercies. One entire side of my face is numb, yet I can still feel his drill sending hot bolts of pain into my jaw. I make unghh noises and wave my hands. "You metabolize novo-caine really fast," he tells me. He drops things and spills water on me. I start thinking he's just out of dental school. He's got a swagger and I can hear him flirting with several other female patients. He leaves me in the chair, suction positioned in my mouth for twenty minutes. "Okay," he says when he comes back, "I'm all yours."

Debra Ginsberg, 42, San Diego, California; author

So Smart

9:00 p.m. After pajamas, story, final snack, potty, and teeth brushing, we are in the tent. Talia falls right to sleep, but Oliver is lively after his long nap earlier. We cuddle. I relish the feel of him, the perk of his voice, his explanations of things. I say, "How did you get to be so smart?" He says, "Because you play with me."

Eve Pearlman, 34, Alameda, California; writer

Takeoffs and Landings

Kitty Thurnheer, 38, Ithaca, New York

A pilot for Mesa Airlines, her passion started when a friend flew her over her family's farm when she was seventeen. "I just started bawling. Flying was something I had to do." She's worked a diversity of jobs—computer tech support, car dealer, stripper, substitute teacher—all the while spreading her wings and eventually buying her own plane. Strong and competitive. The first in her family to go to college. "I didn't know how to go to college; didn't know anyone who had." A feminine tomboy. She's taken jobs on a dare and to prove something to herself. "Once I've finished something, I think, So what, anyone can do this." She was married once, but he walked out. "The only reason I survived is that one day my mother said, 'We're going to build that house you've been talking about.' " So they did . . . on her family's two-hundred-acre property. She and her father cut down trees, sawed them on the family sawmill. She dug her own septic, did all the wiring and plumbing. "Every day I'd say I'm going to kill myself, but first I'm going to finish this house." Boy-crazy growing up, now she's playing traffic controller again to a complicated love life. Future goals? "I think I want to have a kid, but I'm afraid. Will I be giving up my life, my career? I don't know any woman who has a kid in this business."

2:00 a.m.   I get up and take two Advil for my sore throat. I should have bought the antibiotics yesterday and charged the $100 on my credit card.

5:00 a.m.   Why is it, when you *finally* fall asleep after tossing and turning for three hours, the alarm goes off? Ugh. Okay. I'm showered, in my uniform, drinking my second cup of coffee. I shouldn't be drinking this—I'm going to have to make the "walk of shame" to the back of the plane during flight to use the lavatory.

I feel like crap. I can't believe I've been sick for two weeks and am still flying. I only have two legs this morning: Memphis to Charlotte, then Jackson, Mississippi. Done by 10 a.m. if nothing breaks or delays. Then I can rest again. The captain wants to go drinking—I owe him four beers because I let the plane overspeed four times in the past two weeks. It's an unwritten rule with pilots: If you overspeed, you owe the other pilot a beer. The plane is only certified to fly 0.78 mach or 320 knots. If it goes faster than that, this woman's sexy voice comes on: "Overspeed. Overspeed." Research shows men respond best to a woman's seductive voice. It's such a man's world I live in, wearing my tie and my jacket that defeminizes me, but I love every minute of it.

takeoffs and landings   **235**

8:00 a.m.   Airborne, climbing through a beautiful layer of puffy clouds. When I was a kid, there was a commercial of a car driving through a huge poster that read "Exxon." I always envisioned what that would be like, driving through a "wall." Flying into clouds is just like that—as we "drive" right into the clouds. I'm always surprised it doesn't hurt. I have the best job in the world! On this morning's preflight I saw two boxes of U.S. mail get loaded into the cargo bay. I guess that makes me a modern Pony Express mail carrier in my Embraer 145 jet. She's a sweet little jet—holds fifty people and is 98' long and 66' wide from wingtip to wingtip.

9:00 a.m.   Starting our descent into Charlotte from Flight Level 290 (29,000 feet). It's six miles in haze there. This is the busiest time in the cockpit—setting the navigation radios up, planning which runway, reviewing the approach plate (chart) for that runway, and calling Operational Dispatch (the folks on the ground) to let them know we're ten minutes out—all while still flying, making an announcement to the passengers, and watching outside for traffic.

9:07 a.m.   Autopilot fails with an abrupt turn to the right. We reset it and it fails again, so the captain decides to hand fly the plane. As we set up for the approach into Charlotte, my navigation radios fail. Good thing it's VFR (visual flight rules) today. These electric airplanes are great when everything works, but as with any computer, we often have minor software glitches. Thankfully, this plane is reliable, and I like knowing that all the control surfaces are operated by cables. If I lose my hydraulics, I can still manhandle her to the ground, similar to driving after losing the power steering in your car.

9:37 a.m.   On the ground. As I walk to Starbucks to get my mid-morning fix, my lover Jim calls. He's also a pilot and has just landed in Memphis. We've met a couple times to enjoy each other's company. I guess we have what pilots are known for—hungry sexual appetites. On our second trip together, after a few drinks, a back rub turned into something more.

In my complicated life with ex- and current boyfriends who keep wanting to marry me and have children, I love the simplicity I have with Jim. He's incredibly passionate and loving, with no demands made upon me. He asks me when we're going to meet again, since we haven't had a chance to get together in nearly three months. I make excuses, not wanting to tell him the real reason—my period has lasted three weeks out of the month for these past three months. It's hard to meet up with Jim during that one week off, especially now that our schedules conflict.

I guess Jim is really not in a place to make demands, with a devoted girlfriend at home whom he professes to love. Just coming out of a five-year passionless relationship, I felt like meeting Jim was like hitting the Lotto! I've flown to meet him on a couple of his overnights and it's been great, but I beat myself up terribly afterwards, mostly because I know I'm only a piece of ass to him. I wonder why I do it.

Now that I'm in a relationship with my lawyer, Mark, who handled my divorce ten years ago, I'm not sure how I feel about being with Jim. But I've been honest with Mark and told him that I will see Jim if and when I get the chance. I know this will devastate Mark—perhaps I do it to get him to be less serious. For the past seven years, Mark has been my best friend and confidant. He's extremely intelligent and I love big brains. I pursued him romantically since I first met him, always more aggressively between relationships, even asking him to just have an affair with me. He didn't budge until this spring when he and his wife split.

Noon   Delayed departure. Just what I need when I feel so lousy. Twenty people. Thirty-six bags. Cargo: 1,100 pounds. Fuel: 9,700 pounds. Plane empty weight: 26,977 pounds. Total gross on takeoff: 42,226 pounds. All boarded, but can't go. Accumulator failure: emergency brake isn't working. Maintenance is here. Looks fixed. Good to go. Two hours late. Oh no, now we wait twenty-five minutes more for catering!

12:15 p.m.   Mark is on break from trial. He calls to see how I'm feeling. Lousy. He's so nurturing and loving, but I struggle with him being fifty-nine—twenty years my senior. And he's not the "shiny penny" my ex-boyfriend Johnny is. I still miss Johnny, who is one year older than me and never married. We had so much fun together, flying to Oshkosh (the world's largest aviation convention) in my plane, sleeping under the wing. He flies a Citation X for a corporation. We broke up a year ago, but after four years of flying and fun, it's hard not to look back. Even if it did lack passion.

I miss sharing aviation with Johnny, but I'm done with long-distance dating. I always thought a relationship could just "be," but it became evident with Johnny and me that it needed to grow to the next step or end. Neither of us was willing to move to where the other lived, so we both fly and periodically call each other to voice our regrets about our decisions. Bottom line is, we love each other, but we love airplanes more.

Finally, we get our push-back. My leg. I get to fly.

Down the runway, rotate at 123 knots. I love my job. As I pull back on the yoke, I'm twenty feet in the air before

I feel my main gear lift off, fifty feet behind where I'm sitting. Just out of 10,000 feet, the captain has to use the lavatory. By law, the flight attendant has to come to the cockpit. We ring Belinda and she's happy about coming up.

Two women in the cockpit. It's a special and rare moment. "Wow! It's beautiful up here," Belinda says, wide-eyed. She tells me she hasn't been in the cockpit in flight in several months. Again, I realize how lucky I am to have this job with such a miserable aviation economy, so many unemployed pilots, so few jobs. But I've paid my dues. September 11 left me unable to find work as a pilot for two years. During that time I took odd jobs as a carpenter, a bulldozer operator, and a front desk clerk. I wondered if I'd ever be employed as a pilot again. My self-esteem was in the toilet. I hated that the thing I loved most was the thing that I felt had destroyed me financially.

My life savings are gone, and I now have a mortgage on my home, all so I can fly a $20 million jet and bring home $250 a week. Working in software paid four times as much, but I don't miss troubleshooting networks. When I hop in that plane and feel her spirit, I know that I'm doing the right thing, with the best view an office can have. I've wed my job for love not money, and love always wins. I think. I hope.

I float a little down the runway, but the touchdown is soft. As the people get off, I look at them directly and thank them for flying. I have delivered them safely to this destination. Each person is loved by someone. They all have families, a life, a job, but it's just another flight for them. I'm glad they don't know what weather we just flew through before getting them on the ground safely, but sometimes I wish they did, so they'd pause a moment and celebrate *life*.

I do my postflight walk-around, checking to be sure

everything looks good and we didn't unknowingly suffer a bird strike or anything else. A cute old man in a straw hat is pumping fuel in the plane. He hands me a butterscotch candy. I thank him and am surprised as he quickly kisses me on the cheek, then turns back to the fueling panel on the plane. I grab his arm, spin him back around, and kiss *him* on the cheek. He smiles a huge, surprised toothless smile and suddenly I feel alive.

Such a strange, simple encounter. I nearly dance away from him. As I check the nose and nose wheel well, I kiss my hand and pat the plane on the nose to thank her. I believe planes have spirits and thrive on love as much as we do. On the last flight of every day, I give her my thanks.

2:30 p.m. After waiting fifteen minutes for the hotel shuttle (which we forgot to call as soon as we landed), I'm finally in the hotel, in bed. I'm so sick. And I have my damn period to boot! I hate having my period. It pisses me off, and I feel so grossed out. Not to mention the cramps, heavy bleeding, on and on. . . . You'd think I'd be used to it by now.

4:30 p.m. Off to dinner with the captain and the flight attendant at the closest nearby restaurant, which happens to be Chili's. But first a stop at Eckerd's to pick up the antibiotics that my doctor called in. Now maybe I'll get better. This time he called in a prescription my insurance covers. I still can't afford the company's insurance plan, so I'm using the last couple months of New York's free insurance for poor people, which I qualified for last year with my huge annual income of $5,000. Our medical program in this country has SO much to be desired!

I buy the captain the four beers I owe him, thankful for happy hour's two-for-one deals! We have a good time, and Belinda and I try to get the captain to show us his hairy chest, evident from the patch at his collar. It's nice for the two women to sexually harass the guy for a change. The captain doesn't acquiesce but suggests we swap a "flash" for his "flash." This isn't a fair trade, since he has hair on his chest!

7:10 p.m.   Back from dinner with two glasses of wine in me and *finally* I'm feeling no pain. There is some healing in alcohol.

Long phone call with Mark. We talk every night. Sometimes it's good; sometimes it seems like an obligation. Big discussion about Jim. Mark asks if we spoke today. Yup. Mark isn't requesting anything of me, but says gently that if I see someone else, then he can, too. But I take comfort that I doubt he will. So crazy, relationships. I don't know why I am so afraid of commitment. Guess it has to do with marrying someone I worshipped and him leaving me unexpectedly. Ten years later, I still can't seem to trust.

8:30 p.m.   I have a 5 a.m. wakeup call for my 6:55 departure to Charlotte. Tomorrow I'll sleep in my crash pad in Charlotte. Luckily, my crash pad is with three other pilots from my ground school, and we're more like a family than just a fiscal necessity to each other. It's almost as good as home.

Oh well. Tomorrow's another day. More miles to fly, more things to run from. One thing about being on the road—or in the air—you escape reality. No wonder I love this job.

6:00 p.m. I am the starting pitcher and am pretty nervous when I get out there for the first time in months. I do pretty well though—I only hit two batters—but luckily they don't get first base in slow-pitch rules, and my sheepish smile gets me out of any trouble. We end up winning pretty handily after an hour and a half in a low-key game. Terry doesn't curse out the other team, Paul and I don't bicker about whether his comment was critical or constructive, and Karen is giving everyone back rubs. The only debate is where we plan to have drinks after the game.

Suzanne Cope, 26, Somerville, Massachusetts;
associate marketing manager, Houghton Mifflin

8:50 p.m. I ask the DJ if he will play a Shania Twain song. One of my crewmates had introduced me to Shania's music when we were training together for my fifth flight. He's a great dancer and suggested we dance together in orbit, so he flew Shania's album *Come on Over.* The first song on that album, "Man! I Feel Like a Woman!" is even more to fun to swing dance to weightless than it is on earth.

Janice E. Voss, 47, Houston, Texas; mission specialist
astronaut, NASA Johnson Space Center

9:00 p.m. After a looong game of Life, we all count up our money. Both my niece and nephew need help, so I calculate everyone's money. I won by a landslide. I feel kind of mean because I kind of pitted the kids against one another. John and I had high salary cards, but mine was higher. When Katy landed on the "trade salaries with any player" spot, she looked at me and I said, "But I'm nice to you and Johnny said that mean thing to you earlier!" So she took his card instead. That is how the rest of the game went, and I'm sure that is why I ended up winning.

Melissa J. Dyer, 25, Fort Myer, Virginia; staff
sergeant, special band member, U.S. Army

11:45 a.m. As the music begins, Paul throws to me and I do a turnover of the disc to him. He takes it upside down and does a triple-fake catch, then throws two discs out. I nail-delay one of them and do an under-the-leg pull to a flamingo catch. He does a series of rim pulls to his catch. All while the disc is spinning at high velocity. We've gone through the entire four-minute routine with our song eight times already, with another thirty minutes left to practice.

Lori Daniels, 41, Honolulu, Hawaii; assistant
professor and freestyle Frisbee champion

8:40 I have three kids that need to be in two places at the same time, and we are already ten minutes late. I ask the first six times and then finally yell on the seventh time, "Everyone get in the car." Their refrain, "Mom, why do you always yell?" My kids finish putting on their cleats and shin guards, fixing their hair, putting on sunscreen and bug spray, and wolfing down a bag of dry cereal in the car. We drop off my youngest and then race to the next town to drop off the other two at soccer camp. Of course they are in the groups that are on the fields at the opposite ends of the high school. I'm breaking a sweat, and I have yet to work out . . .

Heidi P. Worcester, 42, Lyme, Connecticut; children's book author, mom of three

On June 29, 2004 . . .

46% of day diarists did thirty or more minutes of exercise.

44% didn't do housework.

84% had fun.

~~~~~~

A Refugee Helping Refugees

Adeeba Sulaiman, 43, Atlanta, Georgia

She works as a resettlement specialist for the International Rescue Committee, helping refugees rebuild their lives in America. Born and raised in Mosul, Iraq, the third of twelve children. In 1984, she earned her degree in European languages from Mosul University and speaks English, French, Arabic, Kurdish, and some Assyrian. For years, Saddam Hussein made her family's life a living hell. They were arrested and exiled for two years. Later forced to flee with thousands of other Kurds, hiding in the mountains. In 1991, when the U.S. declared northern Iraq a "safe haven," they returned home to a looted house, "nothing left." She worked at UNICEF, which made her even more of a target. In 1996, the U.S. military evacuated her family to protect them. "I had no choice." She remembers the day she left, hearing the news that Saddam's oldest son had been shot and paralyzed.

God is remembering us, she thought. He remembers our suffering. She and her parents spent four months at a refugee camp in Guam, then came to Atlanta. She misses her siblings, spread across four countries. Work is her social life. She's eager to become an American citizen so she can vote. What does she like best about the U.S.? "The freedom. The liberty. I knew the first night here, I'd sleep in peace. I'm not going to be taken to prison again. I will be grateful for America for the rest of my life."

Midnight I am trying to fall asleep thinking of what tomorrow will bring, since I have many refugees who are without work and need to pay their rent and utilities. How should we convince these people having a job and feeling independent is a very important thing in life? I am having difficult time sleeping this evening due to an allergy. I will see my doctor tomorrow afternoon and hopefully I will feel better.

7:30 a.m. I woke up and rushed to take a shower. My father asked me how did I sleep last night. I said, Very poor sleep and my allergy was worse than ever. My dad was mad at me. He told me, You deserve it since you are not listening to us in seeing a doctor or going to the hospital. You need some rest, and your health is more important than keeping everything in perfect order. I told him, Thank you, Dad, but I could see the pain in his eyes, telling me, Don't come home today without seeing a doctor. I had a cup of tea with some yogurt. I drove to the office and was at work a little before nine. I planned to be at the office earlier, but my condition made it impossible.

9:00 a.m. I turned on my computer and started cleaning the spam e-mails, then walked to the accountant office to check if she prepared the rent vouchers for July. We pay the rent for almost all our refugee clients who arrived in the past six months. Today we will pay the rent for about sixty families or approximately 250 people. It is not that easy in this tight economy.

The accountant asked me how did I sleep last night? I told her very poor, but I am going to see the doctor at 2:30 p.m. My director saw me and said, as usual, "What a smile!" I tried to hide the picture of my pain and tiredness. When I come to the office, I think only of work and refugees, their sufferings, their bitter stories, their loneliness away from relatives, or those who lost dear ones during the war, conflicts, and violence. If you don't receive your clients with a smile or a happy attitude, they will think you don't like them or care about them. When you work for refugees, you work not for the sake of money, but for the sake of helping people. You should have the heart to do this type of job.

9:30 a.m.   I called one of the clients who wanted to talk to me about her medical appointment. I called her into my office. This client is a single mother with five children and one granddaughter. She arrived from the Sudan two months ago to join her eldest daughter, who filled out a form for family reunification for her mother and siblings four years ago. My client waited for five years at the refugee camp in Uganda and lost a daughter there. Now she has the responsibility of caring for her granddaughter.

She also has diabetes, high blood pressure, and some female medical issues. She had thought she would never recover or get better, which was not the case. I had immediately scheduled her a doctor appointment during her first week of arrival so she could have her medication right away. Now today I have to get her temporary Medicaid to get her started with her follow-up appointment. She tells me that she will not depend on anyone from now on and that she has learned her way around. This client speaks good English, and I was impressed with the progress she made in a very short period of time. She has the confidence in herself and was completely different from when I first met her at the airport two months ago.

10:00 a.m. I walked with her to reception. Then I asked the caseworker aide to arrange transportation for ten clients to get their state photo ID. One of the clients showed up for the ID but left all her documents at home. This client came from Liberia three months ago without any family members. Who knows how she got separated from her family? I introduced her to recent Liberian refugees just in case she would like to visit them or socialize with them, but she is isolating herself.

She is not working yet and needs help with transportation and filling out her medical forms. I had asked her a couple of times to come to the office, but she keeps forgetting and does not follow up properly with her English classes or medical appointments or her job interviews. She looks sad and worried. She could be a model—slim, tall, and with large eyes.

I called her inside the office and asked her why she feels so isolated from the rest of the refugees, and why she never responds to my calls. She said that she is always home, but her roommate only relays calls when she needs her to pay her share of the rent or utility bills. I reminded her of how many times we have been to her house, but she was never there. I know she feels uncomfortable with her surroundings, but at the same time, she expects others to do everything for her.

I asked her to be at the office tomorrow, and if she needs a ride to let me know. I will have to pay attention to this particular client, as I can't leave her alone wondering how to improve her life. I am always thinking about how to better assist these people. They are adjusting slowly to life in America, and they depend so much on their resettlement agency since we are their eyes, providing them with orientation and assistance. I left this client at her caseworker's office. Here comes another.

10:15 a.m. This client is from Somalia and has been here four months. He lost most of his family members during the war and now lives with his aunt, who arrived three months before him. This client came with zero English and now is able to communicate well with everyone. He started working and is asking me to move him from a one-bedroom to a two-bedroom apartment.

I called the leasing office about two apartments I had requested last week. The leasing consultant said she won't have those apartments ready but will do her best to move out my client's family by tomorrow afternoon. The client was so excited and rushed to the phone to call his aunt. His happiness and his big smile meant so much to me. When I see clients like him, they inspire me to do more and more for them without any hesitation. He will be a successful contributor to the community.

10:30 a.m. I felt like I needed a cup of hot tea. I went to the kitchen and met my coworker who came for a cup of coffee. We chatted for a few minutes about some work issues. I brought my tea to my office and gave the intern next door a few files to order and expense sheets to update. One of the staff came to my office and we started calculating bills for utilities and rent, since many of our clients share apartments. We have to calculate accurately. It took more than an hour before we finished.

1:15 p.m. My coworkers wanted me to take my lunch with them. I did not have time, but then thought of taking a quick lunch break. While having my lunch, a client stopped at the break room, asking me to pay his bills and rent for him. I explained to him what he should do, but he was unhappy, then walked to the caseworker's office. Clients with high expectations can be difficult to work with.

2:30 p.m. I went to my doctor appointment, even though it was hard for me to get away from the office. The doctor gave me some pills and did some blood work. He said that I would be fine and needed some time for myself and not for work only, and that I have an allergy for which he prescribed some medicine. I was so anxious to go back to work that I did not even stop at the pharmacy.

3:30 p.m. I came back to the office and had two clients waiting for me. Both are single mothers from Liberia, and each of them has two children. The children's fathers were lost during the war. I wondered if I had children on my own, would I be in the same situation? These women don't know where they are heading. They wonder how will they survive in this big modern and advanced world where men and women are treated equally, unlike the society they came from. For one of them, I found an apartment that will be ready tomorrow.

5:00 p.m. A state caseworker who loves to work for refugees called me. I met him seven years ago when I first arrived in the USA. He asked me if we have any openings at the office. I told him to check the website and read about the vacancies. He knows a lot about refugees but not how to work with them. I did not assure him that he would get a job. We have to be careful when talking to desperate job seekers. Sometimes they will take a friendly conversation to mean we are giving a good reference or promising them a job. Looking for a job is not that easy these days.

6:00 p.m. Here comes my after-hours appointment. I gave her that time so she won't miss any work. She came to sign some documents. Her two sons, eighteen and nineteen, live in a refugee camp in Pakistan. They are in the process of joining her after seven years of separation. I spent forty-five minutes explaining what documents she is signing. She told me that she loves me because I brought her good news of her sons. What an afternoon, to be loved by a sincere mother who got separated from her sons during the war in Afghanistan and did not know about them being alive until seven months after she arrived in the USA.

6:45 p.m. I sent tomorrow's schedules to the team I work with. I called my parents and told them I am still at the office, which they didn't mind. My mother asked me if I am hungry. I said no, since I had some fruit and my leftovers from lunch.

7:00 p.m. Here comes one of the staff. We talked about our work and the best way of helping clients. We asked what we could do to achieve more during the normal working hours.

9:15 p.m. On my way home, I saw this sign for the big lottery game—$210 million—and wondered who will win these millions! Should I buy a ticket?! I had this deep feeling not to buy it. I would not win. But if I won, I would get a big amount of it and give it to my agency, especially to pay rents and utilities for refugees for at least six months from the date they arrive.

At home, my parents asked me how did the doctor visit go. I told them I am feeling better and I already took one pill. My parents said that one of our family friends would visit us tonight. I was surprised because it is late. Then I got a call about a client from the Congo who is having trouble with her leasing office. The woman is a single mother of five children, ages one to thirteen. The children wander around and play in the street. The manager at the leasing office said that she would notify the local authority if this client allows her children to play in the street again.

This client was lucky because the person who translated this message at the leasing office is a friend of mine and that's why she called me at home. I told her I would call the client tomorrow and counsel her on how she should take care of her kids, and remind her of the material she got during her general orientation. Now is the time to repeat it to her. The phone call took more than twenty minutes, but it was worth it.

10:30 p.m.   Here comes my friend with her husband and daughter to visit us. She is a Kurdish refugee from Iraq who arrived with her husband and her son seven years ago. The husband is a mechanic and she is a homemaker. When she had her two daughters three and five years ago, I was there, helping her out at the hospital. I knew them from Iraq but did not have this strong friendship then. We visit each other a lot—picnics, weddings, and funerals. I help them with translating forms and any kind of assistance that requires English. They are very sweet people.

My mother prepared some tea and cookies. We spent the last hour and a half having a good time and watching the world news. They left us around midnight. To me, I felt like the time passed so quickly and that I needed my day to be longer.

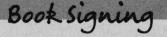

Book Signing

4:45 p.m. The bookstore makes an announcement—there are no more tickets. If you don't have one, go home. I'm pissed. I've been in line for close to twelve hours, since my husband dropped me off at 5:15 a.m. with my lawn chair and "Clinton snacks" (grapes, two bagels, raisin buns, bottle of water). I have spent $26.95 buying Bill Clinton's book from Cody's when I could have got it at Amazon for $21.95. Something in me snaps.

I ask the lady manager whether Cody's has even had a book signing before, and why the hell didn't they just make it first-come first-served, or pass out numbered tickets, or something. The manager admits she screwed up big time. I demand a refund. First she says no, then I say fine, I'll never shop at Cody's again. I probably look like a wild woman and the cops nearby are eyeing me, gauging whether I am a security problem.

The manager suddenly concedes, says she'll give me my money back if I follow her. She leads me to the front of the line and people are shouting, wondering why I get to go ahead. I try to explain that I'm getting a refund, not an autograph. A whole bunch of people follow me, demanding refunds as well. Now I've lost the manager. Near the front of the line security is really tight. The cops have set up a metal barrier, and behind them is a ring of Secret Service agents.

As I try to follow the manager, a cop steps in my path. He asks, "Can I help you?" in a voice that means, Don't take another step. I stammer that I am getting a refund. Finally the manager turns around, realizing she's lost me. She signals to the cop to let me pass. I am still carrying my lawn chair and my bag of bagels. A Secret Service man takes my chair, but lets me enter the store.

I can see the line snaking up the stairs. Bill must be on the second floor, but I can't see anything. I am given my money back and ushered quickly out the door. As I am stuffing my money into my wallet, I drop a penny on the sidewalk. A Secret Service man picks it up, saying, "Here you are, ma'am." I thank him and leave. I am half a block away before I realize that I never got my lawn chair back.

Rachel Crossman, 43, Berkeley, California; substitute teacher

On June 29, 2004 . . .

51% of day diarists read a book.

～～～～

Riot Grrrl Grows Up

Cathy de la Cruz, 23, Athens, Georgia

As a teenager, she was into her generation's brand of feminism, a girl-centric spin-off of the punk movement, only without the macho edge. "A total film nerd," she's worked at the bottom end of the production scale on several independent feature films, "doing all the stuff nobody else wants to do." Now she's applying to film schools while temping. Overly enthusiastic and eager for projects. Being a "whipping girl" to get film work is fine, but there are limits. She quit a reality show pilot after six days—"Worst people I've ever met. Demanding times a million." She's also got her own grant-funded project, an experimental/partially animated documentary about her grandmother, who was sexually assaulted and murdered. "My family never talked about it . . . I went to counseling as soon as I found out." Opinionated. A Hispanic redhead. A hipster? "I'm sure I could be classified as one, but I've just never felt cool." Loves all things feminine, feminist, and fun, whether it's girl garage bands, TV shows like Laverne & Shirley, or dancing to the Go-Gos with her girlfriends. "I would love to get a PhD in girl culture. Maybe I'm what happens when a Riot Grrrl starts to grow up."

Midnight I am at a bar called the Royal Oak in Brooklyn. This is my second time ever in New York. The first time was in January, when I was interning on an independent film. My boyfriend, Will, and I are here with some of my friends, waiting for his friends to arrive.

There are lots of dressed-up girls here. They seem older than me and trying to impress boys. My friend Heather seems jealous of the older girls because she and I decided not to dress up tonight. We opted for comfort. I can tell Heather hates these girls.

The drinks are expensive here. I am drinking rum and Cokes to stay awake (which seems like a joke) and buying Will drinks because he's having bigger money problems than me. Two of Will's friends have shown up. I'm relieved because I was feeling flustered trying to make sure all these different people were having a good time while I'm exhausted, slightly drunk, AND trying to pick the best karaoke song.

Heather's recently titled EX-boyfriend has joined us. She invited him because they're still on "good" terms. He's nice but doing karaoke to sad Willie Nelson songs. He has big, sad, drunk eyes and sings "On the Road Again."

Adam, one of my friends from college, is here, too. Adam just broke up with one of my best friends, Jessica, and I can tell he's a little depressed. I don't blame him. Heather just sang Dolly Parton's "9 to 5." She dedicated the song to me.

She and I both have jobs we are tired of. Hers is just exhausting and mine is just ridiculous. Currently, I'm a glorified telemarketer. I don't actually sell anything, but I call people and disturb their dinner to ask them to take a market research survey. Often people hang up or yell at me.

My turn comes and I sing Lesley Gore's "Maybe I Know," which I'm sure was more like a performance art piece than anything else. I don't really know how to sing, am maybe tone deaf, and probably just look like a punk girl trying to do a sixties girl-group song for kitsch value. But I really like the song.

My boyfriend shows me up because he sings "Hot Blooded" by Foreigner and is like a stripper on stage. Will was once called the "Karaoke King" by a snobby Seattle alternative weekly, so he really must be some kind of karaoke god. We leave soon after because Heather—who Will and I are staying with—tells us she really needs to go to bed. She is, after all, a nanny.

1:30 a.m. Heather and I buy an organic Amy's cheese pizza and put it in the oven at her apartment. We all drink lots of water. She's so much thinner than me, and I know I shouldn't be eating this, but whatever. I'm on vacation. I give Heather my phone card and she half-drunkenly calls her current boyfriend in Italy. He's there for the summer. I imagine him in a cobblestone room somewhere beautiful, picking up his cell phone. I obviously have never been to Italy. I tell Heather she can keep my phone card since I have a cell phone. She tells me I'm the best. She has cable and we watch Dave Chapelle's show and eat our natural pizza.

2:15 a.m. Will and I finally go to bed in Heather's room. Will wishes I would hurry up and go to sleep.

8:00 a.m.   I wake up because I always wake up early after I drink. And besides, I'm not quite comfortable when I am sleeping in someone else's bed. I try and go back to sleep. My boyfriend kind of smells. He smells the way something tastes when you leave it in the refrigerator uncovered, a little touched by everything mixed together in a slightly stale way. I don't mind though. I probably would if we didn't love each other. I'm sure I smell, too.

8:45 a.m.   Heather's alarm in her bedroom goes off by mistake. It's faint, so Will doesn't wake up, but I wonder if this means Heather's not getting woken up in the living room. I know she shouldn't be late to work, but I also know she may think it's worth it to sleep in after a late night of drinking.

9:00 a.m.   I hear Heather moving around outside our bedroom and finally she knocks. She is shocked that I locked the door. It was just because I always lock the door and not because of anything funny. Heather comes in and gets some money. I actually like that she trusted us enough to leave money in her bedroom. Heather's a really good friend.

9:30 a.m.   Will and I are hot (no air-conditioning). We see a huge spill in Heather's living room and think maybe her cats, Leon and Pinta, peed. I call her and she says the cats spilled their water. For not getting much sleep, Heather sounds so pleasant. There's cat hair everywhere in her house, and her cats are the biggest cats I've ever seen. I think about how supposedly a goldfish grows to the size of the tank it's in, and how if you throw a goldfish in a lake, he'll get huge.

I am grateful to Heather for letting us stay here. She saved us so much money. I don't take a shower because I'm just going to feel dirty as soon as I walk outside and start sweating.

10:00 a.m.   We find a ticket on my car for parking in a no-parking zone that is only a no-parking zone for like an hour and a half on Tuesdays and Thursdays. This is my third parking ticket since I moved from Texas to Georgia with Will four months ago. Up until then I had never gotten a ticket of any kind.

Will and I go to a nearby hardware store to make copies of Heather's apartment key. I make the mistake of asking the hardware people (older, maybe considered elderly) for directions to a vegan restaurant I'm pretty sure is in Manhattan. This was dumb because a bunch of their friends walked in and it just became chaos—a bunch of Brooklyn old grumps directing us every which way but there. I feel like they basically told us to just give up, but I think they were really trying to be helpful.

10:15 a.m.   I call information on my cell phone and get the number for the restaurant I, embarrassingly enough, read about on the Internet. I get directions. It's on the Lower East Side.

10:45 a.m.   We get a little lost walking to the restaurant, not surprisingly. We see lots of hipsters who look like models. My boyfriend thinks the hipsters here are shameless, but I don't think he and I are exactly that far off from them. I always joke about clothes I see in fashion magazines and how real people would never wear them. Real people do wear those clothes in New York City. I have argued with my boyfriend before, trying to explain to him that he is a hipster. He always disagrees, which I think might be part of being a hipster—denial.

11:02 a.m.   We finally make it to this cute little vegan/vegetarian restaurant called Kate's. A friend told me this is the best brunch deal in Manhattan. We end up ordering lunch, though. I order iced green tea (I try not to drink coffee unless I really have to stay awake). The man and woman sitting directly next to us are obviously slightly famous in the theater world or something. The woman seems nice and talks like a former professor of mine. She talks about leftist politics and traveling and about not getting enough credit for her work. I'm trying not to listen, but it's hard since Will and I are eating and not talking. The man she is with seems happy to accommodate her needs at the theater he owns.

I call my friend Adam to make plans. He was still asleep from our night of drinking. Will and I eat veggie burgers that are amazing and French fries that seem like a treat and just what we needed.

12:05 p.m.   We walk to a bookshop that lots of my friends recommended. It's so new and nice and overpriced. I wonder who can afford to buy new books.

12:20 p.m.   Outside, we call Will's pals, Lou and David. I wonder what we look like to others, and then imagine we probably aren't being noticed by anyone because there are so many people here.

12:40 p.m.   We start walking to Union Square and talk about how we dislike New York, but see how it does have some appeal, just not for us to live here. Everything seems so dirty. We keep almost getting run over, sometimes to the point where I feel genuinely lucky when I make it to the other side of the street. We hold hands for a bit. Will usually hates holding my hand in public. I really believe him when he says it's because he walks faster than me and not because he doesn't like to. Because I have a fairly recent memory of being here (less than six months ago, when pretty much all I did was run errands) and Will doesn't, I feel like he and I finally need each other equally.

We sit on a bench in Union Square waiting for Adam to arrive. I talk on my phone to my other male friend in town, who happened to be my first kiss. I don't think of him that way anymore, obviously, but I always feel this forced bit of nostalgia (he was my first kiss, that's special, etc.) whenever I have to introduce him somewhere. Will is just about to meet his friends. Even though he actually used to be a cartographer, I'm worried about him getting lost.

I decide to walk to a shoe store. Someone says my name and taps me on the back. It is a friend of mine from college, Tim. He is on his lunch break, and we randomly go to his office across the street and catch up for a few minutes. Tim is covered in tattoos, but he is the office manager at a book publishing company and is the boss of "normal" people. The whole thing seems weird, but I know anything is possible in New York.

1:15 p.m. It turns out the ringer to my cell phone got turned off and Adam has been trying to call me for the last few minutes. Tim walks me back to Union Square. I introduce him to Adam because one of them works in publishing, where the other one is trying to get a job. I get antsy because I am afraid I am not going to have time to go everywhere I want to go. Adam and I head to SoHo.

1:45 p.m. We get mildly lost. Adam, who has been living in the city for a couple of months, feels like he's letting me down. I assure him I am happy to be in his presence and would be really lost if I didn't have a friend with me. We go through a few typical Hello Kitty, cute stuff, Chinatown-type stores, and talk a lot about Adam's ex,

Jessica. I wish they were still together, and I'm pretty sure they do, too.

2:05 p.m. We get to the clothing store I love the most, Built by Wendy. I don't have much money and am up to my ears in student loans, but there is only one store that makes clothes I really, really like, and this is it. Whenever I go into stores like this one (stores where the cheapest thing costs $50), I feel fake; like the people working there will just know I shouldn't be shopping there. Maybe they will lecture me and say, "Shouldn't you be buying art supplies or books or GROCERIES?"

This isn't even that upscale of a store, but I really can't afford it. I don't have a clothing addiction, I really don't, but at this store I feel like I *have* to buy something. So I search and make something seem perfect just because. This is truly frivolous spending. Adam is slightly concerned and reminds me to not live beyond my means. I spend $200 on a shirt with some loose threads (not exactly a sign of superior quality) and a skirt on sale for half the cost. I think it was a return.

3:00 p.m. Adam and I get lemonade at some café that just seems fake and only for tourists. Then we go to another store I love, H&M, where everything is kind of cheap. I tell Adam I shouldn't buy anything, so I look really quickly and find a top and blouse for less than $40 total. I wanted shorts, but I get a shirt that's too tight for me (they didn't have any larger sizes) and another shirt that looks like a piece of art and seemed really New York. I guess stupid magazines really have affected me.

3:45 p.m. I ask Adam if he will go vibrator shopping with me. I'm slightly embarrassed, but this is my one chance until who knows when to stop by the wonderful

this day in the life 262

Toys in Babeland. Adam jokes that he will accompany me but feels that a straight female friend would never be expected to accompany him to buy a pocket pussy. We laugh and proceed to get lost in a swarm of cyclists and annoying hipsters.

We pass one store that just looks too hip for me, the kind of scenester that pretends to be New York cool/hip and Brooklyn tough. One of the sale flyers on the wall says, "For all you sluts, this is on sale." I didn't find the wording offensive, but I just knew that store and I have different sensibilities.

4:00 p.m. We find Toys in Babeland, and I know instantly what I want: the waterproof Nubby G. It's probably the best battery-operated vibrator around. I highly recommend every woman have a vibrator and try out something simple like the Nubby G. Though I really want the vibrator that is disguised as a rubber ducky.

4:35 p.m. Adam and I go out for pizza. I love New York pizza. I don't know if loving fashion, vibrators, and pizza makes me trashy, but if it does, I guess I don't care. Adam informs me this pizza place was once featured in an episode of *Sex and the City*. We think about shelling out thirty bucks to go on the actual Sex and the City tour but quickly realize due to our dwindling funds and lack of interest, we should just wait on that three-hour tour.

5:05 p.m. We go back to Union Square and meet up with Heather. I give her the copies of her key Will and I made earlier, except for the one Will kept for himself. We joke that we sure hope they work. I am exhausted and decide to take the subway solo back to her apartment in Brooklyn.

5:35 p.m.   I am so happy to be alone in this comfortable apartment (well, with the giant felines of course). I thought for a split second that maybe I'd go to the Curves down the street and then quickly remember, I'm on vacation. I'm embarrassed I go to Curves, but that's a different story. I make phone calls and seal plans.

6:30 p.m.   I buy organic watermelon and blue tortilla chips to take over to my friend Ash's apartment. I also buy a huge case of bottled water for Will and me. We are really funny about drinking cloudy water. Small, college-town Southern life has spoiled us.

7:00 p.m.   I take the subway to Ash's place. Ash is my best friend from high school and lives in a very normal, unhip part of Brooklyn. A rat climbs up the subway stairs with me. Surprisingly, I see Will as soon as I get off the stop. He looks frustrated and is on a pay phone. I'm worried he lost his wallet or something terrible. It turns out he lost his address book. I feel so bad for him. He is wearing this brown-and-white tank top and flared seventies pants. He wrote all the phone numbers and contact information he could remember on an Aldous Huxley book, which is the most HIM thing he could've done.

7:30 p.m.   We walk to Ash's apartment building. She acts cute, pretending to be a magician or something, and lets us in. It feels like we are climbing a million stairs to get to her apartment. I'm not complaining, but I know Will just had one heck of a tiring day, so it seems almost comical to be climbing all those steps together.

7:35 p.m.   Ash and her boyfriend, Chris, make us vegetarian chili. She and I eat chunks of cheese while Will looks sweaty, sits in front of their fan, and makes phone calls to his

this day in the life   **264**

friends on my cell phone. We eat and soon after, Will, who just looks so tired and miserable, runs off to meet his friends.

Less than five minutes later, Ash and I spot the marked-up Aldous Huxley book with all Will's important information. We give each other a crazy smile and run after him to the subway. By some amazing force, we catch him and literally throw the book into his hands. I love Will.

Once back and calm, my friends and I drink beer, gossip, and giggle. I feel drunk, but it is just the exhaustion and heat. Ash's boyfriend plays a video game the whole time, but it doesn't seem rude or anything. In fact, I love Chris a ton. I truly wish our get-together could last longer, but I am sleepy and don't want to take the subway by myself any later at night.

11:00 p.m. I arrive at my subway stop and walk to Heather's apartment. I'm not scared, but I remind myself to swing my arms and take up space; don't stare at the ground.

11:15 p.m. I feel guilty because I planned on spending more time with Heather, especially tonight because she was packing to go back home to Texas for a week. She doesn't seem to care, though. She goes around her apartment making semifrantic to-do lists. She hints that she wants to borrow my car, and I hint that it isn't a good idea. I love Heather.

11:45 p.m. I make a mental note that my friend I called earlier (the First Kiss who is really so much more than that, and I should stop giving him that title) isn't going to call like he said he might. I really don't care. I am tired and just want to feel carefree for once. I sit in Heather's living room and giggle with her about vibrators and other girl talk. I really love my friends. Then we wait for Will to come home, since those goddamn keys we made earlier completely didn't work.

9:30 a.m. Getting up in the morning, poor and with a fat body, makes getting dressed feel daunting and humiliating. Didn't these jeans fit last week? Better opt for the sweatpants. Hell, I work at home, an empty apartment for most of the day. People on the TV can't look out at me from Comedy Central and make cracks about wearing the same shit I went to sleep in. So who cares? If only it was winter. I'm sure I'm not the only fat person who finds it easier to be fat during cold seasons.

Hannah D. Forman, 23, Auburn, Washington; college student and Microsoft test editor

8:00 a.m. Support group from office gets weighed. Let's see, before stepping on scale, remove shoes, earrings, and jewelry. (Oops, gotta run to ladies' room first.) DANG! Just one pound off. Well, I have to remember my goal was really just to not gain since I stopped smoking. Lord, what I wouldn't give for a doughnut and a cigarette.

Nancy Day, 57, Catonsville, Maryland; patient billing systems analyst

I am so excited that I am almost ready to move. In Ohio, no one will know I have MS. No more odd looks because they know I can't deploy when I joined to "fight and defend." (I am trying to make the best out of defending the home front.) No one will know that my son Spencer's birthday is one week before my wedding anniversary. No one will know that Devin and I had so many problems, and no one will know that I gained so much weight and wore the biggest size uniform they make. Now everyone will see what I want them to see.

Dawn L. Banks, 27, Alexandria, Ohio; captain, U.S. Air Force

8:57 a.m. Jon, who plays alto sax in our band, just e-mailed a really great band pix taken at a gig we had last week. The first thing I look at in the picture are my arms. I'm very muscular and self-conscious about my big arms. I have a Big Arm Strategy, though. For most gigs I wear this really nice black front-zip, sleeveless dress shirt with my best push-up bra and a thick, black faux leather bracelet. The theory is, at least one or both of those things will pull the audiences' focus away from my big arms. I wonder if it works. Maybe people just say, "Hey, check out the woman with the big arms *and* big breasts *and* big bracelet."

Judy Fine, 34, Keene, New Hampshire; musician

I got to the water park at 10 a.m., swam three-fourths of a mile, and sunned in the lounge chair. I know the sun is bad for you, but I put on sunblock and read my novel. I rarely have an opportunity to read during the school year. May the Lord forgive me for what I am about to say, but He knows what is in my heart, so I might as well say it—I have never seen so many fat people in all of my life. I am not talking about twenty pounds overweight. I am talking OBESE! I feel bad about my body much of the time.

Bobbie Trowbridge, 46, Statesboro, Georgia; teacher

our bodies, ourselves **267**

Better get up. Hot showers are God's gift to mornings. If I don't turn sideways, I look thinner. I'm glad no one's home. I don't want anyone to see me naked . . . I'm thirty pounds overweight, and I've got double chins, a flabby waist, and wobbly underarms. Yuck. The good news is, I lost three pounds this week. Not having time to eat and being totally stressed out is working wonders for my "diet." I put on black stretch pants and a bright lime green T-shirt with a female M&M on it. I'm not going anywhere, no client meetings today, so I can wear what I want. I make myself a fresh pot of coffee and have a piece of rhubarb pie for breakfast. Then I take my pills—Synthroid, Detrol, Zoloft, and Claritin—one to keep me alive, one for bladder control, one to keep me sane, and one for my lousy sinuses. Breakfast of champions. The notepad Mom sent me last week says it all—"Aging and Raging."

Stacie Stevens, 48, Anchorage, Alaska; graphic artist
and landscape designer

On June 29, 2004 . . .

28% of day diarists were on a diet . . . 40% of those were watching carbs.

22% ate fast food.

~~~~~~

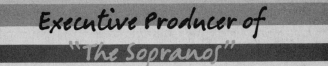

Executive Producer of "The Sopranos"

Robin Green, 58, New York, New York

Her writing career started at Rolling Stone *as the only female contributing editor on an all-male masthead. At thirty-two, she graduated from the Iowa Writers' Workshop. Ten years later, a former classmate working in television saw her byline on a restaurant review and remembered liking her short stories. Would she want to try writing a script? Enter a new plot twist in her career. TV writer. Producer. Winner of Emmys, Golden Globes, and Peabodys. When she signed on to* The Sopranos, *it had just been picked up by HBO after having been turned down by every broadcast network. "We took a huge pay cut to work on it because we really loved the show. It's a lesson in following your heart." Heart and work have often overlapped. She and her writing partner, Mitchell Burgess, go back twenty-seven years. They've collaborated professionally for twelve. Two years ago they got married.*

"It just became apparent we were a pair. It was a profound thing to make those promises and formalize what has been going on for years." A party girl. Childless. Eleven years of therapy (dealing with a temporary split from Mitch and the loss of her father) was "absolutely essential." Does she feel successful? "Yes, but I haven't fulfilled all my ambitions." Maybe she'll paint or write a play. "I'm content, but I also think I missed out on a lot."

6:45 a.m. On Tuesdays I make sure to wake up a half hour before Mitch to take Fosamax, a medication for osteoporosis. I was diagnosed two years ago. You have to take the pill on an empty stomach—not even coffee—with eight ounces of water, then stay upright for a half hour, no lying or bending down. Why, I forget, but I do it anyway.

I go upstairs with Evian and pill. Our bedroom is downstairs in what in New York City is called the "garden level," meaning it's half below street level. The room is dark, like a cave, and quiet, perfect for sleeping. Upstairs are the living room and dining room and a tiny galley kitchen. I sit looking out the French doors, which open onto a veranda with steps down to a private garden, a real luxury in New York. There's a nest full of robins chirping away.

We have the yard for our two seventy-pound mutts: Al, thirteen, and Lulu, twelve. We brought them with us from California when we came to the East Coast to do *The Sopranos*. I own a house in L.A. in the hills above Sunset Strip, but we are renting here in Greenwich Village, the bottom two floors of an 1832 Federal townhouse. I always wanted to live here. I came here after college and worked for a while as Stan Lee's secretary at Marvel Comics, but then I lit out for Berkeley in the sixties. I didn't want to miss that. But now here I am. Amazing. I don't know if we'll return to California when we finish *The Sopranos,* but that's not until the end of 2005.

7:23 a.m. Mitch woke up when I slid back into bed. We briefly told each other about our dreams. Mine was a sex dream about Bill Clinton. Believe me, a total surprise. In Mitch's dream, his recently deceased father appeared, unfurling his belt to give the kids a whupping. Mitch went upstairs to make coffee.

In a short while he'll come back down with the *New York Post* and *New York Times,* two cups of coffee, and an orange wedge in his teeth for me. I bought him a tray one Christmas, but that's too hardcore for him, I guess. The coffee is another luxury. We have it shipped here from Graffeo in Beverly Hills. It's just the best there is. This business with the coffee every morning, I think it's these little rituals that are our greatest pleasures, mine and Mitch's. I consider myself very lucky to get coffee in bed each day, and I love reading the paper next to Mitch. It's my job to arrange his pillows before he comes down. And here he comes now.

9:15 a.m. Just got back from walking the dogs. It is a spectacular summer morning, clean and cool and sunny. But the truth is, I love walking the dogs through the Village in all weather. In L.A., too, at the dog park, it's my favorite part of the day. An anxiety-free zone. I'm free just to be. No one expects anything of me but to pick up the dogs' poop.

I walked them down Washington Place past Sheridan Square (which is really a triangle), around the periphery of Christopher Street Park where transvestites sleep it off on benches, lunatics feed the pigeons and mutter, office workers stream obliviously by on their way to the subway. The dogs are so happy to be out, which makes me happy. They love New York. There's so much food littering the sidewalks, though now, with the low-carb craze, pizza crust and bagel pickings are conspicuously slimmer.

On our way home, we passed Mitch on his way to the gym. He asked after our walk, then gave me a kiss and continued on. At home, I fed the dogs, finished the paper, did my chores. The housekeeper doesn't come Tuesday (or Thursday), so I make the bed and tidy up. When *Sopranos* is in production, she comes every day, mostly to let the dogs out into the yard. When we're working on story at the studio, it's a regular 10:00–7:30 job, but when we have a script in production, one of us has to be on the set at all times and those days are fourteen to sixteen hours, sometimes eighteen. When we're working so hard, it's great to come home to a spotless house.

This year, *The Sopranos* is on hiatus and we're working at home. We have a deal with HBO to develop a new series. They approved our idea, so we're working on the outline for the show now. We'd already spent two whole months on another idea about an immigrant family in Astoria, but we just couldn't make it work to our satisfaction. We weren't connecting with the characters.

After we gave up on it, we sat here in our dark, garden-level office, time wasted, year ticking away. We talked for days about different stuff and then Mitch said, "What about this?" At first I didn't see it, but then he explained what he meant and a whole world opened up. I think when he had the idea, he saw that whole world all at once in all its possibility. This is a better idea than the other one, more specific. He knows these people, or people like them, intimately.

Most TV shows are franchises—cops, doctors, STAT! Emergency! Get the truck! We're drawn to family shows, but finding a fresh take is a challenge. They tend to be "soft." That's what makes *The Sopranos* so genius because you have all that gangster action, life and death, though it's really a family show in disguise. A hard act to follow. Soon Mitch will be home from the gym, then we'll start in.

One thing I have to say, when I was out walking and thinking about the beautiful day, the thought crept in that it was on just such a glorious morning, also a Tuesday, that disaster struck the World Trade towers. We had just flown out to L.A. the night before to do research for a script. One plane flew very low right over this house, our upstairs neighbors later told us. And I thought when I was on the street a few minutes ago, will we in New York never again be able to fully trust a glorious summer morning?

I am full of so many emotions about September 11, personal and political. I'm angry, I'm sad. And I worry about our country, our place in the world, our national soul. Enough for now. Here comes Mitch. I have to get ready for work.

2:20 p.m.   We worked from 9:30 until lunch, went for a bite up the street, came back and worked some more. It's been a difficult day. We spent some time evaluating the work we'd done yesterday and found it flat, boring. We decided to try another approach, a different place to start the story. We have a big, dry-erase whiteboard on the wall in our office/guest room, and on this we outlined new scenes leading up to this big thing we know for sure is going to happen to this family.

Creating a show is quite different than going on a show for which the pilot has already been created, which is how we came to both *Northern Exposure* and *The Sopranos*. In those cases, you walk into a world already made, characters and conflicts already drawn. This is the blank page. The whiteboard. It's awful. It's difficult. But as Mitch says, if it were easy, everyone would do it.

So we are struggling. We came back from lunch and looked at the morning's work, and again, boring. How to tell this story? There must be a way. There better be a way. We erased what we had. It makes me feel so defeated I want to scream, but this is the process. You sit there thinking and it doesn't feel like you're doing anything, but it's the only way to get anywhere that we know of. At *The Sopranos,* the four or five of us sit there for days, weeks even, just trying to come up with ideas for the next episode, never mind the subsequent days and weeks plotting it out and writing it. And this is on a show already launched and successful. This is the process, I know. I still want to scream.

So I am going to Pilates. That was the plan for today, anyway. I go three times a week, *Sopranos* or no, or I just can't keep my strength and energy up. Pilates is the most efficient and un-boring exercise I've found, and I've tried 'em all. I try to keep in shape. I'm five foot seven and have a weight limit I try not to go over, 135 pounds. I'm pushing it right now, so I'm eating mostly fish this week, very few carbs, lots of vegetables, and this will bring me back from the brink.

Gotta go change, then walk the twenty blocks to class. After that, I'll take a subway back down and meet Mitch at The Grey Dog, a coffeehouse on Carmine Street where, as a favor to a bigwig at HBO, we agreed to meet with and advise a young aspiring writer. And tell him what? How jammed up I felt working today? How disheartened and blue I am about work right now?

5:10 p.m. He turned out to be a great kid. Tall and funny, with a nice, open face and no 'tude. Regular, in spite of the fact he went to Harvard! He plans to move to L.A., and I think he'll do fine there.

Mitch is out walking the dogs. I just caught up on my e-mail. Frankly, I'm full of bad feelings, negative thoughts. I feel guilty that I didn't work harder today. I'm worried about the project, failure, letting HBO down when they've been so supportive, my reputation. Could it be that I'm tired from Pilates, from the day in general? Do I really deserve to be tired? Is anybody else out there having thoughts like these right now? Only one thing to do—what I usually do at this hour during these months of working at home—take a hot bath.

9:00 p.m.   Here is the pile of mundane details from this evening. I went around the corner to 4th Street to the Korean nail parlor to see if someone could wax my legs. How's that for prosaic? But no one was free, so I'll go back tomorrow. On the street coming home, I ran into a guy I knew forty years ago who said I looked exactly the same. Ha! But I knew what he meant. I do look essentially the same, just a lot older! And a lot happier. When I knew him I was so young and confused. While it was nice to see him, it also reminded me of an unhappy time and, frankly, I was glad finally to continue on my way home.

Mitch and I went to dinner early, around 7:00 at Pearl, a restaurant around the corner on Cornelia Street. When Mitch arrived in New York to get our apartment set up, before I came from L.A. with the dogs, he discovered it, called me and said, "You're going to love this place. It has all the stuff you've been missing in L.A.—Ipswich steamers and lobster and little necks." He was so right. The place is perfect, has a 27 rating in the NY *Zagat* guide. Amazing for a little seafood joint. And the perfectionist owner, Rebecca Charles, has become a good friend. She was, in fact, the sole witness at our wedding.

I'm in the office now, of course, at the computer. Mitch just came in and sat down, and said, "How you doing? I'm not watching, just taking off my shoes." The room is also his dressing room. In New York, every space serves several purposes, at least in our price range. About our price range,

I realize how privileged my life is—all these luxuries in my day, the excitement and fulfillment of my job now (well, maybe not today), and the financial rewards, all of which are considerable relative to other times in my life and jobs I've held—temp secretary, waitress, factory worker. I became a well-paid TV writer late in life, so I appreciate every luxury and know how lucky I am.

I also have a sense of much that I've missed in life. At the end of the day, I'm still stuck being me, a mixed bag, which I guess is apparent. Before I say good night, I just want to say what I had for dinner: little necks, Caesar salad, a boiled lobster with drawn butter, a few glasses of Gascon. And to say that when I came home from dinner, I spoke with my nephew on the phone. He and his wife live in my California home now while she finishes film school at UCLA. He teaches high school at South Central, and they are expecting their first baby in November. He said they had an ultrasound today and the heartbeat was strong. He also reported that my house—a mid-century modern with glass walls and views of L.A.—seems to have survived its three-day fumigation tenting for termites.

After I spoke to him, I came downstairs and checked my e-mail. There was a message from my mother (eighty-seven years old next week; we just got her set up for e-mail last month) who said that my brother and his wife are having dinner for everyone Saturday night. They live in Vermont in a beautiful house on a mountaintop. My nephew and his wife are coming; also, my niece and her family. Mitch and I will be there, too. We'll head up Saturday morning with the dogs. Hopefully we'll have our story outline done by then.

Wish You Were Here

I called my mother, like I do every night between 9:30 and 10:00. At first, the call was just to catch up every day. Then, when Dad died, the call became necessary. Now the call seems to be something that she has come to expect, but I don't know what she gets out of it. She tells me about her day. I don't really tell her many details about my day because at times it doesn't feel as though she is listening. But I don't blame her, really. She has been riddled with cancer, is all alone after losing her husband of forty years suddenly, and has to deal with getting rid of Dad's vintage cars before she can move to a smaller place. Every single time I talk to her I am reminded of her angst. Sometimes she cries. What can I say? Tonight's call is fairly uneventful, but before she hangs up she says, "Love you," like she always does, but then adds in a choked voice, "I wish you were here." Yes, Mum, I know. But I don't want to be there, with all those feelings of misery and loss. I end up torn between my mother and my husband. This feeling just sucks.

Tammy Raabe Rao, 34, Arlington, Massachusetts;
graphic designer/photographer

Cocktail Hour

5:30 p.m. Have my martini with *Lou Dobbs*, except he is on assignment and I never felt the same about his replacement, so I switch to TCM to watch Cary Grant, my all-time favorite idol. Isn't it great to have him, sometimes young and always gorgeous, even though he is long gone? Mmm.

> *Ann Taylor, 78, Nichols Hills, Oklahoma; community volunteer and former mayor*

Orientation

12:30 p.m. I hold an information session for parents whose children are going to be freshmen in the fall. Parents are so strange. I can't believe that they expect us to police their children while they are in college. "My child is allowed to have overnight guests OF THE OPPOSITE SEX?" asks an Indian father. He reminds me of my dad, overprotective and perpetually concerned. "Yes, sir," I say. "They are eighteen." He huffs and puffs for several minutes. It's the opposite sex part that bothers him. I joke to myself about how my parents were so concerned about boys, while I was having sex with other girls.

> *Ahoo Tabatabai, 26, Cincinnati, Ohio; diversity education program coordinator*

Semper Stinky?

5:00 p.m. Filled up a fifty-gallon trash can with water. Tomorrow, they are shutting off our water again. This time until Friday. Yippee. Glad I worked out extra today. I won't be working out if I know there are no showers. But at least SSgt Fig and I will have water to wash up. There are going to be some stinky Marines around here. Oh well. Baby Wipes are gold when this happens.

Angela C. Mink, 32, San Diego, California; combat correspondent, United States Marine Corps (serving in Iraq)

Roommates

7:30 a.m. Today, like most days, my roommate has gotten up before me and made coffee of the store-brand variety from the groceries we share. I have most likely purchased this very tin in a moment of cheapness and refused to throw it out for similar reasons. Lately, in some new yuppie form of acting out, I have taken to buying $9 per pound Italian roast, grinding the beans, and brewing my own pot in secret while she is in the shower. I feel guilty about not sharing, but even worse that I am hiding all the evidence. I'll just blame this on the fact that I am an only child. I sip my secret gourmet coffee and watch *The Today Show*, calling the weather forecast to my roommate as she applies makeup. I occasionally make faces, as if my coffee is merely mediocre, to keep up my charade.

Suzanne Cope, 26, Somerville, Massachusetts; associate marketing manager, Houghton Mifflin

Jimmy Who?

7:45 p.m. You see so much at the local transportation center. There's a concert in town. It's some guy name Jimmy Buffett. Allegedly his concerts attract rowdy individuals interested in getting drunk and disorderly. Anyway, that does not concern me; I am ready to head home.

Taiye M. Oladapo, 24, Philadelphia, Pennsylvania; program administrator, UrbanPromise Ministries

Mother Hen

Jenee Guidry, 30, Houston, Texas

Plan A was to be an attorney, travel, and stay single. Instead, a friendship in college turned to love, they had a couple kids, got married three years ago, and had two more babies—all before she turned thirty. What happened to Plan A? She laughs. "I ask myself that question every day." Seriously, "He turned out to be such an example of what a husband is supposed to be. It just went from there." Growing up, his family was like the Cosbys'. Hers wasn't. Separation. Dysfunction. She changed schools thirteen times. "I was more the parent to my parents. I took care of everybody." She has two sisters. The youngest "is more like my daughter." The other is her best friend. "We always had the attitude, if we couldn't depend on anyone else, we'd take care of each other." Now she's "happily content." Surprised she's okay with being settled. Thinks having four kids is "hilarious." She loves how each one is so different and makes a point to treat them all individually. An emotional sponge. "I absorb other people's problems and want to fix them." Dominant. "It's Jenee's way or no way." She's studying for the LSATs, while her husband is applying to med school. Competitive. "No way I would let my husband die without my having the same number of degrees, even if I have to be eighty and in school."

12:01 a.m. I am so tired. Carryn, my four-month-old, will not go to sleep. I have nursed her, rocked her, sang to her, and bounced her on the pillow. She has passed her bedtime and is fussy. I had a "date" to meet my husband at the gym after he gets off work. I am dressed and ready to go but can't leave until the baby is asleep. My seventeen-year-old sister, Whitney, is supposed to be helping out with the kids this summer in exchange for a used car, but I guess that is only during the commercials and between phone calls. At this rate, she'll be lucky to get a bus pass.

12:30 a.m. Still rocking the baby while searching the Internet. I am looking for ways to streamline the household by giving the kids age-appropriate chores and hoping to find free charts that I can download to enforce my new merit system. In this system, you are rewarded for above-and-beyond behavior; not good behavior because that is always expected.

1:01 a.m. Carryn is asleep. Desperate to get some alone time with my husband, Cliff, I ask him to ride to the all-night Wal-Mart to get some dog food for our two huge dogs in the backyard. We spend $100 a month on dog food. I really just want to escape the house without kids, even at this late hour. Cliff is tired and thinks I am nuts, but he misses me, too.

1:24 a.m.   We are leaving for Wal-Mart and I am falling asleep. We discuss the plans for the weekend and how I need to buy presents for three birthday parties. I am sick of birthday parties and tired of wasting money on toys. I think after you clean up toys so many times you resent toys.

2:08 a.m.   I am in the parking lot of Wal-Mart, wondering, Is this what parenthood has reduced my marriage to?

2:41 a.m.   Cliff and I are preparing for bed. I take a shower and throw on a T-shirt and my pj shorts. He is off work from the pharmacy tomorrow and likes me to watch TV with him, but I do not get an off day, so no, I am going to sleep. Our sex life is almost nonexistent. Maybe that has something to do with the fact we know sex = children or that my T-shirts and shorts are no longer sexy. But, on second thought, his T-shirt and boxers are not exactly making me feel the fire. Plus, if I even kiss my husband, Caitlin (two) will knock on the door wanting her daddy. And if that isn't bad enough, little Cliff (four) knows how to pick the lock with my car keys.

My husband is looking at me funny, and I am going to sleep before he tries to get friendly. I feel guilty but am exhausted. Good night or rather, good morning.

7:03 a.m.   Carryn wakes to nurse and I want to sleep. Yes, we will accomplish both goals in bed. My husband pretends not to hear her, but sometimes I wake him up just so he can see my job is twenty-four hours a day.

8:13 a.m.   She fell asleep nursing earlier, so here we go again. I just need thirty more minutes of sleep.

this day in the life   282

9:28 a.m.   Carryn is nursing again and this time she is really eating. I hear the pitter-patter of little feet down the hall. Caitlin and little Cliff want cereal. Little Cliff is demanding to go to baseball practice, but it is raining. Bj just wants to find the Xbox. They will continue to come in and out of our room to demand we wake up, or to jump on the bed, or turn on the television, or just crawl in bed with us. Let the day officially begin. My husband is waking up, and Carryn is going back to sleep.

10:48 a.m.   I have served bowls of Apple Jacks and oatmeal and plates of waffles. Our grocery bill is outrageous. I would like to shower and get dressed, but Carryn is attached to me at the hip. I need to get the kids dressed. We are interviewing contractors to remodel the kitchen and bathroom. We have had some really ridiculous offers, and I am not in the mood to keep haggling. How can one estimate for the job be $7,000 and another be as expensive as $48,000? I am at my wit's end. This is my last interview and then I am squashing the project.

My husband is playing video games with the kids since it is raining out. He is yelling loudly because Bj beat him at NFL Blitz. I don't care how many degrees he has, Cliff is the biggest kid here. We are very competitive in our house. None of my friends will play Monopoly with me because I have been known to flip a board or two, and we definitely do not let our kids win. If you lose, you will try harder next time. And when you finally do win, you can take pride in your hard work.

I remind Cliff the contractor will be over at 11:30 to discuss our addition.

11:28 a.m.   The kitchen needs to be cleaned, but that is okay. Mom will get it. Sarcasm. I think my can-do attitude has been taken the wrong way. I usually do everything, and now they just take it for granted. My kids do, anyway. My husband thinks he is the best housekeeper in the world. He makes everything "disappear" into the closets, but that is not cleaning, that is cluttering and stacking.

The contractor calls to reschedule. This seems to be an unproductive day. I would like to get more done as far as errands and housework, but my husband is not always on the same page. I also would like to be alone for a minute or more, but I will get a break when I get one. No time to complain.

12:49 p.m. I am trying to leave to go downtown to do errands. My husband wants to bring the kids, but I do not. My sister, Sharon, can watch them, so why bring four kids to the courthouse when all I need to do is change the name on the deed to our property from mine to ours. Big Cliff thinks he does not get to see the kids enough because of his work schedule, and I think I get to see the kids *constantly* because of his work schedule. At least he is the type of father who is concerned about spending time with them. He does not like to be separated from his peers. Ha-ha.

1:11 p.m. We finally leave without the kids, after a lengthy conversation explaining that I need a break and that he can take them later to the movies or somewhere they would actually enjoy, rather than a trip downtown. On the way to the courthouse, we stop to pay the registration fees for our son's new private school for the fall semester. I really do not understand why a four-year-old's tuition is so high.

2:51 p.m. I get the deed transferred and pick up my sister's birth certificate, plus I register my business name. I have been trying to accomplish this for six weeks. I really want to start an event planning business or just decorating for parties, but it cannot interfere with my family. I feel like I can do that with minimal intrusion if I plan in advance and take jobs at my convenience.

3:47 p.m. I am in the car with my husband driving. Can I just say I am busy and exhausted for every hour? I had to pay $3 for parking. I hate parking downtown. Now my kids are taking turns calling my cell phone, each asking one question or saying one thing.

"What are you doing?"

"When are you coming home?"

"Somebody hit me."

"Can I eat this?"

I hate that ****ing cell phone. (I can think the "F" word, but I won't use it.) That cell phone is like a GPS system for everyone I do not want to talk to.

4:30 p.m. We're back at home, but the kids are still with my sister. She will be dropping them off soon. Sharon complains she needs an SUV just to drive all my kids around. My husband is watching television and bugging me about getting my oil changed and cleaning out my school bus (Suburban). I am trying to figure out what I can get done before the kids or the contractor—who is on his way—arrives. God help me.

7:15 p.m. I get caught up with the contractor. We discuss the floor plans for the bathroom. I want to reverse the bathtub and add counter and cabinet space. My kitchen will also get cabinet space, as well as granite countertops, plus I want to close in a huge window and change it to a pantry closet. I also would like to install a double oven. I really want a more functional kitchen, since this is where I seem to spend my life, but it is all contingent on the price.

I am tired. Caitlin tells me if I yawn again I need to go to bed. Children are wonderfully simple. I just realize I have not had a bite to eat. My husband wants to take the kids to dinner. Bj wants to know how to prevent pimples. Hygiene! Something ten-year-old boys lack! I explain about dirt and bacteria and show him one of my husband's many textbooks on skin conditions. The two-year-old is chasing the four-year-old with an ugly doll because she knows he is scared of dolls. Caitlin has my dark sense of humor. She is hilarious.

9:17 p.m. I am hiding in my Suburban to get some peace and quiet. Carryn is with me getting some tummy time and playing with her feet. My entire family is knocking on the car windows, asking me what is wrong. They think this is funny. I tell them to get away from the window, and then the kids jump on the running board, laughing hysterically and screaming, "Don't leave us. We love you." I guess you have to love kids like that.

11:01 p.m. Doing laundry. Does anyone have as much laundry as me? There are laundry baskets everywhere, and I think my dryer is going out. I do not feel like comparison shopping for a new one. I wish I could just go buy the biggest and prettiest one I see, but my husband would have a coronary. He is the cheapest man I know, except when it comes to his kids. His new tradition is to have diamond solitaire earrings custom-made for our daughters. He is a sucker for those girls. Plus, the boys get top-of-the-line bikes and remote-control cars.

11:59 p.m. I am so tired. No, my husband is not helping with the laundry. He is playing with the baby and asking, have I finished his medical school application? And the world keeps turning.

this day in the life **286**

Haifa, Israel 12:01 a.m.   I go outside for a final cigarette on the stone stairs outside our door. It is only twenty steps from the street to the door of our first-floor apartment. The city is like San Francisco, on a steep hill, overlooking a bay. Nothing is flat. The midnight air is finally cool. My sweetheart is watching the 12:00 news. Today, two were buried, killed in a terror attack. The dead include a four-year-old boy. They bury them fast here, usually within twenty-four hours, often on the same day they die. Unlike the U.S., our news programs bring the blood and the body parts into our homes, to push home both the brutality of their deaths and the personal insult we are encouraged to feel when Jews die. Is it so we can work up a more frothy revenge ethic?

Batya Salzman Levy, 47; English teacher, Berlitz School of Languages

Kabul, Afghanistan 3:02 p.m.   Made it to the bike place. Not a shop, really, but a place. It's so crazy because I had to take a driver with me to guard the car while I shop, so that no bombs are placed under it. And I had to take a man with me because it is not considered safe for me to shop alone. I haggle for my bike, and once the lights are removed, I save myself $20. I try out my Dari, explaining to the bicycle man that I will not need lights because I am not allowed out after dark unless I am in a car and accompanied. Oh! The fear people live under! It drives me crazy because I don't feel afraid here.

Tanya Abadia Weaver, 34; humanitarian worker,
Shelter for Life International

Peshawar, Pakistan 7:30 a.m. I peel the mangos from my neighbor's garden to make a smoothie and open a box of black tea that a colleague brought me from her vacation in Zanzibar. What a combination. I give some mango peels to my impatient rabbit, Mr. Mango, and toss the rest in the compost. I've been extra vigilant about composting after watching the street children foraging in the trash, competing with the stray dogs and the many ravens, trying to get to it before it is incinerated. I am still tortured. By composting, do I deprive them of some of their only food?

Pilar Robledo, 34; program coordinator, International
Rescue Committee

New York City 8:00 a.m. Moving company arrives to give me an estimate to pack up my apartment and move everything into storage. I hire them on the spot. $1,300. My life will now be stored somewhere in Harlem until I decide what to do. En route to work I walk down 3rd Avenue and then cut onto Fifth Avenue on 28th Street where I get an iced coffee and a yogurt at Café 28, a favorite neighborhood joint near work. This day has the same crispness as 9/11, a day that began with bright blue and ended in a somber, surreal mix of browns, grays, and reds. This move is bringing me back to 9/11 and my homelessness for the three months after the attacks. Do I shake it or let myself feel it?

Carey Earle, 38; CEO, Harvest Communications

Baghdad, Iraq 1930   I can't believe I spend half my day e-mailing for work; then I come back to my room and spend the evening e-mailing my family and friends. I stare at the wall at my kids' drawings and pictures. I don't want to be here. I look at my photo album. Erin will be seven when I get back! I remember what she said before I left: "Mommy, when you get back from the war, if you're still alive, will you tell me who won?"

Terry Besch, 43, Frederick, Maryland; commander,
U.S. Army Veterinary Corps

Fez, Morocco 4:15 p.m.   The intense desert heat boiled the water in the radiator, and our bus chugged to a halt. An unscheduled adventure squeezed its way into a packed itinerary. We piled out of the bus and ran across the highway to the shelter of a welcoming olive grove. Some sought the comfort of the olive trees' shade, and I enjoyed the fire energy of the sun. As the mechanic tinkered, we followed Rabbi Analia Bortz's lead and sang an old Jewish song about Abraham, our father, then an African melody with the words, "We are marching in the light of God." Someone ran back to the bus to get two drums, purchased earlier that day in the market, and our singing became bolder, accompanied by rhythmic drumbeats. Jews, Christians, and Muslims singing together in an olive grove in the Middle Atlas Mountains, "Peace is attainable; peace is simple."

Tayyibah Taylor, 51, Atlanta, Georgia;
publisher/editor, Azizah Magazine

Sister of the Holy Cross

Dorothy Anne Cahill, 91, Kensington, Maryland

Growing up, her mom was Protestant and her dad was Catholic, but religion was never a big issue. In high school she transferred to Holy Cross Academy and had her first contact with nuns. "It didn't take long for me to fall in love with the whole gang of them. They were the most joyous people I knew, and they worked like dogs." She's been a nun for seventy-one years. Much of her work life was spent as a teacher, but the challenges of educating high school and college students in the sixties ("it was against their principles to listen") prompted her to pursue another interest—nursing. "I got my Medicare card and passed State Boards the same year." She still works part-time at Holy Cross Hospital, though she no longer works as a floor nurse. Years ago, her convent switched from habits to regular clothes, but she chooses to wear a veil at work. "People feel more free to approach a Sister. They trust us." *A published poet. She's traveled extensively through Europe and the Middle East. Her great loves are the Washington Redskins, her family ("the Sisters can't get over the loving attention they give me"), and her religious community. "It's been a great ride, believe me. This isn't an easy life, and you don't choose it for that. But it was joy that attracted me, and it's been joy ever since, even amidst tribulation."*

6 a.m. When the alarm went off, my first thought was the usual one—Why don't I retire? A thought which faded by the time I brushed my teeth.

My day begins in a definite routine, probably just as well. Otherwise, I would be sure to omit something important. I head for the coffeepot in my convent's kitchen. Today of all days when I need the comforting assurance of caffeine, the pot is empty! I return to my bed with my rosary beads and prayer booklet to have my "coffee hour with God," sans coffee.

This hour is a cherished time. I get up an hour before I need to just to have this quiet time for prayer and meditation, to count my blessings and to pray for God's blessing on my day. I must admit that today's prayers paid special attention to the "job" before me of keeping a day diary, and a prayer for all the other diarists in this project. I wondered if they were busy at it in the wee small hours from midnight on. I am not a night person. I used to think I was a morning one, but now I seem to be gravitating to a noonday one.

What struck me during my prayer time was a quotation from a booklet providing a thought for the day's meditation, which stated, "We each have our stories to tell, our crosses to bear, our lives to live. We are different from each other in many ways, but we all serve the one loving God."

My usual prayer intentions are pretty demanding of God. I ask each day for PEACE—peace in the world, in my nation, my church, my religious community, my workplace, among my friends, in my beloved family, my home, and in my heart. And if that isn't enough for the Almighty to handle, I also throw in my eyes, ears, and teeth that I can keep what is left of them until I die.

7:45 a.m. I am dressed and ready for work at Holy Cross Hospital. I sit near the front door awaiting Sister Barbara Marie, who will drive me there when she goes. This is surely my biggest cross, having to be dependent on someone else to take me where I need or would like to go. And I hate it! But at least it gives me some lessons in humility, which I must admit I sorely need.

My trip to work focused on thoughts about the deplorable condition of our street, while wishing there were some wonderful things I could write about. How exciting is the fact that they have been working on the street for months, for what I do not know. And from observation, I think they probably don't know either. It seems that their task is to dig a hole wherever it will most impede traffic, look into it, and then refill it only to dig up the same hole a week later. This morning, my driver mused on whether they will be finished in our lifetime. Maybe hers; surely not mine.

8:30 a.m. Once I get to work at the hospital, all thoughts of retirement disappear. I love being here, and although my job description has changed since I arrived eighteen years ago, I am still on the pediatric ward. Having let my LPN license expire, I am now doing many other jobs utilizing some of the skills I acquired during my forty-three years of teaching. Part of my role while traveling the halls doing errands is to help people have a good experience in the hospital. I see myself as a goodwill ambassador when riding the elevators, here for people who may need to talk, and easing their worry.

Today (unfortunately) was an unusually slow day. My boss is out sick, and much of my daily activity is generated from her office. Since I couldn't come up with any creative thoughts, I was forced to drown my sorrows in a few games of computer solitaire! But don't tell!

My ride home was via the hairdresser's. My driver had an appointment and I go where the car goes. It's a long walk otherwise! However, it works out pretty well for me, as she parks right in front of a Dollar Store where I entertain myself while waiting. This proved especially providential, as I was able to pick up a few picnicky things to take to the beach, where I will be going in a few days with my family. I just hope I will be "coordinated" by the time we go, with my turquoise thermal coffee cup, jigsaw puzzles, blue jeans, and mystery novels. One thing I have learned for sure is that when you are old, it takes twice as long to do half as much!

Each day when I get home from work, I try to make a brief visit to our chapel. Somehow in the busyness of the day I haven't given too much thought to my Friend. So before I go to my room, I take this time just to say hello and thanks for another day.

2:00–4:30 p.m. These hours are spent in activities like checking e-mail, playing computer games, reading (at the Dollar Store, I picked up several mystery novels set in a fictional abbey in historical England), and clearing off my desk—an eternal job it seems, since it is always in disarray from the piles of charity requests, catalog gifts, coupons, magazines, and books that I have amassed during the week.

4:30 p.m.   I check my mailbox. A real, genuine letter is a rarity and an object of delight. Of course, if I would ever get around to answering my backlog of communications, I might expect to find an improvement in that area. I have always hated writing letters and found e-mail a delightful gift from God before I reached senility!

4:40 p.m.   I am in the chapel for a few minutes of prayer before Mass. I like having Mass at the close of the day instead of the early morning, which it was for the greater portion of my religious life. First, if it isn't a workday, you can roll over and snooze a bit longer if you want! The second reason is that it brings a quiet closure to most of the day's activities.

After our dinner, most of us disperse to various enterprises. For me, this involves a game or two of Scrabble, usually with Sister Vivian. For many of the Sisters with whom I live, it is the TV for the news and game shows. Tonight it was an early preparation for bed. I attended a birthday party for my niece the night before and was up way after my bedtime (9 p.m. is usually my limit), so I was glad to be turning in earlier tonight and to put an end to this very ordinary day.

But what is probably my most important thought of all is, ordinary or not, I am grateful for another twenty-four hours of life; for the love of family and friends, and the opportunity to serve God even with my now-limited capacities.

With appreciation and in loving memory of Dorothy Anne Cahill, who died October 26, 2004.

On the Job

11:52 a.m. Finished the voice-over and am on my way to the 15th floor of the FUSE Network offices for a meeting. Lots of changes. It's the second day of our brand-new live show, *Daily Download*. I am feeling the pressure from the producers, and they are feeling the pressure from the VPs. Already have a knot in my stomach. I come upstairs and our talent supervisor is going through tapes, looking for new talent. Even though he tells my cohost and me that they are looking for *additional* talent, it still makes me feel a little insecure. In this business you just never know. I try to hold my head up and stay focused.

Marianela Pereyra, 24, Jersey City, New Jersey;
VJ/DJ, FUSE Network/KTU radio

11:34 a.m. Great, I was talking in my office with a co-worker about how a manager in our company doesn't like me, and I didn't realize she was sitting in my boss's office. I have been sweating this situation because I know my voice carries and she must have heard. I guess I'll be hearing about this later. Oy!

Laurel Brightwell, 31, New Orleans, Louisiana;
advertising/media representative, Harrah's Casino

8:50 a.m. Thank goodness for pig PMS. It's good comic relief. Kelsey, the babirusa (a rare type of pig from Indonesia) is in heat again and screaming at me for her food. If I wasn't a seasoned keeper, I'd swear she was dying by the sound of it! All right, all right, I'm going as fast as I can. Cut me some slack. These are the hands that brought you into this world, little girl. How soon they forget.

Jeannette Beranger, 39, Providence, Rhode Island;
zookeeper, Roger Williams Park Zoo

2:30 p.m. We wrap up the meeting. Client tells us good job and walks us to the elevators. Boss and I get to our cars. She seems somewhat determined to stand here in the parking lot and talk through details of the plan, but I'm really not interested. Especially since I know we'll only have to do it again after she's given it some thought. I listen politely but begin taking baby steps backward toward my car. I nod. Take baby step. Say, "That's what I was thinking." Take baby step. Why isn't she getting the hint?

Kimberly Gavagan, 35, Mendham, New Jersey; project
director

1:30 p.m. Off again to Anson's first appointment with his new doctor. I was organized and brought some Creative Memories paperwork with me. So glad I did because the receptionist noticed my folder and told me she loves to scrapbook. I gave her my card and got her address to mail her a summer workshop schedule. You never know where a new customer will come from!

Nancy Dorsey, 48, Warwick, Rhode Island;
occupational therapist and Creative Memories
consultant

1100 Amputee wound rounds with multidisciplinary team. I am the sole orthopedic surgery representative today. We visit Spc N.'s room. He looks twelve. His entire family surrounds him, but it looks like they have all run out of words to say. He looks deflated, like the fragmentary wounds all over his body have allowed the life air to slowly drain from his now wasting body. I am asked to look at his draining wounds on his back and chest. They will heal, but he will carry grotesque scars. The nondamaged skin is soft, like a baby's skin. I am not sure if his eyes are flat because he is another TBI (total brain injury) patient, or if that is the look of defeat, hopelessness. I wish I could do more than just give suggestions on how best to cover his skin graft donor sites.

Amy Ross Schroer, 29, Washington, D.C.; orthopedic
surgery resident, Walter Reed Army Medical Center

On June 29, 2004 . . .

33% of day diarists were late for something.

5% wore panty hose.

~~~~~~~

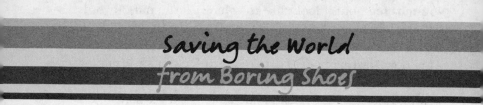

Saving the World
from Boring Shoes

Ashley Dearborn, 29, New York, New York

A shoe designer based in New York City, she doesn't do basic black. "My idea of a black shoe is one that has a huge red lightning bolt across the top." She's been drawing shoes since she was twelve, filling notebooks and notebooks. "Shoes have magical properties. Regardless of a woman's shape or size, a hot pair of shoes can convince her that she's a fox." It's been two years and three collections since she went to Italy in search of a shoe factory. Now her handmade creations can be spotted on celebrity feet. "Beyoncé bought four pairs!" It took a few years to hit her stride. After graduating from Cornell, she worked as an event planner and copywriter at the Wall Street Journal, *trying to leave for three years. "They kept offering more money." Finally, she went to Parsons to learn how to handcraft shoes, then left to get retail experience and investors. Her biggest challenge? "In Italy, it's a man's world. I'd hear the shoemakers talking trash, calling me crazy. Plus, the sample guy would say my designs were absolutely impossible and should cost a million dollars. They didn't think I would last, but I kept coming back. I think I've finally won their respect." A thrill seeker. Fiercely optimistic. Her favorite shoe is called For-Ever. "There's a rainbow that wraps around the entire foot with clouds across the instep."*

8:43 a.m. Wake up and drunkenly walk Chump (my Pekingese pup).

9:17 a.m. Realize that sort of tipsy drunk feeling is transforming into full-fledged hangover as I take a whiff of Chump's food while feeding him. The night prior I had been to several discothèques with an amazing Roman guy and, as expected, drank too much.

9:19 a.m. Decide that McDonald's hash browns will save my ass.

9:27 a.m. Successful execution of said McDonald's trip.

9:35 a.m. Frantically get my apartment/showroom/office ready for the pending arrival of the six people from *Vogue*. Irini has already written the article about how I started my shoe business, which will appear in September's issue. Now they want photos to go with the article. Remorse concerning last night's antics sets in. You would have thought that I would have laid low, knowing that today was my photo shoot. I am such an ass.

10:00 a.m. *Vogue* photographer shows up and I haven't even showered. Great.

10:08 a.m.　　The rest of them arrive—two makeup girls, two stylists, and a hair gal.

10:30 a.m–3:30 p.m.　　Rocked out with the *Vogue* folks. Had a helluva time with costume changes, new hair-prep techniques, and smolderingly sexpot makeup. Went through four outfit changes. Stayed away from black as instructed by the stylist, who told me Anna Wintour doesn't like it when subjects wear black. I hope they end up using the photo of me in the pink lace top and pencil skirt. Love that top and it looks really great with the tangerine orange "Flashbacks," my current fave from the fall collection. The Flashbacks are so great; comfortable. We had an amazing crew. So much fun, until the end when I realized that you won't even see the coolest part of the shoe in the photo. The back has a copper lightning bolt going down the heel. Missing that is really a shame. Oh well, the color of the shoe is pretty terrific.

3:31 p.m.　　Walk Chump again. Poor Chump had been holding it for quite some time.

4:08 p.m.　　Place phone call to my new store in San Francisco, Beau, to find out developments as to the health state of my partner's brother-in-law, who had been in an accident, rendering him possibly brain damaged. Feeling so fortunate to have lived this life as full and completely as I have. I am so sad for his family. They are all wonderful people who don't deserve an ounce of unhappiness.

4:37 p.m.　　Get a phone call from a guy in Colorado I'm sort of crushed out on that I'll see this upcoming weekend at a mutual best friend's wedding in Oregon. Have heart palpitations thinking about him and his hotness. He's been sort of sweating me for a couple of weeks. Daydream for a minute and wham . . .

4:51 p.m.   My horrible, asshole, cheating-dog ex calls to say nothing again. This happens a ton these days. I ask him when I can drop Chump off for his stay while I'm in Oregon. I really dislike my ex, but the dog was his, too, kind of. Okay, not really, but because I'm sort of a softie when he says he misses Chump, I try to accommodate him. He tries to tell me to behave myself while I'm at the wedding, and I tell him to go fuck himself and that he's not the boss of me anymore. Like he ever really was. Well, maybe a little.

5:05 p.m.   I thank my lucky stars again for granting me the power to break up with said ex. He's a manipulative bastard, and I have been nothing but the happiest girl in the world since leaving him. I also have begun to realize that I have been emotionally abused by him for the last two of the three years we were together and that being constantly disappointed, berated, snapped at, told I'm not attractive, ignored, and lied to are not parts of a happy relationship and that Chanel bags don't make up for said abuse. I do like them, but they don't make up for it.

5:06 p.m.   Start getting butterflies about new boys in general. I've been really fortunate to have met three amazing ones in the last two months and have been dating and making out like crazy. It's super fun. Have a San Francisco daydream involving this really, really great guy. There is something about him that makes me feel safe, really cared for. I rewind our interactions from several nights prior over and over, and each time I do I get a mini hot flash. I sort of think he's gonna last. I am not one to ever jump the gun, but I can see him in my future. It also doesn't hurt that this

San Fran guy is starting Fordham Law School in New York in the fall.

I have to play it cool, though. I've only known him for a week, so I e-mail him instead of calling. In my e-mail, I invite him to my house in the Adirondacks in a week and a half, post the Oregon wedding. Whoa, I've got a great couple of weeks ahead. I am totally boy crazy. I sort of know full well that the San Fran guy's attendance in the Adirondacks will be a near impossibility. I *really* lay it on thick about the merits of the house. He's a bird lover and so I double up on the bird references. Of course, during the time in question, he's triple booked—going to Texas, Vegas, and L.A. with old friends. Who am I to even attempt to dissuade him from such plans? I do it, anyway.

5:08 p.m. Start packing for my five days in Oregon, while talking to my friend Jeff, the groom. I find out that the first night there will be spent at *The Shining* lodge (where the movie was filmed). Gives me a chill. He also tells me that the first night's party will be themed "Après Ski, 1978." Get really stoked to dress up. Have hilarious reminiscing moment of a present from Jeff, a plastic toy named Wee Boy that was presented to me on a road trip. When you pulled down his plastic shorts, his penis shot water. Amazing. I am so excited to see all of my favorite college guy friends; I can't even wait.

5:14 p.m. Return the day's work-related phone calls and write an e-mail to my Italian production team in Rome about a change in schedule for the most current shoe samples. Also get back to *Lucky, ELLEgirl,* and *Teen Vogue* about sample requests and field comments and questions generated from my website.

5:59 p.m. Finish laundry, keep packing.

6:07 p.m.   Ex calls again to say nothing—maybe we'd still be together if he ever called me while we were dating, but then I flip back to the good-riddance side of the coin.

6:09 p.m.   A friend calls to ask me to meet him for a drink at Café Noir, a sceney Spanish restaurant that can be really fun during the summertime on weeknights.

6:45 p.m.   Get bombed on Chardonnay.

7:20 p.m.   See the girl who interviewed me for the *Vogue* piece weeks earlier walking by and run after her to say he-he-hello.

About 9:00   Switch to champagne.

10:00 p.m.   San Fran guy calls me to tell me that he's gonna come to the Adirondacks. I decide that I adore him and slur those very words.

10:08 p.m.   Hang out with friends in my kitchen consuming more liquor unnecessarily. Realize that this will be my MO for the next five days in Oregon and get a headache just thinking about the pending bodily abuse.

2:00 a.m.   Go to sleep after setting my alarm for 8 p.m. rather than 8 a.m. Wake up to alarm dog, Chump, the next morning, and repeat steps one through four.

12:50 p.m. The baby just nearly choked on apples while she was sitting in her high chair. That's the thing about being a mom. It's impossibly mundane and then, with no warning, you have these episodes of high drama. And I am such a great player in this scene. Imagine what a comfort it must be for Sabrina to have her mother standing over her screaming, "She's choking! She's choking!"

Jan Stinchcomb, 37, Austin, Texas; adjunct professor

5:21 p.m. Paddy, twelve, complains about his foot as he finishes his supper. Yesterday, he cut it when he jumped off his scooter. He was barefoot! We soak and douse it with lavender oil and apply Band-Aids. I remind him to keep it clean or it will get worse and he might end up with gangrene. He wonders what that is. Just wanting to get my point across, I tell him that they amputate gangrene limbs. He replies with, "Yeah, but that wouldn't hurt because they put it to sleep first." How can you reason with someone who thinks this way?

Jill Canillas Daley, 36, Lebanon, New Hampshire; special education assistant

1:07 p.m. No sooner do we leave my mom's house when the fights automatically start in the back of my minivan. Sean is pulling Meghan's blankie away and she screams at him shrilly, "It's mine. It's mine!" I struggle to keep my eyes on the road. Mechanically, I fall back into Mother Mode, telling Sean to give it back or he'll go to his room when we get home. It took all of thirty seconds for my patience to be eaten away after three days of a child-free vacation. Pathetic!

Maureen Quinn Salamon, 37, Long Valley, New Jersey; homemaker

8:00 a.m. Juliet, four, finishes her breakfast and comes up to inform me that she would like another birthday. I tell her she only gets one a year but that Daddy will be having a birthday soon and won't that be fun. Apparently that is not what she wants to hear and informs me that Daddy does not need a birthday and storms off to her room.

Kathleen Korosec Holmes, 38, Overland Park, Kansas; realtor

11:20 p.m. The phone rang next to my bed. IT WAS LAUREN! She's at camp and only had five minutes to talk on someone else's cell phone. I hadn't talked to her in weeks and the first thing out of her mouth is, Did I send her boots? She's selfish and independent and everything I guess an eighteen-year-old should be. I had a million more questions, but she had to get off the phone and said she'd call again tomorrow. She damn well better. I told her I loved her and went back to sleep.

Sherry Salant, 47, O'Fallon, Missouri; journalism teacher and author

8:45 p.m. My fourteen-year-old daughter comes into the room. "Do you have any condoms?" she asks. Condoms!

Though coming from my daughter I think this is a benign question. "Condoms?" I ask. She answers, "I need eighty condoms so each person in my health class can touch one, feel it, and experience it." (I hope not!) I learn that her health teacher, to whom I have given various health teaching materials, asked Emily to ask me about condoms.

Elizabeth A. Rider, 52, Chestnut Hill, Massachusetts;
pediatrician

6:00 a.m. My husband, Bruce, is perky, ready to start his, er, our vacation. While we wake up and get ready to head out of the Comfort Inn, we're watching that horrible HBO documentary on child beauty pageants. Bruce and I are appalled and terrified by the hyper-driven parents and the creepy made-up children who all look like tiny Dallas Cowboy cheerleaders from the mid-'80s. Our four-year-old, Sabine, on the other hand, is enchanted by the fancy costumes and makeup. Yikes!

Susan "Zan" Meigs, 40, Austin, Texas; English
instructor

On June 29, 2004 . . .

30% of day diarists spent quality time with their kids.

45% sat down with their families for dinner.

~~~~~~

A Medical Secretary
with a Motto

Faizbano Rayani, 51, Stafford, Texas

"Be the best, be the first, and be on top." Those are the words she lives by. "Why should you complain? Just do your best and if it doesn't happen, then don't cry over it." A hospital secretary, a gift shop owner, and once a Cub Scout leader, even though she doesn't have any sons. She loves a challenge. Growing up in Sukker, Pakistan, she was the only girl in her city who went to university and then to work. "Always bold, so bold!" In Pakistan she had her dream job as a teacher but an unhappy home life. Married to an abusive husband for nine years, with two daughters. "The kids were hit more than me." Soon after she and her family moved to America, she found the courage and support to leave her husband: "I always thought if you marry someone, then you die in that house." She remarried another Pakistani within a year of her divorce, the cousin of a former student of hers. When

her second husband proposed, she answered, "Let the family decide." His mom in Pakistan called her mom in America, and that was that. "It was arranged, but not arranged." After twenty years in Texas, she considers herself more American than Pakistani. A perpetual committee chairwoman, volunteer, and doer. "I look forward to doing a good turn every day, and when I do, I feel an inner happiness."

4:30 a.m. After going to bed after midnight, my husband woke me to help him find his stuff and pack for his business trip to Dallas. I was dreaming something good, but I got up so fast I forgot my dream. Half asleep, I had to pack his things, make tea, and get his vitamins out with a glass of water on the kitchen counter. As with all Desi women (*Desi* is an Indian word for people from the Indian subcontinent: Pakistan, India, etc.), I am given instructions by my husband on what to do and what not to do—"Make sure you pick up the dry cleaning." "Call the store and get the list." "Go to the wholesale market. Buy the stuff and price it."

Being an educated woman with leadership roles at work and in the community, it would be calling trouble if I said he doesn't have to tell me what to do and not to treat me as if I am his child. I just say that I know what I have to do and I always do it anyways.

He just left for two days. I will live peacefully. Thank God.

5:45 a.m. Time to get ready for work. As I only have a half hour, breakfast was out of the question. I think of my motto: To be the best, to be the first, and to be on top. I shower, get dressed, and run, taking my jewelry and socks to put on while I'm on the bus. It is so ironic, I can drive seventeen miles to the hospital parking garage in a half hour, but it takes me another half hour to go by bus from the parking garage to the hospital itself, which is hardly a four-minute drive.

6:20 a.m.   I drove eighty miles an hour most of my way. After listening to the traffic and weather report, I said my morning prayers, which lasted 'til I reached the parking garage. I once was told you are lucky if your mom is alive, for mothers always pray for their children unconditionally. I was doing the same for my daughters. I prayed for my older daughter, Henna, twenty-four, for passing her research statistics test with good grades that morning, and for my younger daughter, Sharlene, twenty-two, who has just come back from her training as an auditor. I am so proud of her today. She will be the youngest of all the employees in her company to get such a promotion.

7:00 a.m.   Oh no! I just missed the bus by a few seconds. The driver did not see me through his side mirror. I guess he was simply rude as well, because there was another lady right on his side, but he did not stop. While waiting for another bus, I put on my jewelry and socks. Here comes the bus and I get on. The bus is either too hot or too cold. You better be prepared. Good, I have my sweater with me.

7:20 a.m.   Finally, at work. Started the computer, clocked in, and got my coffee to break my fast. I like the coffee we make at work and never miss a day. I drink tea at home only if I am making it for someone, otherwise I can go without tea or coffee for days. Another secret: somehow this coffee keeps me regular.

Oh my God! It is my dear and only sister's birthday

a medical secretary with a motto   **309**

today, but I can't call her from work because it is long distance to Dallas. I called both my daughters to make sure they call her. My sister has been there for me through all the thick and thin of life. She has been the greatest support, but unluckily bad things happen to those who are very nice. She has an immune system disorder. There is no cure for it yet. She is on steroids and has become so fat. She was so pretty when she was young; I used to envy her. I pray for her all the time. The thought of her suffering makes me cry.

7:30 a.m.   I jumped right into the load of work. My schedule today is kind of exciting. After running the reports for my director, who thinks I am a computer guru, I have to prepare and print colored posters for my department's "Employee of the Month" and "Birthdays of the Month" celebrations. I have been cochair for the pharmacy department's Spirit Committee since January 2001. Tomorrow is the last party my cochair and I are going to be organizing, so we are going to be giving out Letters of Appreciation to all our members on the team.

My creativity has been at its height today. Certificates look beautiful and professional. The exciting part is that, although I will be stepping down from the Spirit Committee, I have been appointed to the Partners in Caring Committee for the hospital, which is an honor. This committee arranges programs for hospital employees like blood drives, fund-raising for employee assistance programs, the scarecrow contest, etc. The committee had a clothing drive where I made sure our department participated and was recognized.

Most of my day went to preparing for the department celebration. Working at the hospital is fun. Maybe not for everyone. But, to me, it is somewhat like a dream come true. Now this is funny. I always wanted to become a doctor, but guess what, I get depressed even when I get pricked. It was out of the question to become a doctor or a nurse, but working around them gives me a sense of fulfillment.

I usually walk in the afternoon for about ten minutes while I am doing my 12:00 prayers. Someone told me once that if you pray at noon when the sun is on your head, your prayers are heard. Well, I like to pray all the time and this is the best time, doing two things at once. I look foolish with my high heels and walking, but I don't care. I do that all the time. I need to remember to bring a pair of walking shoes.

My day at work passes so fast, and I am always in a good mood. I never take my job as if I am working. I always think I am learning something new all the time. I am also privileged to attend the weekly supervisors and managers meeting with the director of the pharmacy department. At this meeting, I learn a lot of leadership techniques and management skills, as well as an understanding of the administration of the department.

Today we discussed the Annual Behavioral Expectations form—how each supervisor would judge his staff according to the workload they have, what questions to ask on one-on-one evaluations, how would they deal with the staff member who always does his best, and one who just did his best one time around. It was a good learning experience. Except when the salary-adjustment part came. I was sent out then, as it only had to be discussed with the supervisors.

4:00 p.m.   Now it's time to go home, but I can never go straight home. We own a gift store I have to take care of—buying, hiring, training, payroll. We always have had a business. This gift shop was an opportunity we got two years ago, and I agreed to help my husband out. Actually, it was his idea because he wants to keep me busy with his things some way or the other so that he can bully me. I have a new employee at the store I have to check on.

As soon as I clocked out, I called my sister on my cell phone to wish her a happy birthday. Both my daughters had already called her.

4:25 p.m.   On my way to the gift shop, I had to talk to the program manager for our upcoming festival in celebration of Imamat Day of our spiritual leaders of the Shia Ismaili Muslim community. As a board member for the social welfare of our elderly members, I am supposed to prepare the seniors with a group dance we are to practice every evening after the religious ceremonies at our *Jamatkhana.* I also had to talk to the lady who called me about finding a job. I made a couple of phone calls to people who would know of any job openings. I feel the pain of people when they ask me to help and I can't. I try to go out of my way to help them.

Traffic is so bad downtown. I had no choice but to drive slow. It has already started to rain. My store is inside a car wash. All month it has rained except for five days. It is hurting. I tell my husband to get rid of the store, but he thinks it will do well at Christmas. It didn't last year and I don't think I can do justice with it because, as my motto is to be the best, I have to give 100 percent, which I don't have the time to do. And how much can an employee do on her own, unless you find a loyal one?

4:50 p.m.   The minute I get inside my store, I got a message from Sharlene asking if I could go with her to choose a gift for the 25th wedding anniversary of her best friend's parents. Her friend lives in Atlanta. Sometimes I wonder whether she looks forward to going there more than she wants to come home to me. Seems like I am jealous. We went to Galleria Mall and got her an engraved silver capsule. By this time I was starving. We ate McDonald's—spicy chicken sandwich. No wonder I am gaining weight.

7:20 p.m.   I was late now. I had to go home and fax the list of participants for the Going for Gold program for seniors at the Golden Club. I also had to clean up a little. Talked to my uncle, whose youngest daughter at thirty-eight is suffering from arthritis and diabetes. Doctors want to amputate her legs. My aunt is suffering from Alzheimer's and Parkinson's at the same time, and my uncle, ninety, takes care of them. I wish I could help him.

7:40 p.m.   Attended a conference call at home for my Going for Gold program. Since it is an Olympics year, we have five rings—life skills, health, asset preservation, family harmony, and fitness. We do seminars, and whoever attends these earns ten points each. At the end of the year, if they earn 100 points in each ring, they get a bronze medal; 125 points, a silver medal; 150 points, a gold medal. Being one of the content developers, I have to prepare two new topics for the seminars.

8:25 p.m.   Left to go to *Jamatkhana* where I was going to meet the seniors, but the rain was so bad only two people showed up. I was upset but couldn't help it. I myself didn't feel like going, but duty comes first. I am a uniformed volunteer at our *Jamatkhana*. Our motto is "Work no word." When we give honorary service, we do not complain. I think that is the reason we Ismailis are so successful. I did meet some new people. One more lady asked me if I could find her a job at the hospital. I hope God helps me find her one.

9:00 p.m. Came home. There is no cooked food, and I am in no mood to cook. When my husband is not here it is supposed to be my holiday, right?

My hubby just came home unexpectedly from out of town. His deal did not go through and he came back hungry. I cooked kebabs/cutlets. He wants to show off every little thing he does and hammers on what I did wrong in the past and how I don't pay attention to what he says, etc. I don't like anybody putting anyone down, so how can I tolerate it when he wants to put me or my daughters down?

After dinner, I cleaned the dishes and put a load of clothes in the washer. I usually wash clothes every weekend, but last weekend was hectic. There was a wedding and a party. And I had to be at the store both Saturday and Sunday all day because my new employee was going to start working Monday.

Made phone calls to all the Golden Club chairs to submit their quarterly reports for the social welfare board.

11:50 p.m. Thank God the day went by well. It was hectic enough, but I would rather have a hectic day than sit around and waste time gossiping and window shopping. My daughters always ask me, "Why don't you ever chat with people like other mothers do? You are always busy with meetings and conferences or you are volunteering."

I am in bed, thinking, What am I going to wear tomorrow? What will I say in my speech to the Golden Club? I had to pray before I went to bed. Oh, what a day a woman has being a wife, a mother, a volunteer, an employee, an employer, and herself. I hope I can wake up at 4 a.m. to meditate. Thank God I am going to sleep a little earlier than last night.

Miscellaneous Moments

You Are Joking, Right?

1:03 a.m. On the phone with my boyfriend, I happen to open the drawer where my journals are kept and discover they are missing. These were the journals that were the subject of a huge argument this weekend because he "found" them and read them without my permission. The journals included references to my past love relationships. "Honey, where are my journals?" I ask. "In a landfill," he replies. "What?" He repeats, "In a landfill, I guess." I begin to feel a knot tighten inside my stomach. Unmotherf*ckin' believable! "Please tell me you are joking. You are joking, right?" All I hear is, "I'm sorry."

Vonda L. Marshall, 39, Brooklyn, New York; field attorney, National Labor Relations board

But Do They Really?

6:05 a.m. Plop on wig. No way can I face that curling iron this morning. How can such a little bit of hair take an hour to curl? Best thing I ever did for myself was getting this wig six months ago. And everyone loves it. At least they say they do (hmm).

Nancy Day, 57, Catonsville, Maryland; patient billing systems analyst

Oprah

8:45 a.m. I turn on the *Oprah* show as I do most mornings so I can have company while eating breakfast. I remember meeting her in person twenty years ago when I was in her studio audience. (It was *AM Chicago* then.) Her guest was a hairstylist and he was doing makeovers. I asked him some questions, so I got to be on TV. Afterwards, I chatted with Oprah and she complimented me on looking younger than my sixty years. We had our picture taken together, and she said she'd like me on a future show about women who age well. Oprah, I'm still waiting to hear from you.

Goldie Bulgatz, 80, Morton Grove, Illinois

Mean Girls

12:45 p.m. My friend Bex is here. Time for "therapy," thank God. I go first as client, exploring why I hate this woman Carry who has moved into my social circle. No, I really hate her. I'm twenty-eight and haven't hated like this since I was much younger. Of course, it has to do with early hurts. It always does. I realize that Carry reminds me of my two best friends in fourth grade who stabbed me in the back that year and left me for dead. Bex suggests that it's possible that Carry might not be those girls. I consider the possibility that she might not stab me in quite the same way.

Stephanie Abraham, 28, Temple City, California; substitute teacher

Get the Flip-Flops!

8:17 a.m.   At the shower trailer, I realize I've forgotten my flip-flops and debate going back to my room to get them. This would mean crossing a gravel lot, jumping over a two-foot-wide irrigation ditch, crossing a major two-way divided road, hopping over another two-foot drainage ditch, and finally scampering down and up a four-foot-deep trench. I decide that I don't have time and reluctantly take a very quick shower, imagining all the horrible things growing on the shower floor. I try to stand in one place and rationalize that I have seen the cleaning lady scrub the stall floor at least once in the past two months.

Cathy Wilkinson, 30, Lacey, Washington; commander,
28th Public Affairs Detachment, U.S. Army (serving
in Iraq)

Lethia Cobbs, 36, Long Beach, California

She works ten-hour days, four days a week at a university as an alternative media specialist, converting textbooks to e-texts for blind students. Discontent. "I have a job, not a career. What I really want is to write poetry and fiction." And play the fiddle. She took violin lessons as a kid, then picked it up again two years ago. "It takes me away from the television, it keeps me creative, and it keeps me humble." She dreams of busking at the 3rd Street Promenade in Santa Monica. Her favorite music? "I'm the only black person I know who is really into bluegrass." She's been living with her fiancé for eight years. Why haven't they set a date? "When I procrastinate"—she laughs—"I don't play at it." Her family sees her as an underachiever. No house, no desire for kids, a nonchurchgoer in a family of Baptist preachers and deacons. She sees herself as a dreamer, a drifter. "I'm searching for the things that will make me happy." She does stand-up poetry. Took up kayaking. Cut off her dreadlocks, then started locking again. "One of my favorite creatures is the butterfly because it metamorphoses. I'm always changing. I'll get interested in something and, at first, I'll say I can't do that, but then I'll end up doing it."

6:20 a.m. The alarm clock went off and interrupted a dream that I was having that made no sense. I dreamed about Wimpy from *Popeye.* In the dream, I kept asking my friends, Why did Wimpy continuously beg for burgers? How come he would pay you on Tuesdays? Was Tuesday the payday where he worked? I spent the wee hours working on the logic of all of this until the alarm broke my obsessive pattern.

7:00 a.m. Oh my God! I don't want hair anymore! Hair is too much. Hope I can work up the courage to do away with it this weekend. After ten years of wearing my hair down to my elbows in dreadlocks, you'd think I would've learned about hard work! I do not feel like twisting the roots to maintain it, and I don't want hair longer than my ears, period. This weekend it goes. But what if I have a funny-shaped head?

7:56 a.m. I'm sitting in my car waiting until my favorite song ends. I don't know why I've become attached to sad songs. "Ghost in This House" by Alison Kraus & Union Station always makes me contemplative. I'm in this zone right now where I think I can sing. If I can't sing, just don't tell me 'til the song ends, chil'.

8:15 a.m. Good! There's not a soul in the office, so for now I can live in this silence. I was going to put a CD on, but no. This is the kind of silence that needs to be held close. I don't even get this kind of peace at home anymore. The maintenance man installed a fire alarm that beeps every forty seconds, so even the stillness of night is gone. I can converse in my head right now, turn that dream over in my mind and wonder what the heck was going on.

10:30 a.m. On my break, I like sitting here near the women's center on campus because my friend Barbara has trained one of the birds to eat from her hand. I get to breathe right now and wish I were somewhere else. It's not that I hate my job. I just don't care for it either. Still, I try to find something to make the day tolerable. I feed the blue scrub the cracker from my hand. It needs food and shelter, like me. It's too easy, this comparison I'm making. The blue scrub does not hate or love the work it does to live; it just does it. I take this thought back to my desk where I scan, convert, and edit books for Braille or e-text.

Noon I go out to my car to take a nap. Of course I begin drifting off to sleep wondering why Wimpy is always broke.

2:00 p.m. Blah, blah, blah. Endless paperwork that stopped having meaning hours ago. I attempt to contact the publishers for electronic text, and they take their sweet time. For the students, having their books in an accessible form makes a difference in whether they pass or fail. Still, I feel empty inside. What I want is meaning of some kind. I don't know if I'm describing my work or my entire life.

I've been curled up over my keyboard and my chest hurts from this posture. I want to think of something else while I'm here. I want to remember the last poetry reading I attended or the last song I listened to that made me both happy and sad. I push myself on by remembering how bad the economy is right now and that I should be thankful for what I have. Sometimes, just having a job has to be enough.

4:00 p.m. I finished working with a student who's preparing for the Writing Proficiency Exam. I like the individuality of the work and when I can help the students overcome their issues with writing. I am also thinking of chocolate. I have exactly $6 to my name until payday. Hmm, choc-o-late. Is it a hobby or necessity? I'm in the mood for some bluegrass. At least I can punch in an Internet station. I end up listening to Lightning Hopkins, "Penitentiary Blues." It's the moans and groans of this song that pull me into it.

6:00 p.m. One hour to go. I'm counting the minutes like I count pennies in my jar, thinking of the blue scrub bird flying around outside. Is she thankful that her day is almost over? Then again, it doesn't end if you're a mother. My mother called today to ask me to bring a bag of ice. She also wants food, every day. She hates the food in the board and care. I am worried about her. I don't know if the schizophrenia is getting worse or if she has any of the other issues that happen to old people. I had to tell her I only have $6 until payday. I wish she'd ask how I'm doing or something like that.

So forget about my day ending. I have to see about Ma. I was thinking about squeezing in some fiddle practice, but by the time I get myself motivated it'd be time to go to bed. Work-Ma-Home-Sleep. I am stuck on the wheel.

7:33 p.m. I want to be at home, stripped of these hot clothes and, oh yeah, my hair. The wrong, and I mean the *wrong* time of the year to start locking your hair is the summer. Your hair becomes a well-insulated wool cap. I walk up to the steps of the residential home, and Ma's sitting out-side waiting for me. I sit down beside her and we watch the sun go down. "Did you bring food?" she asks me. I just turn and face the sunset. From our view, there are no special colors, but there is a stillness that holds us together.

8:18 p.m.   I got to get out of this bra and these work clothes. It's burning up in our apartment. Cooking doesn't appeal to me at all, so I grab a bowl of cereal. My fiancé is home on the computer as usual with the TV blaring. We kiss and settle into our seats; his at the desk, while I sit on the couch. We don't say much. I don't know how to get the ball rolling to human interaction. I want something to laugh at. I need to laugh, but not at something on TV. I need it to come from something organic. I put on Cesaria Evora and I smile. Now I am closer to that sunset.

10:07 p.m.   Part of me just wants the day to end right now. I am going to sleep to dream about everything I desire coming into fruition. Maybe my life is my own fault. I don't know. I just know that dreams allow me to make it through the days.

A Walk at the Zoo

12:30 p.m. Oh boy. My husband, Bobby, just radioed me to tell me that his ex-wife, Debbie, and grandchildren are on their way to the zoo and wondered if I could walk around with them.

2:45 p.m. It is 84 degrees and I am sooo sweaty! We walked all through the animal trail. Debbie was sweating profusely and breathing hard by the time we got to the cheetahs. Bobby was in an electric wheelchair so he didn't notice my pace. I did try to keep it slow . . . I DID! But I didn't stop for a rest. I guess I should have, but this was the first time that Debbie had been to see me at work, and Bobby's family is always bragging on Debbie and how she cooks, cleans, and sews. She is Saint Betty Crocker. They all still live next door to each other and never understood why Debbie and Bobby got divorced. I didn't really try to show off on the walk, but I guess I did a little.

When they got ready to leave, Debbie asked Bobby and the kids to stand together. She handed me her camera and asked if I could take a family picture. I don't think I cut off her head.

Yvonne D. Lemons, 44, La Vergne, Tennessee; program coordinator, Nashville Zoo

323

Exotic Dancer

Lisa Oppedyk, 25, Portland, Oregon

Some of her friends were nude dancers, so, she thought, why not give it a try? She needed the money and besides, she'd applied for jobs at the mall, the movie theater, Starbucks. Her anxiety about working a "regular" job always got in the way. At her first dance audition, "I was so scared, not of stripping, but that the club manager would reject me and crush my ego." Now she's learning pole work for her act. "One day, no one was watching, so I just spun around. It was the best feeling, exhilarating." She grew up on a farm in small-town Oregon. As a teenager, it was a relief to move to a bigger city when her parents split. A punk phase. Ten tattoos—crossbones, hellfire, barbed wire. "They don't fit my life anymore. I feel pretty mainstream now." A morning person. A rape survivor. A feminist. "I'm not saying stripping has empowered me, but the ability to make money empowers me. And getting over my body issues enough to be naked on stage makes me feel em-powered." At work she wears lots of pink and white. "My customers think I'm really sweet. What they don't know is that I have frequent fantasies of kicking their asses." She likes road trips with friends. Cats, but not kids. She's saving for massage school and wants to gear her practice toward sex workers. "It would be perfect 'cause I know where it hurts."

8:00 a.m. I just woke up. I don't have to be at work until 2:00 this afternoon, but I like spending lazy mornings around the house by myself.

10:00 a.m. I've been watching TV and reading the paper. Neither is holding my interest. During a commercial, I made myself a bagel and iced coffee. The coffee may have been a bad idea, as I'm getting nervous about my first day back after a ten-day vacation in Lake Tahoe and San Francisco. I'm afraid that I've forgotten how to dance in that slow, specific style that most of us do. When I first started dancing, it took me some time to master the moves. I was incredibly awkward, but one day it just clicked and my body took over. I have a feeling it's like riding a bike and that I can't have possibly forgotten how to dance in only ten days, but I'm still nervous.

12:15 p.m. I'm home again after giving my housemate a ride to work. She dances at one of the same clubs that I do, but not today. I like working with her but worry that it's damaging our friendship. She's super competitive and gets really upset when I make more money, and I almost always do. I'm a lot better at carrying on conversations with the customers, which is at least as important as how I look or how well I dance. She despises the social responsibilities of this job, and I don't blame her because a lot of the customers are annoying, rude, or just plain boring. Some customers do come in just to look at us, but many are there for other reasons—they're lonely, or want to "get to know" us.

I have an hour and a half before work, so I need to shower soon. There's a lot of preparation involved in stripping. I need to shave everything, do my hair and makeup, stretch my legs so I don't get sore muscles, make some food to bring with me, and repack my work bag. I tend to bring just about all of my work outfits to every shift, even though I usually only end up wearing two or three a day.

I don't have a lot of actual stripper clothes, which can cost around $50 to $100 per item or set, despite being cheaply made. Most of the things I wear at work come from the lingerie section of Goodwill. It takes a lot of picking through racks filled with gaudy lace teddies—cheesy attempts to spice things up in someone's desperate marriage. I also shop the regular clothing sections. I love sparkly fabrics and even something that initially looks hideous and outdated can sometimes be altered into a cute, new outfit. A baby blue sequined dress that was probably worn to some junior high school dance in 1992 can become a miniskirt that looks fabulous with thigh-high fishnets under the flashy stage lights.

2:00 p.m. I arrive at the club fifteen minutes before we open to give myself time to get dressed and do any finishing touches on my hair and makeup. I don't need to look perfect; it's not like I work at some top-tier gentlemen's club. Most of the clubs in my city are just neighborhood bars that happen to have a stage and a couple dancers. The one I'm at today has a small diamond-shaped stage in the middle of the room. There's a pole in the middle of the stage, and around its perimeter is a narrow counter where the customers can set their drinks when they sit at "the rack"—what we call the chairs that line the stage. Strip club protocol requires each customer who sits at the rack tip at least $1 per song. We do three-song sets in which we generally end up nude by the end of the third song.

I'm almost always at the club before my coworkers and today is no exception. The other dancer hasn't even shown up yet, so I'm sure I'll have to go on stage first, as usual. No one wants to dance during the first set because it's almost guaranteed there won't be any customers.

Usually, I sit at the bar and talk to the bartender for a few minutes before I have to get on stage, but today she is busy taking money out of the video poker machines. I particularly like this bartender. She is queer and one of the few people here who knows that I am, too. It helps to have her around, to know I have a witness to the bizarre, hetero-sexual mating rituals I participate in all day long; someone who knows that it's all so funny and fake.

It's funny to think that I was once unsure if any clubs would hire me and my size twelve body. The fact is that most of the dancers I know have various "imperfections"— stretch marks, chubby bellies, cellulite, tattoos and piercings, bruised knees, and other wear-and-tear from work. I'd like to say that I came into this business on my own terms, but the reality is the rent was due, and a competitive local job market coupled with some mental health issues left me feeling like I didn't have much choice.

That's not to say that I don't sometimes enjoy the job, but in reality it's pretty boring most days. Taking my clothes off for money doesn't feel dangerous or bad *or* fun and exciting. It's just a job, and like any other job, it's frequently a pain in the ass. But unlike any other job I've ever had, I actually kind of miss it on my days off. And there are definitely perks: instant cash; a higher wage than I could

exotic dancer 327

possibly get at any other job; I get to dress up and wear cute shoes; and I get paid to DANCE!

Well, the bartender is heading toward the door with her keys. That means it's time for me to pick my songs on the jukebox and get on stage.

2:45 p.m. I was right, it is like riding a bike. How could I even think I could forget these movements? I've got it down like a formula:

1. Bend over and slowly run my hand up the inside of my leg.

2. Turn around so my back is against the pole and slide down into a squat.

3. Crawl seductively toward the customer.

4. Arch my back and writhe around like it's sooo hot.

5. Always smile and make eye contact.

It's the same thing over and over, but the customers never seem to notice the repetition.

3:00 p.m. Tuesdays are not typically busy, and I don't expect to make a ton of money today. Most of the few customers here are busy playing video poker. There's one guy who is really into me. He sits at the rack every time I'm on stage. Now he's talking to me in very broken English. I'm not sure, but I think he is asking me to marry him. My tactic is to laugh uncomfortably and say, "Thanks, but no thanks." I get a marriage proposal once or twice a week, and some customers actually claim to love me.

5:00 p.m. I'm hiding out in the dressing room for a few minutes, feeling pretty ready to go home, but the shift is only half over. The guy who wants to marry me bought me two strong margaritas earlier, and I feel a little bit drunk. I usually limit myself to one drink per shift because dancing in my impossibly high heels is hard enough when I'm sober, but I was feeling irritated at the slow day and the money I'm not making, and tequila seemed like it might put me in a better mood. I'm not sure if it's working yet.

5:35 p.m. On my way to the jukebox, a customer drunkenly stumbles into my path and asks me to do a table dance. Whenever we're not on stage, we're expected to try to get customers to buy these private dances, which are where the real money is since we charge $20 per song. I hate to beg customers to buy dances—it feels weird and tacky—so I don't do it much, but I miss out on a lot of money.

I agree to this customer's request because I've made next to nothing on stage yet, but first I check in with the other dancer who has already given him a table dance. She says he is okay and didn't try to touch her or anything. Apparently he's a regular of hers, so she knows his bad habits well. She tells me I shouldn't turn my back on him because she's seen him try to grab dancers when they're not looking. I'm glad she was nice enough to give me this advice. Many dancers wouldn't. We're all essentially in direct competition, and catty, bitchy behavior is common.

I decide to take him to a more open area where there's brighter lighting than the corner with the leather couch where we usually do our table dances. I remind him, no physical contact. I can tell he's pretty drunk, and by the time he gets himself situated in the chair, the song has already started. I spend most of the song standing on the bench over him, with my feet on either side of his legs and my crotch inches from his face, slowly gyrating my hips and watching him carefully to make sure he doesn't try to touch me.

exotic dancer **329**

I can never figure out why men are so intrigued by female bodies, but it doesn't bother me. I hope they'll learn something from staring at mine and put the information to good use with their wives and girlfriends. Before I know it, the song is over and I put my clothes back on and accompany him to the ATM to collect my $20.

7:00 p.m.   Two of my regulars come in, both about my age. Most of the younger guys aren't into me; they seem to prefer the skinnier girls. Older men generally have more appreciation for my broad hips and fleshy thighs. Dancing for people my own age always makes me feel a little uncomfortable, like it's too close to home. These two guys are nice though. One of them brings over a Jell-O shot for each of us, and I sit on the stage for a song while we suck them down and talk about the weather, what they were up to that day, what kind of music they listen to. It is nice to have a break from dancing, especially since they continue to put dollars on the stage. They say they saw me at the movie theater a few weeks ago. I wonder if they saw my girlfriend with me and figured out that I am queer. If so, it doesn't seem to bother them.

7:20 p.m.   I had my first foot fetish customer. I'd been hoping for one for a while. They seemed so simple, but I actually ended up feeling kind of annoyed that he *only* wanted to look at my feet. I was wearing my amazing silver-sequined platform heels, and I know they draw a lot of attention, but still, this was kind of ridiculous.

8:00 p.m.   I'm finally off work. The tiny dressing room is chaotic with the shift change and four half-naked girls getting ready at once. The night girls are a lot friendlier with each other because they work three to a shift, so when one is on stage the other two can hang out and talk. The night girls are loudly talking shit about certain other dancers who think they are too good to work at our club. I try to keep my mouth shut, even if I agree with what's being said. I'm still pretty new at this club, and I don't want to get on anyone's bad side. Mostly I keep to myself.

I just have to pack up my stuff and trade my money at the bar for bigger bills. I have a stack of $1 bills that is about three inches thick. I love the ritual of smoothing and stacking each crumpled bill so they each face the same direction and organizing them in groups of twenty. It's so satisfying.

Around 9:30 I walk with my girlfriend and our housemate to the bar around the corner from my house. Tuesday is queer night, and pretty much everyone I know comes here. We like to go early before it gets crowded so we can find a table.

9:45 p.m. The drink line at the bar is so long that we order a couple pitchers of beer so we won't have to wait again. We spend the evening camped out at our table in the corner, saying hi to friends and running out to the dance floor when the DJ plays a song we like. It is such a relief to come here after work, after a day spent pretending to be straight and flirting with men that I'm not attracted to in any way. I can finally be myself and make out with my girlfriend and dance how I want.

11:45 p.m. It was a fun night, but my girlfriend is a nanny and has to get up for work in just over six hours, so we left early and are home getting ready for bed.

Nine-something p.m. Downstairs in Merkin Concert Hall. I watch Toshi Reagan on the monitor. She starts the show with "Tangled Up in Blue," and she is a powerful force. Then I go to the bathroom (the dressing room is crowded with mostly male musicians) to change out of my shorts and sandals into some shiny white pants, a light brown knitted halter top, and strappy shoes—a few notches up from my usual gig wear, but this is a special occasion. Ollabelle is rehearsing just outside the door, and they sound wonderful. Marc Anthony Thompson sees me in my new outfit and says, "Bling bling."

Right before it is time for our song ("If You See Her, Say Hello"), my band and I go upstairs. I exchange a few words with the host/MC on stage. Quickly he gets to the inevitable question, "Was your dad, Harry Chapin, influenced by Dylan?" I tell him I believe that he was, like so many of his generation. I also tell him that my dad had taught my mom to play Dylan's "Blowin' in the Wind" when he was her guitar teacher in the mid-sixties (this was how they met).

The whole interview is so quick and cheerful that when I go to my mic to sing, I realize I am far away from the desired mournful mood of the song. The band jumps right into the intro and there we are. It's a challenge for the first few notes to switch gears, but I think I get there. Steph, Pete, and Jamie play beautifully. In our rehearsal earlier that week, we had focused on creating a sort of climax in the fourth verse—"I've never gotten used to it"—before breaking down the intensity in the fifth and final verse. Tonight, I'd say our interpretation overall is subtle and quiet.

During the final applause, I'm always a bit unsure of how quickly to exit the stage. I say thank you, smile, wave my arm to acknowledge the band, and try to maintain contact with the audience. After we get off stage, the crew and other musicians say complimentary things. At least two people tell me they were moved to tears by the song, which I hesitate to believe. (Music is my love, but I don't know if it ever makes me cry!) But of course it is great to hear.

We listen to the rest of the show, then I go back on stage to join the other artists (Vernon Reid, Joan Osborne, Jesse Harris, etc.) for a finale performance of "I Shall Be Released." Joan sits behind the drums and provides a simple backbeat. I sing a harmony part on the choruses. The group finale thing is always a little corny, given the swaying, sing-along tone of it all, but fun in its unrehearsed looseness. The audience of about 450 people gives us a huge amount of energy and love (or at least gives it to us as proxies for Bob Dylan).

Jen Chapin, 33, Brooklyn, New York; singer/songwriter

Ellen Jean Lynch, 38, Kearney, Nebraska

Location: North Arabian Sea. Mission: Deliver Marines to Iraq. Her job is to supervise the ship's electrical shop, fixing relay panels, instruments, and other helicopter components. She's a mother figure to the guys in her shop. "I'll chew their butts out if I think I have to. Doesn't mean I don't like them. I just have to mold them." She grew up in a three-bedroom mobile home in Nebraska and worked as a nurse's aide after high school. Now she lives in a mobile home on water. "I joined the Navy to get out of farm country." Met her husband at a bike hangout in Tennessee where she was stationed for electrician school. She rode a Yamaha, but he had a Harley. "This guy's for me!" They married seven months later. Two kids— fourteen and eleven—they named the first one after her, Ellen Jean Lynch II. She's been in the Navy eighteen years. Twenty-one months to go until retirement (but who's counting). *"The Navy is for younger people who can keep up."* Thanks partly to the job, she's only seen her kids two weeks a year over the past three years. *"I e-mail them every day and keep their pictures on the air-conditioning pipe over my rack."* When she retires, she'll return to Nebraska and her old job. *"Being a nurse's aide is more rewarding, 'cause it's helping individuals versus helping a nation."*

0245 Up and at 'em. Oh, oh, oh, it is hard to get up this morning. Tired from staying up late to work on an X-rep part (transformer). We needed to fix it and get it back to the squadron. Enough of the tired thing. Get your tush moving. It needs the gym, especially with this ship's fattening foods.

0255 Finally, I climb out of my rack. Yep, this top rack is fun to climb out of, three bunk beds high. I try to be quiet for my shipmates who are sleeping below and beside me. I have to put my feet on the edge of the racks to help me climb down. MA1 (master-at-arms) Fritzgerald does not like it when I do that. You hear everything that goes on in the berthing, since it is pretty small, about forty feet by twenty feet, with forty-five women sleeping in it. I must look funny getting in and out of my rack. I am a barrel of laughs this morning. Boy, I miss my soft waterbed.

0310 Made it up to the gym. Thank goodness the ladderwell to the gym is right beside my berthing and I only have to go up two flights. It only takes a few minutes to get there. I see some other people working out. They believe in torture, too. As I jog on the treadmill, I dream of being on my own farm and not on this ship. Hey, my dreams work on getting me through the morning routine. Before I know it, my workout is done.

0445 I feel much better now. Head for the shower in my berthing before anyone else wakes up and before the head (bathroom) gets crowded. I hate having only two shower stalls for forty-five women, which can mean a ten-minute wait. Oh, I hate the lack of privacy. People see you get in and out of the shower; I feel like a flasher some days. Stop thinking. Just hurry up and grab a cup of coffee and relax.

0600 I hear, "Reveille, Reveille, all hands heave out and trice up, smoking lamp is lit in all authorized places. Breakfast for the crew." I head to the chow line. The wait is not too bad this morning, only twenty minutes. I grab my usual two boiled eggs, fruit, and two glasses of milk. You know, I am tired of breakfast stuff for breakfast all the time. I would like some sweet potatoes or tofu once in a while. I eat by myself 'cause my friend/bunkmate waits until the last minute to get up and get ready for work.

0700 Head to the electrical shop. No one is in here yet, so I check my e-mail. Of course, nothing from the kids again. It's been two weeks since they e-mailed me. I guess that is what happens when you choose a Navy career along with motherhood. The motherhood part gets neglected due to duty. I feel like I don't have a close relationship with my kids because I have been gone on deployments most of their lives. I guess I can't blame them for not writing to me.

I stop and think about how happy I am that someone else, an AT1 (aviation electronic technician), now takes the Production Control meetings. As for me, I don't miss them. All they are is put-downs on how stupid we are according to the khakis. I would give up my leading petty officer position to avoid those meetings.

this day in the life   **336**

0720   AT1 is back from the Production Control meeting. All she has to pass down is that securing General Quarters will be at 0730, uniform inspection at 1045, and that I have urinalysis observer (pee-pee watcher) duty from 1000 to 1500. I am glad that this gets me out of uniform inspection, but on the other hand, it is not thrilling to watch women pee in a bottle.

0732   I hear the General Quarters bell, so I hurry to my repair locker to get my equipment to help fight a fire or stop flooding and to get Zebra set for my area (close all fittings, including water, air, etc., and hatches). Then I put on my SCBA (self-contained breathing apparatus) and get ready to set fire/flooding boundaries if I need to. (For fire boundaries, you surround the room with hoses. For flooding boundaries, you put plugs and braces over the holes.) After ten minutes of standing around, the damage control (yellow hat) guys tell us that since this is only a drill, and due to the 95-degree heat, we can put away our SCBAs. I am happy that we can down dress.

After putting my SCBA away, my repair locker decides to hold training on damage control by asking questions to each other.

"What is a class Charlie fire?"

"An electrical fire."

I ask, "What type of extinguishing agent do you use for a Charlie fire?"

Someone answers, "CO2."

0930   General Quarters is secured. Time to get some water. I am dry.

1000   Muster for pee-pee observation as I sing, "Oh what fun it is to ride on a one-horse open ship." Yes, I have to watch people pee for drug testing, what fun. I read my sheet of dos and don'ts and sign it. Do watch the urine leave the body and go into the collection bottle. Don't let the person stick her fingers or any other object into the urine, which could contaminate it. The master-at-arms senior chief gives us observers a brief and blunt speech. She tells the males that they are meat gazers and the females that we are snatch watchers, or whatever we want to call it. Boy, this new Navy has no couth.

1200 Not too bad of a morning on the observer watch. Only ten customers. I take a chow break. They are serving meat lasagna, white spaghetti noodles with meat sauce, breaded fried eggplant, peas, white rice. Fattening crap again. Oh, I miss low-fat meals, complex-carb meals. I eat only wheat pasta and nonbreaded nonfried veggies. No wonder Navy people are fat. I decide on the peas and some fried eggplant and two glasses of milk. Of course, this ship only serves 2 percent milk. I miss my skim milk. This is killing me. I am eating extra fat—thirty fat calories per glass to be exact—by drinking 2 percent milk instead of my skim. Try not to die a thousand deaths. The deployment will be over soon, and I can go back to my healthier eating.

1230 Back to pee-pee observing out on the hangar bay. Oh boy, what a joy. I have just one customer waiting, an AE3 (aviation electricians mate) who works on the flight deck. The guys have about ten waiting in line. Maybe I'll smile and ask them if they would like fries with that. No, that would get me in trouble. Keep quiet. I only give the instruction on what to do. Pee in bottle. Keep your bottle in my eyesight at all times. Other than that, no talking.

1430 The senior chief hands me back my ID card and tells me the other two girls can cover me. So I head back to the shop where I find the guys working on another X-rep. I jump in and help them work on the transformer.

1755 Finally done with the X-rep. Since we don't have the capability to check it in the shop, I go to Production Control and tell them I need them to call the helicopter squadron and ask them if we can use one of their helicopters to plane-check the part.

1810 AE3 and I meet up with the Marines that work up on the flight deck. It sure is hot out here, maybe 98 degrees. They help us verify that the transformer works on one of their helos by checking to see if it's converting AC to DC. Thank goodness it checks good. Good job to all.

1815 With the MAF (maintenance action form) paperwork signed off and no more parts to work on, everyone heads to chow. I decide to check my e-mail instead. I don't need another fattening meal today. Hey, I got an e-mail from the kids' father, but none from my kids. It makes me sad that my kids don't e-mail but once in a blue moon. Of course, their father doesn't make them or encourage them. He don't make them do nothing. He believes he can win them over to where they like him better than me by being their buddy and not being their father.

That's what I get for marrying a lazy use-you-to-the-hilt man. I hate him for refusing to work. I hate his stupid excuses that "No one will hire me when they find out you're only going to be stationed here for three years." Lazy goodfor-nothing. Everyone else's spouses work for a living to help with expenses. Why can't he? It takes two paychecks when one of you is in the military. But no, he can't see that. Instead he keeps going in debt further and further instead of helping out or living within a certain income. Oh, he makes me mad. Enough of that. I have a headache.

1835 It's that time of day again. AT1 heads up to Production Control for the meeting. Again, I count my blessings I don't have to take that put-down meeting anymore. AT1 complains about the meetings a lot, says that they are stuffy. I believe it's getting to her like it got to me. I will pray for her to get the strength to handle it.

1910 AT1 is back. A typical meeting. Nothing to pass out. I count my blessings that it is time to go to bed.

2015 Finally done with my nighttime routine of showering, brushing teeth, and defrizzing my hair with K-7 hair moisturizing lotion. I put on my black sweatpants and sweatshirt to get comfy. Nowadays, it takes a little too long to get ready for bed. It must be the old age, as I stare at my gray hairs. A few more pop up every day. Remind myself, only about two more years of gray-hair-causing routine. Enough of worrying—time to climb in bed.

2018 I tell the kids good night and say a prayer for them. Maybe tomorrow I will get an e-mail from them.

5 a.m. I woke as usual. After the bathroom, back in bed, as usual clicked on CNN to see what terrible thing had happened overnight. Strident-voiced anchor Carol Costello, whom I really like, announced the transfer of civil authority to a transitional Iraqi governing council. It took place two days ahead of schedule for fear of disruption. An Army convoy was ambushed in Baghdad this morning. Three of our soldiers were killed and more wounded. It's so terrible. And then Carol said, "Move over, Michael Moore, Spider-Man is coming." I cringed and shut the damn TV down and pulled the cover over my head.

Barbara Bick, 79, Vineyard Haven, Massachusetts

8:25 a.m. I arrived at work. I started reading my e-mails and the *New York Times* online. There was an editorial by David Brooks. He wrote an article about how the country is becoming more politically polarized, either staunchly conservative or very liberal. One of his points is that in order to combat political isolation and polarization, more Americans need to travel around the country and see other walks of life. He wanted there to be an "ambitious program of national service." I wrote to tell him that it already exists and it is called AmeriCorps.

*Melissa Myers, 23, Miami, Florida; AmeriCorps
VISTA volunteer

9:30 p.m. Check e-mail. After thirty-five years on the air, I can't get a job. I've done forty applications. Ageism. One guy said, "No one needs an old broad." I'm living in the wrong country.

*Sally Jessy Raphael, 61, New York, New York; host of
the* Sally Jessy Raphael Show, *1983–2002*

2:30 p.m. I met with Radia for our language exchange, her practicing English with me and me practicing Arabic with her. She picked McDonald's as our place to meet because it is air-conditioned, especially since she wears hijab, leaving only her hands and face showing in public and covering everything else out of modesty and respect for self and for God. She appreciates a cool spot in such sweaty weather. I couldn't stop thinking about the consulate's warnings to stay away from American-identified places, yet I didn't suggest another spot. The air-conditioning was just so tempting.

*Mandy Halpin, 22, Boscobel, Wisconsin; Fulbright
Scholar studying in Morocco*

6:30 a.m. President Bush is on the TV and my husband watches. I begin to ready the house and me and make my work list. The president is in Turkey at NATO. The terrorist topic is a heavy burden on the world. Sometimes it seems so remote from Iowa. Protection of our people and places we love seems more assured in the Midwest.

Joni Axel, 61, Muscatine, Iowa; attorney

9:30 a.m.   Awakened by my partner, my WIFE, thanks to Massachusetts Supreme Judicial court ruling allowing same-sex marriage! "Do you want coffee?" Those are the magic words to get me out of bed.

Mel Andrade, 39, Roslindale, Massachusetts; nurse

0630   I had just enough time to press my BDUs before first formation. All us medics were accounted for and the cannon went off. I always get a surge of pride when I hear the cannon and I watch the flag being raised. It makes me so proud to be an American solider.

Nikki Shaw, 21, Ontario, Oregon; combat medic, U.S. Army (serving in the Headquarters Company in the Old Guard, Washington, D.C.)

2023   All systems are go. We lift off. The sun is setting, the moon is rising, the sky is blue, and the weather is good. Simply gorgeous. As we pass abeam northern Maine, it is not quite dark towards the west. We are at 35,000 feet. It appears to be dark for those whose feet rest on terra firma on the East Coast of the USA. I see fireworks being set off below us. Very pretty. I think some are celebrating the Fourth of July early, either that or their barbeque is completely out of control.

Connie J. Tobias, 54, Loudon, Tennessee; pilot, US Airways

On June 29, 2004 . . .

77% of day diarists knew who they were going to vote for in the next election.

〜〜〜〜〜

Resilient, Even as a Kid

Roberta Blain, 57, Eden, Utah

A college counselor, she works with at-risk students, drawing on her own experience of rising above a childhood of poverty, abuse, and neglect. Her dad was an alcoholic; her mom—now dying of lung cancer—has bipolar disorder, as do three of her five adult kids. The family is enrolled in a bipolar study at Johns Hopkins University. She jokes, "It's our way of contributing to science." She's always been upbeat, despite circumstances. "You're either optimistic or pessimistic and that doesn't change." She became a college freshman at age forty-four, returning to school after her divorce, with two teens at home. "I was on the single destitute mom scholarship program." Graduated with straight As, then went on to get her master's. She remarried twelve years ago to a retired Air Force officer with seven kids of his own. A close-knit family despite adversity. My kids "put me on a pedestal. I know that I am loved." An organizer. An activist. Cofounder of the Utah Federation for Drug-Free Youth. A Mormon, she and her husband plan to serve together on a church-sponsored mission. Never satisfied with the status quo, she's always looking for a better way. "Everyone tells me I can't be all things to all people, and intellectually I know that, but the Little Engine That Could, that's just me."

Midnight Today's entry in my day planner reads, "ALASKA!" and, "Fun, fun, relax, relax, catch lots of fish. Yes!" Alaska is where I'd planned to be right now. Instead, the only place I've been going is back and forth on the forty-five-mile round-trip to my mom's assisted-living apartment to take care of her while she is dying of lung cancer. At seventy-six, she has decided to let the disease run its natural course because she doesn't want to lose her hair!

She's already gone two months beyond the time she was expected to live. I put so much into that first month, when she started actually getting better briefly; I was taken off guard and left with little energy reserve. I'm totally exhausted. So, I'm here, and my husband is in Alaska with his daughter on MY dream vacation! It's not important anymore, and I'm too tired to care. ZZZ.

8:30 a.m. Oh, I don't want to get up. I stagger blurry-eyed to get my stupid pills. I need them so I won't have pain today (esophagitis and IBS). Can't afford to be sick, got duties. Geez, I'm a mess at fifty-seven. Menopause messed everything up. I've been falling apart ever since. And trying to do both work and take care of my mom is probably what gave me the shingles a few weeks ago. I don't have to go to work now because I'm on family medical leave.

resilient, even as a kid **345**

8:32 a.m.   I crawl back into bed to finish experiencing the typical morning hot flashes. The bed looks like I've been wrestling with all five pillows. The cool satin sheets feel sooo good, though my husband hates them. Just before I woke up, I was dreaming about my oldest son's bedroom in my old house. In the dream, it was empty and dusty, just like his life. Rather symbolic, considering the house in the dream was lost in the divorce thirteen years ago, and my gay son, too, has been lost for years to drugs, alcohol, bipolar, and hepatitis C. Why am I thinking such depressing thoughts when I've got other priorities to worry about?

This morning time is my medicine to gain the strength to face the rest of the day, helping my mom leave her life. After twenty-three years of watching over her with her severe bipolar, I'm tired. She's tired. Why is she suffering this hell after the shitty life she's had to live (as my youngest daughter put it)? Enough pondering. I've got to get moving. My gosh, it's getting late!

10:00 a.m.   Why did I think showering last night would save me time? I'd better not just throw something on like I have been doing. I'm going to make an effort for Mom. It seems a disservice to go to her all grungy, since she's looking at me all day. I'll wear a blue blouse and my pretty topaz necklace that she can stare at when I'm leaning over her. I put on makeup, comb my hair with an actual comb, add some cute flowered socks to keep my feet warm in the freezing studio apartment (in which my mom seems to roast). I may be the last face she sees.

10:20 a.m.   Breakfast is the usual banana, lactose-free milk, wheat toast and peanut butter (no fried egg today), and a passel of multivitamins and other pills to fight cancer, stay youthful, keep going . . .

10:25 a.m. Gulping down my food (standing), I take a quick look at *For Better or For Worse,* the only comic I read. I'll take the paper with me today. Mentally, I pat myself on the back for resisting ice cream cake for breakfast. That and the sherbet and root beer Popsicles will have to wait until I descend on them when I get home. The marshmallow Circus Peanuts go with me. I'll allocate two per day for when I need a boost. What am I doing—trying to put on the weight my mom is losing? Weird.

10:30 a.m. I load a couple pillows in the car and throw a toothbrush and makeup into a bag in case I have to stay the night. So what if I sleep in my clothes?

10:35 a.m. Grabbing the beautiful bouquet my stepdaughter gave me when she and her dad left on MY TRIP, I put it into a box in the car to keep it from tipping over during the winding drive down Ogden Canyon to catch the freeway.

10:45 a.m. I am running SO late and now, I've decided to stop by a mortuary in town. It's a new one that's not real fancy like the one I originally had planned to use. They took care of my stepdad's funeral, and I'd like to give them more business.

It's a totally gray day without the usual puffy white cumulus clouds Utah produces so well. Darn. The clouds are high like one huge, dingy, flat sheet. The sun peeks through for a minute as I take the turn around the lake. Looking across the water, I see the boats are causing ripples that bounce the light. I think how our lives do the same thing. From any small point, ripples of whatever we send out affect everyone and everything somehow. We cannot NOT influence others by our actions. I remember my teens saying, "What does it matter what I do; it's my life!" I couldn't explain it to them back then.

resilient, even as a kid 347

Rounding the bend, crossing over the dam, I head down the rugged canyon into town. It's like riding the back of a snake. The river is flowing slowly, and the waterfall at the mouth of the canyon is a trickle today. It all depends on how much water the farmers are using miles away.

11:15 a.m. I start crying at the mortuary. While the lady is copying my mom's funeral plan, I look out the window and am astonished to see my youngest daughter's sister-in-law with her husband! They have lost so many people in their family these past two years. I rush out to see who died this time. It is her husband's grandfather. He was not very old. I tell them how sorry I am, then I get out of there as fast as I can. I can't stand it! Death is coming at me from all angles!

11:45 a.m. I arrive at Mom's assisted-living place and sign in. Walking down the long hall to her studio apartment, I'm dreading this. As I enter the room quietly, I see she is pretty much the same as I left her last night—just staring, looking miserable and scared, bed cranked up, tugging at her oxygen tubing, hating it all. She tells me she fell on the floor. She didn't know where I was and was going to find me.

I give her a kiss and reassure her I'm not leaving until time for bed for the both of us. I pop in a Richard Clayderman CD so we can listen to piano music, and she says, "Music." I ask her if she wants me to turn it off and she tells me no. Thank goodness, because even if she often wants it entirely quiet, I need the music to calm my jangled nerves.

11:47 a.m. I get maybe a two-minute reprieve and she wants me to sit her up. She says it hurts her to sit up, and I ask her why. She says she doesn't know. She's up thirty seconds and wants down again. She can't read her body anymore and asks me if she is okay, thinking she's hot, then cold. Every few minutes the covers are on, then off, and it goes on and on and on. She reaches for my arm. As softly as a feather, her fingers run up my arm and she holds on to me for dear life, literally. Her biggest fear is being alone.

11:49 a.m. Now she's taking off her socks. She'll ask to put them on in a few minutes. It's been like this for three months. She tries to cough, but she's so weak it sounds like she's crying. Now it's, "Cover my feet." I say, "I have, Mom." We do this three times in the space of thirty seconds, and she gets tired and gives up, so she can concentrate on something else bugging her that isn't necessarily real.

She hasn't eaten in three days and is drinking very little water. I've read the hospice literature on what to expect as the body shuts down. She's following it like a script. She isn't sure what the sensations in her body mean, so she looks at me confused, expecting me to fix it. That's the worst part! I feel helpless, and I break down and cry because she's so frustrated and I can't stand to see her suffer like this!

11:50 a.m. She's saying "buttons" over and over now. I take off her blouse since she's pulling on it and put her into a soft, cotton pajama top. She likes that. As I lean over her in bed, she says, "Beautiful flowers," referring to the ones I'd brought from home. Then, looking at me with this desperate expression, she says, "Don't worry about me."

I say, "I'm not worrying about you. Are you worried about something?"

"Yes."

"What are you worried about?"

"Your hair is tickling my face." I burst out laughing. She is still staring at me with that pained expression.

11:55 a.m. The "Help me!" cries are tearing my heart out. She has no clue what she needs—other than just to escape the damnable torture somehow. The shifting and pulling on the bed continue incessantly.

Noon Ah, lunch. I eat my allotted two Circus Peanuts for the day (comfort, yum), and read a timely newspaper article about how few people know to use the free hospice services if they have six months or less to live. I'm thankful we knew. It's hard to believe all the stuff for which hospice pays and the equipment they've brought in for Mom's comfort. I asked them to be with me the day I told Mom she was terminal. A waltz tune is playing, so I'm dancing around the room. Mom thinks I'm silly, but hey, things need to lighten up. Is this behavior sacrilegious?

12:05 p.m. My oldest daughter, Cailin, just walked in. My girls are all like little sunshines, lighting up any room they enter. She kisses Mom. "Hi, Nana, how are you doing?" We shift Mom up to the top of the bed for the millionth time. Cailin brought nail-painting stuff to do her toes up for July Fourth. She decides to do stripes of red, white, and blue. I ask her to do my toes, too. We're talking and giggling as Mom is asking for help. How awful are we or what? Cailin does offer to paint Mom's toes, but she shakes her head. She keeps asking us what we're doing on the floor because her short-term memory is shot.

We walk on our heels and waddle like ducks around the room as we try to take care of Mom's needs. Cailin hits her toe on the wheelchair and messes up her stripes. She repaints it. Mom steps on my nails when I'm trying to get her back into bed with a bear-hug technique, but my nails are dry.

12:50 p.m.   Cailin and I talk in whispers about which picture to use for the obituary and marvel at the beautiful photos of Mom before we knew her. She's perfection on the outside. I placed the photos on the wall to remind everyone she wasn't always this little wasted body with white hair. She's a unique person who had a life! People look at her picture and ask if that gorgeous woman *was* Aloa (named after the song "Aloha Oe"). How sad. Old age is the great equalizer.

1:00 p.m.   Cailin leaves for home. If I even try to walk somewhere else in the room, Mom is calling with a loud whisper, "Don't leave me." I sit her up thirty seconds and put her down for sixty seconds. Up and down, up and down; in the wheelchair for two minutes, back to bed, and then to the bathroom two seconds after I get her all settled in bed (she doesn't have to go). She's saying she has to go pee pee, and I tell her she's got a catheter and she *is* going. She looks so perplexed and says she has to go the other way.

I'm exhausted lifting, adjusting. It's heartbreaking. I'm feeling frustration, even anger; the emotions are like a roller coaster out of control. "What a Friend We Have in Jesus" is playing (I decided to put on hymns). She likes that kind of music. Music does things to and for people. "Aloha Oe" was playing at a picnic I attended a couple weeks ago. I got all choked up. There isn't going to be another Aloa. That song shot my whole day.

Mom pops me back to the present with a weak call, "Roberta, help me." Button fixation again. "Roberta, help me."

"Oh my gosh, Mom, I can't!" "Abide with Me" is playing

now. It's one of the songs she wants for her funeral. There's no reaction on her part, but I'm crying.

3:12 p.m.   Daughter number two, Sallyann, arrives and goes through the "Hi, Nana" routine. Her past CNA experience helps immensely, as she is continually teaching me little tricks to save my back. She also monitors the meds really well.

As we jump up and down taking care of Mom, we talk about a bipolar study our family volunteered for. Sallyann (also a phlebotomist) drew blood from Mom a couple weeks ago to send off to the National Institutes of Health and Johns Hopkins. We talk about how great it'd be to find the gene markers and understand the disease better, perhaps even develop new medicine. Wow, would our family ever benefit!

We girls understand why we're going to such great lengths to keep Mom in her home and not at a care center. She hasn't ever been able to live her life like a normal person. It always got interrupted with a mental crisis, and often others made the decisions for her. No more strait-jackets or mental hospitals with electric shock treatment. We cry when we talk about how unfair it is she's suffering so much now and admit we've both been praying she just goes in peace. I guess we feel guilty about that, but it isn't like we want her to go for our convenience.

4:30 p.m.   Sallyann goes home to her family.

4:40 p.m.   A CNA brings in a menu. I put Mom's glasses on her and she looks at it. I am telling the CNA she hasn't been eating for the last four days, but Mom begins shaking her head and saying she wants some food!

5:00 p.m.   When the food gets here, I lay it out on her tray as she sits in her wheelchair. I watch her start to eat and it freaks me out. Oh no! She's eating! I thought the last was getting near and she's eating. Doesn't she know she's extending her suffering? I can hardly stand watching her shovel it in—feeling both guilty for my thoughts and angry at the same time. That urge to survive is so strong. The mind says, "Live!" but the body is trying to shut down. That food will probably buy her another week of hell on earth. Well, we can't starve her. It's her choice. Anything she wants except what she really needs—death. I'm crying uncontrollably and have to go into the bathroom.

When is the last supper? Dear Father in Heaven, I pray, why can't she go home to you in peace and joy? Do I want her to die to end her or my suffering? I've said good-bye a million times and administered to her needs second by second each day. At times I've collapsed due to exhaustion, and my daughters stepped in when I got the shingles, taking shifts. I still feel the prickly needle pains in my arms and chest. I'm so tired. Isn't she? I sound so selfish, so uncaring.

5:15 p.m. I clean up dinner, which has to happen right now, according to Mom. She never was able to wait for anything without getting agitated. She usually had nothing better to do but sit, yet she'd get upset about waiting for appointments or for me to do an errand. Her self-centeredness is part of her illness, and I haven't let it drive me over the edge, though I've dangled off a few times.

5:18 p.m. She's obsessing over her teeth now as I clean them and put them back in. She insists they aren't in! Help me! (That's me this time.) My neck muscles are starting to spasm. I start reading some little thought cards in a box by Mom's bed. This bugs her. I choose one and read it to her, anyway, trying to get a point across: "Suffering produces perseverance; perseverance, character; and character, hope.

resilient, even as a kid **353**

And hope does not disappoint us, because God has poured out his love into our hearts." (Romans 5: 3–5). She's just staring at me; it doesn't seem to register or mean anything.

5:30 p.m. I say out loud, after moving Mom again, "Oh, my arm hurts."

She says, "That's because you pull and pull . . . I'm sorry."

"I am, too, Mom, but it's not your fault."

"Don't let it hurt me."

"I won't."

"Take this off" (the blanket).

"You want it off?"

"No, take this off."

Here we go again.

6:00 p.m. I turn on *Little House on the Prairie,* which Mom always liked but doesn't really follow since she's lost that ability to stay focused years ago.

6:45 p.m. I start the bedtime routine—cleaning and soaking of teeth; putting on pj's, ChapStick, and lotion; and kisses on the forehead and tip of her nose. I ask permission to go home for some sleep when she goes to sleep. There's more adjusting and readjusting and discussing with nurses and aides on what to do to calm her down; then more med adjustments.

7:00 p.m. My youngest daughter, Karalee, shows up with her husband and my ex-husband. We all visit while Mom fades in and out. She was good for about five minutes of recognition and whispered one-word responses to questions. Now she's probably hearing us but shows no response. We ask if she wants us to leave so she can sleep, and we get a faint but definite "Yes." Hallelujah! I'm outta here!

9:00 p.m.   I'm eating at Marie Callender's with Karalee and her husband. We don't talk much. Karalee buys.

10:00 p.m.   I hug everyone good night and head for home over Trapper's Loop in the mountains, past the downhill ski site of the 2002 Olympics. I'm listening to the Book of Mormon on CD, which almost lulls me off to sleep, even though the segment is about an ancient prophet explaining to his errant son about the state of a person when they die and where they go. Good thing to know. Within a few miles of home, I almost fall asleep at the wheel.

10:45 p.m.   As I pull into the driveway, the car lights illuminate the garbage can my neighbor put out for me. How nice. I open the car door and a blast of cool night air hits me, so refreshing. The three-quarter moon, peeking through breaks in the cloud cover, has a ring of soft light encircling it.

Inside, I gather the garbage, then take it to the can. Looking up at the stars, my soul reconnects with the elements, and I feel the stress leaving my body. All in this universe is connected. We are all in this together. Isn't life so worth experiencing! Every day, driving in and driving back in the gloriously breathtaking scenery, I thank Him for all of it. And I marvel at how creative He was with creation. Earth—the ultimate masterpiece—all for us to *live*.

10:50 p.m.   It's been a breathtaking day for Mom, too. The nightmare of losing one's air little by little is playing out. Why couldn't/wouldn't she quit smoking? I read the rest of the newspaper and end my day with a sweet bite of ice cream cake I had to have. Then I shower and pick up a phone message from my husband saying he had called at 10:00, sure he would catch me at home. I do one last-ditch effort to locate my long-lost brother and son, so they can be notified of the impending death. I send an e-mail to the county for whom my brother works and check the county jail sites to see if my son is there (which would provide an explanation for his disappearance).

11:58 p.m. I flop into the disaster of a bed I left this morning. The whole house is a mess, and I don't care. Kneeling for a quick thank-you prayer and please bless my loved ones, the troops, and everyone with whatever Thou knowest they need; especially watch over the moms (my husband's mother is ninety-nine and in a care center) so they won't experience any unnecessary pain. I quickly realize my mother has been spared a great deal of pain through her ordeal. There's a blessing.

I roll back out of bed a second later when I noticed the ol' esophagus wants a chew of Gaviscon to get through the night. I feel good and realize I'll make it tomorrow and all the tomorrows it takes. I'm glad I made the effort to be more presentable today—just remembered, at different times today, Mom said she liked my pretty blue blouse, pointed to my necklace as she enjoyed it, and told me my hair looked nice. Wow! I presented a daughter she could enjoy.

Night, night, Mom. Sweet dreams and I love you.

Miscellaneous Moments

Pink Slips

7:40 a.m. *Good Morning America* drones on in the background as I shower and think about the day. After ten years of working my ass off as a teacher at Spelman, I'm getting 86ed—kicked to the curb, not on tenure track, been there too long, administration change, blah, blah, blah. Mostly, I worry about money. I have figured out tentative budgets through age sixty-five—if we sell the house; if I get another job; if something happens to my husband; and considering social security (ha!) and pensions, etc. Every purse and tablet in my office and house has a slip of paper with my budget calculations. As the warm water cascades down my aching back, I calculate mentally. Maybe God has some greater work for me in store. Now, if I could only be really sure there is a God. Get your ass in gear, Joan.

Joan Foster McCarty, 55, Decatur, Georgia; stage manager and assistant professor, Spelman College

Out the Door

I try to get Hermione's jacket on her, but she won't give up the milk in her hand. I have to wrestle the milk away, get her jacket on as quickly as possible, then give her the milk back. Only now she won't take it. So I set it down. Then she collapses on the ground. I go to the coat rack and retrieve my U of M hockey jersey. While I was getting it, Hermione decides to pick up her milk and start drinking again. I get my backpack, her day-care bag, and my purse and keys, and go to pick her up. She starts yelling for her Dora the Explorer doll. I get it and head for the door. She starts yelling for her Boots the Monkey doll. I get it and head for the door. She starts screaming for Elmo, but we're late and I have no hands left. We get out the door by 5:53 a.m. We're due at day care at 6:00.

Melissa J. Dyer, 25, Fort Myer, Virginia; staff sergeant, special band member, U.S. Army

CALL ME!

4:07 p.m.   I call two of the commercial agents I freelance with just to leave that message, that pitiful message that says, "Hey, I haven't heard from you in a while. I'm available. CALL ME!" But of course the pitiful message has to sound upbeat and positive. I just wish I could be signed with an agent (meaning working exclusively with one) so I can stop freelancing with all of these different people who barely know who I am. I am just one actress of many and not taken care of and groomed. I want to be taken care of.

Sheaquan M. Datts, 29, Brooklyn, New York; legal assistant/actor

Poets and Writers

12:24 a.m.   I have finally gone out and purchased two copies of *Poets & Writers* magazine. I am on the cover. Me! Samina Ali! My god, does this mean I am a writer? After reading this magazine for twelve years, after aspiring to be like the writers inside of it, after sending off selections of my own writing to the contests and anthologies advertised in the back pages, I have now come to take my place among them, to be on the cover. I cannot stop staring at the magazine. I hold it inches away from my face, then at arm's length. I set it on the dining table, then on my desk right next to my computer. Is this possible? Could I really be on the cover? Well, there I am. It feels strange. Like an out-of-body experience. I am here and there at the same time. I am in shock. I guess this means I have arrived.

Samina Ali, 34, San Francisco, California; writer

The Few, the Proud . . .

6:00 p.m.   Headed over to CSSB-7 barracks to watch the second season of *24* on DVD with the guys—Nelson, Gunny Mac, and Gunny Ski. Nelson's wife is having a baby in a couple of weeks, and he is going home to be with her. I don't think she knows yet. That is so cool that his command is doing that for him. I'll miss him though. They are my brothers, the big jerks. I have to think of a good prank to play on Nelson before he leaves.

Angela C. Mink, 32, San Diego, California; combat correspondent, United States Marine Corps (serving in Iraq)

Rosanne Cash, 49, New York, New York

From the crown princess of Nashville to a celebrated career as a folk musician and songwriter. She's the daughter of the legendary Johnny Cash but started out a reluctant star. "I saw how fame affected my dad, the life he led, the exhaustion, how it pulled our family apart. It just seemed horrible. He handled it with more grace than anyone I've ever known." She's still private, but no longer reluctant. "I don't believe the myth anymore that success destroys you." Married in 1995 to her second husband, musician and record producer John Leventhal. Mom to four daughters and one son, ages twenty-eight to five. She wanted a sixth, even though pregnancy hormones did a number on her vocal cords. She couldn't sing for over two years, prompting an identity crisis. "I thought my voice was permanently trashed." Far from it. A working mom, she adjusts tours around school schedules. "I never agonized—

Oh, I'm giving up this great opportunity to go on a fourth-grade field trip. The kids are always first. That's just my instincts." She's published children's books, short stories, and essays. A social activist. A Francophile. Obsessed with her Scottish ancestry and the roots of the melancholy minstrels in her family, including herself. A stickler for good manners. *"I don't believe you can have it all, but you can have what's important to you."*

2:20 a.m. Jake, five, comes in the bedroom, crawls over my head to get between me and John. It takes me an hour to get back to sleep. Thinking about Dad.

4:40 a.m. Jake is pushing John to the edge of the bed, so I pull him towards me. There is still time to have a dream about Dad.

7:50 a.m. I'm up. Frustrating dream about trying to prepare a meal for the kids who are complaining that they're hungry, but I keep breaking the dishes. I feel kind of miserable, flulike for two weeks now. Dr. Cohen said all the blood work would be back today, so I'm seeing him at 3:45. The kettle is on. Tea makes anything and everything better.

8:20 a.m. I just read two Psalms aloud to Dad. In the last few months of his life he loved for me to read them to him, both in person and on the phone. I still do it, hoping they reach him in the other world. Last Sunday, I read aloud to him and when I finished I said, "There you go, Dad." Then I got up and turned on the radio to the gospel and blues show, and Sister Rosetta Tharpe was singing. I was startled and delighted. Dad always said that she was his favorite singer. Hearing her out of the blue was like he was letting me know he got the Psalms.

8:35 a.m. I'm staring at this returned package on the kitchen table. For some reason, the post office returned the Annie Leibovitz book yesterday that I sent to Claire and Gerald in Paris LAST MARCH. The world is going to hell.

9:25 a.m. Got Jake dressed and fed and examined his new book with him on prehistoric sea monsters. Then John took him to camp. They went on the bike today. It's beautiful outside. I have the door open to the terrace, and there is a little breeze blowing. Blue skies and the hydrangea in the garden are in full bloom. Just feeling that breeze makes me grateful for my life.

10:30 a.m. Coco, my daughter Hannah's close friend and my sometime assistant, came over to answer the basket of mail, photo requests, auction requests (it's unbelievable how many organizations hold "celebrity" auctions to raise money), and edit down 2,200 e-mails on my website. I should probably have had Coco come more often in the last few months, but I didn't have the heart to keep reading the messages of condolences, although I appreciate them. And, truthfully, after the nasty e-mails I got after the "Musicians United to Win without War" press conference, I just got discouraged about reading e-mails from strangers.

I don't understand people who would rather attack than have a dialogue. None of the people who disagreed with me about going to war in Iraq said, "Well, I'm all for attacking Iraq and I think you're wrong and here's why." I would have respected that. But so many of them just wanted to call me filthy names and accuse me of hating my country and loving Saddam, for God's sake. I actually wrote a few people back, respectfully, trying to open a conversation, but it was a futile exercise. I guess I don't seem like a real person if they only know me from television. So Coco, who is so much quicker on the computer than I am, is here vetting for me.

I keep sneaking upstairs to watch a few minutes of my movie-on-demand, *Love Actually.* Hugh Grant: my guilty pleasure. Got an e-mail about a concert during the Democratic Convention. My name has been suggested as a performer. I'd love to do that. I hope it happens. I am so alarmed at the corporate infiltration in government, among so many other erosions of democracy, that I would do just about anything to help defeat this administration. Yeah, I'm sure that a couple of sensitive verses from a depressing song from me would just crumble the whole house of cards.

11:00 a.m. Phone calls and e-mails re: house parties for Kerry; meeting in L.A. at Capitol Records; travel to L.A. in July; and Canada/Northwest tour in August. I feel tired just looking at the schedule. My fifteen-year-old, Carrie, and her friend May finally arise and go directly to the back garden to lie on towels in the semi-shade. They are reveling in the free time, their languor, their little half-bare bodies in the weak sun. I disguise how adorable I think this is. Teenage girls are so heartbreakingly self-conscious. I just want to wrap them up like babies.

12:30 p.m. Ate a salad and blue chips for lunch with Coco. Reading my most interesting mail with her—a request for a pair of my pants to turn into a handbag for a charity auction; lyrics written in tribute to Dad to the melody of "I Still Miss Someone" (approximately number seven hundred in Songs Written About Dad, which have been sent to me since his death); a letter from a soldier in Kuwait who simply wants "to see how my family is doing" (God bless him); and a letter from a guy who wants me to

eleven number-one hits **363**

know that I'm "easy on the eyes." A normal batch. No marriage proposals, death threats, or tongue-lashings about my politics today. I sign a stack of photo requests, go search up a pair of pants for the auction (the Pringle Army pants I ordered from Scotland, which were a nice idea, but make my hips look like a billboard), and write a short note to the soldier.

1:30 p.m. Went to get Jake at camp. Walked down 8th Avenue, stopped at the bank. So many tourists in the city, especially since the Gay Pride parade on Sunday, ESPE-CIALLY in my 'hood—a center of gay culture. When I got to Jake's classroom, he was talking on the play phone. The teacher said he was calling me to come get him. We took a taxi home.

Sheilah, my dear friend and sounding board for all things maternal, and her kids come over. Jake and Will, happy as clams, immediately strip to their underwear in an impulse of five-year-old liberation. The teenagers leave and go downtown. I'm still not used to the lazy schedule of summer, as far as the kids go. But all sense of laziness will disappear once the tour starts. I'm seriously ambivalent. It's always great once we start playing—there is something liberating or emotionally transformative about it—but the other twenty-two hours of the day are brutal.

Too much travel lately. In the last six months: three trips to Europe; a few trips to Nashville on family business; shows to various spots on the Eastern Seaboard and Texas; California for a week in April; and the trip I enjoyed most, a week in the Virgin Islands. But I feel depleted and like I've been running as fast and hard as I can for the last year to avoid feeling what I feel when I stop. So much sadness.

I can hear G.E., my friend, neighbor, and guitarist extra-ordinaire, playing his guitar. Single notes are wafting up through the garden. Three guitar players live around me in close quarters: John, G.E., and Phil next door. Sometimes when they are all playing at once and guitars are coming through every wall and floor and window, I just want to scream at them to at least play in the same key, for the love of God.

2:45 p.m.   Kids are making me a little nuts. Blue paint on the floor, clothes strewn everywhere, mail soaked from the garden hose. Periodic demands for Pokémon movie, which I deny. Television on such a beautiful day seems like sacrilege. Both Sheilah's kids and Jake are now running around stark naked. I don't feel so good. Looking forward to the escape to the doctor in thirty minutes.

5:40 p.m.   Back from the doctor. I like him so much. He wears cool shirts instead of a white jacket. Unfortunately, his office is in SoHo, aka Fashion Theme Park. It's incredibly crowded. It used to be bad only on weekends. When I lived on Mercer Street in the early nineties, it was still relatively civilized during the week. Now, Tuesday morning is the same as Saturday afternoon. Anyway, it appears that I have a wicked virus. He told me to take a vacation. Why didn't I think of that?

6:30 p.m.   I'm lying on my bed. We just ate takeout. John has a gig tonight with Joan Osborne. I wish he were not going out. I feel kind of fragile. I hear sirens outside. It is a beautiful, clear evening. It's hard to imagine the sheer volume of suffering in the world going on this very moment. But I do. Imagine. My own suffering seems very small, relative to an Iraqi woman, for instance.

I miss Dad so much. The shock of losing him ten months ago is wearing off, but once in a while I am still hit with that sense of incredulous panic. But the grief, that doesn't wear off in the slightest. I suspect it never will. The song I wrote a couple months ago, "The World Unseen," has a line that says, "I am the list of everyone I have to love." How true that seems just now.

I miss June, too. How can a person take up so much energetic space in the world and then be so completely gone? She never went more than a couple of seconds without chattering, laughing, coddling, or "puffing," as she called it. Making things nice for people. Making the world bend to her wishes in the most charming way possible. She was a wall between me and my own mortality, like my father was, but with less emotional tension because of our lack of blood relation. As those walls fall away, and my mortality comes into clearer focus, I miss the comfort of my elders protecting me from the unknown.

But, looking to the next generation, I have spoken to all my children today: Caitlin in Santa Monica; Chelsea in Nashville; Hannah in San Diego; and of course the little ones are here. It's a good day when I connect with all five. I feel a sense of completion on those days. A day is so long. But if a day is so long, why is it that a decade goes by in a heartbeat? A child grows up in an instant, but the hour between dusk and night is endless. How does that happen?

7:30 p.m. Reading my book, *The Secret Life of Bees,* while Jake watches *Peter Pan* next to me. I did not do any work today (beyond the obvious child-wrangling). I did not write or sing or play a note. I put no effort into all my looming projects with looming deadlines, or the new record, or the series at the Rubin Museum, *Acoustic Cash,* which will have me talking and singing with a new guest each week on some subject that relates to Tibetan art, religion, or culture. (The first subject: The Wheel of Life. This is not ironic.)

And I haven't even thought about the two books due: my memoir for Viking and the new children's book for

HarperCollins. Nothing. A slow, meandering day. A Tuesday that felt like a Sunday. I feel guilty. I feel guilty for feeling guilty. Damn. I thought I got rid of the Catholic school imprint a long time ago.

9:35 p.m.   Read Jake three books: a story by Isaac Bashevis Singer; a book about sea monsters; and the ubiquitous *Berenstain Bears*. It's so beautiful having children in your forties. I read to my older children but not as much or as obsessively. Jake and I get on a subject, like dinosaurs, or sea creatures, or volcanoes, and we completely exhaust it. I love that about Jake and my relationship with him.

I still lie with Jake every night until he falls asleep. Maybe I shouldn't now that he's five, but children eventually pull away. He's my last, so I'll let him make the first move. I wouldn't trade anything for the conversations we have when we lie together waiting for him to fall asleep. He tells me he loves me "infinity times infinity." We pray, we draw letters in the air and guess what they are, and we sing. Oh man. This will all last such a short time. College is just around the corner.

10:28 p.m.   Tired. Should I go for Hugh Grant again or read something to enhance my mind?

10:56 p.m.   Can't do Hugh again. Don't have the energy. Carrie is downstairs watching the Food Network, a program about cheese. How adorable is that? At fifteen years old, she still calls me Mommy.

11:14 p.m.   Waiting up for John. The day is almost done. Nothing exciting happened. That's probably a good thing. Tomorrow I'm being interviewed by yet another author writing another book about Dad. I don't mind. I like talking about him now. Maybe he hears. Talking about him is a way to talk with him, I think. And the respect these writers have for him makes me happy. When you lose a parent, it is such a sweet comfort to have people speak highly of them, to cherish them with you, to acknowledge their work.

Just because Dad belonged to the whole world doesn't change the really personal need for small commiserations, even if the commiseration will be published and sold. I'm thinking of that old Celtic lullaby "John O'Dreams" and the last line, "All things are equal when the day is done." But are they?

Ring of Fire

7:00 p.m.   My son drives me to rent *Cold Mountain*. He rents his own movie—a Quentin Tarantino. I think about a June Carter song, a song she wrote for her granddaughter. The refrain is a warning to the granddaughter, who has gone to Hollywood to be a star, to stay away from that Quentin Tarantino because he "makes his women wild and mean." What a loss the world has suffered in losing Johnny Cash and June Carter. What a lesson to be learned from their story of passion and torment and loyalty and undying love. Would that we all could fall into a "ring of fire" like theirs.

Marian Carcache, 50, Auburn, Alabama; English instructor

12:39 a.m. I spent the last hour playing a computer game. I told myself I'd stop before midnight, but got sucked in. A war game no less.

Hollie Rose, 39, Connecticut

1:15 a.m. Finally, I put my head down on my pillow after putting away the last items I brought back home from the baby shower for my much anticipated, already much loved, first grandchild.

Laurie Denenberg, 57, Connecticut

1:30 a.m. I am naked except for watch and clogs, washing dishes. I can't sleep and I've already tried drawing in my studio, but everything seems to come out wrong.

Lauren Weinstein, 29, New York

2:20 a.m. Look at the clock and calculate—if I fall asleep immediately, I'll get almost three hours more sleep. I try to keep from looking, but am compelled.

Susan E. M. Young, 43, Pennsylvania

2:32 a.m. I FOUND THE SECOND PACIFIER!

Julia Litton Steury, 32, Minnesota

2:48 a.m.   The menopausal witching hour. The only others awake at this time of night are the coyotes.

Susan Bowers, 55, California

3:00 a.m.   I ask the god and goddess to please watch over me as I meditate in the cool night air and calmly try to picture purple and blue light surrounding my body.

Samantha Thomas, 34, North Carolina

4:27 a.m.   My beeper sounds. "Can't wake baby up." I'm up like a shot and call the parents back immediately.

Elizabeth A. Rider, 52, Massachusetts

4:30 a.m.   I awaken to the sound of a cat puking. I wonder which one it is and hope it's not doing it on the bed.

Midyne Spear, 47, California

6:00 a.m.   I turn on the Disney channel, plop both kids in my bed, and try to do something with the frizzy hair I'd convinced myself was fine not twenty minutes ago.

Annmarie Donnelly, 33, New Jersey

6:00 a.m.   Tai Chi on the patio. Grasp the sparrow's tail . . . white crane spreads its wings . . . embrace the tiger and return to the mountain . . . repulse the monkey . . . snake creeps down . . . golden rooster stands on one leg . . . add a new move—swat the mosquito.

Brenda K. White, 50, Kentucky

6:45 a.m.   Put on the leather and RIDE! Leather jacket, leather chaps, leather boots, leather gloves. (I'm wearing a whole COW!)

Cindy Phillips, 42, New York

7:00 a.m. Jump on the scale and get three different weights! So which one is it? I'll go with the lowest one.

Tori Mason, 41, Tennessee

7:05 a.m. Walking the lake, I pray the rosary. Several years ago a nun told me that a rosary can be prayed anytime, anywhere. So I took her advice and no longer pray in the privacy of my bedroom.

Diana Chavez, 54, Colorado

7:14 a.m. Toto and Betsy, the black rhinos, are truly God's works of art. So awesome, even though Betsy is cycling and charging at me.

Tammy S. Schmidt, 38, Missouri

7:30 a.m. Aboard the Long Island Railroad. I follow my ritual—the *New York Times* in this order: business, sports, arts (for my true addiction, the crossword puzzle).

Sue Rodin, 56, New York

7:30 a.m. Preparing to leave for Tikrit from Mosul. As we were awaiting transportation (the driver was late), the base was heavily hit by mortars very close to the airport where we were to leave out of.

Karen Banuelos, 46, California (serving in Iraq)

7:30 a.m. Finish writing my paper while eating half a tube of raw cookie dough.

Rochelle Spencer, 26, Georgia

7:30 a.m. Chore time. Horses are here to get feed and put in the barn with fans on them. My husband, Marty, thinks I spoil them too much.

Sindi Jandreau, 37, South Dakota

7:38 a.m.   Shit, I've got the flu.
Barbara K. Ige, 38, California

7:45 a.m.   On my way out the door I kiss my husband, pat our dog on her head, and remind my husband of his "honey-do" list—honey don't forget to pick up the laundry today, get stamps, and mail the bills . . .
Margaret A. Seime, 62, Tennessee

7:59 a.m.   All coffeed up and raring to protect some community from environmental harm.
Jean Belille, 48, Colorado

0800   Okay, I'm in charge of the safety of the ship now. Time to put everything out of mind and lock it on.
Caitlin Sharbono, 23, Colorado (serving on the USS San Jacinto)

8:03 a.m.   Clock in at work. Damn, late again. Should 180 seconds REALLY matter in the scheme of things?
Dawn Neptune, 33, Utah

8:15 a.m.   Toilet and crossword puzzle. I spot the address for my meeting this morning written in pencil on the lid of the tampon box.
Paula Austin, 36, North Carolina

8:15 a.m.   Check in at the dental clinic on base so I can have a cavity filled. Gave my husband's social security. It's bad enough I am only a number to them, but to add insult to injury, I don't even have my own number.
Lolly Horvath-Dandeneau, 28, England (married to a staff sergeant in the U.S. Air Force)

8:30 a.m.   Head to breakfast in the cafeteria at the Olympic Training Center. I am so thankful for the cafeteria because it means I don't have to cook.

Tara Nott-Cunningham, 32, Michigan

8:30 a.m.   Between Nathan, the drill sergeant, and the crabby baby, I just want to go back to bed and hide under the covers.

Anne-Marie B. Nichols, 39, Colorado

0835   Crisis mode. One of the winch computer monitors goes awry, all readings are flashing red.

Véronique Robigou, 45, Washington (on the research vessel Atlantis)

0900   Help a patient getting into his leg. He is a little frustrated by the process of socket changes.

Janet Papazis, 41, Virginia

9:00 a.m.   We are touring our winery with friends—new bottling equipment, barn, gardens, new vineyard, and the vision of our "work-in-progress." Talking irrigation, garden funk, and grandchildren.

Marcia Arnold, 57, New Mexico

9:15 a.m.   My friend Jean calls. Her ninety-seven-year-old mother caused a food fight at the nursing home she's in.

Carolyn L. Mazloomi, 56, Ohio

9:17 a.m.   Copier jams mid-copy. Restart even though sign on copier says not to turn it off. Whatever. I need copies. It craps out again.

Cindi Harrison, 34, California

9:30 a.m.   Washed my car and had my hair done all in anticipation of my mammogram and possibilities of a negative report too often on my mind.

   Sandra Greenberg Silverglade, 65, Illinois

9:40 a.m.   Finally leaving the house. Changed into three different pairs of pants, and I'm not even thrilled with this outfit, but I don't really care anymore.

   Amy Greenberg, 32, Missouri

9:55 a.m.   The words coming from the cabin are not reassuring—something about a wind shear. The stewardess announces that our plane is brand-new, only fifteen days old. Is that a good thing?

   Taylor Collins, 54, Delaware

10:00 a.m.   A bride calls looking for services for a late 2006 wedding. Please. Two-and-a-half years away. I'm just trying to get through this week; don't talk to me.

   Carol Marino, 50, Virginia

10:20 a.m.   Arabic class is not going well, but *alhamdulillah*, it is now break time!

   Mandy Halpin, 22, Morocco

10:50 a.m.   Driving to my meeting, I pump milk. I do one side at a time so both hands are still on the wheel.

   Kimberly Gavagan, 35, New Jersey

11:00 a.m.   The kids call from two different phones. My desk phone rings. My cell phone rings. Both at the same time. Sometimes technology is a bad thing.

   Marta Martin, 45, West Virginia

11:30 a.m.   A schizophrenic support group. There are only two of us. The meeting is short.

>   *Lora Lafayette, 41, Oregon*

11:45 a.m.   I check e-mail and see that I have pissed off my mom and initiated a Silent Treatment War. My mother and I do not know the meaning of conflict resolution.

>   *Vicki Cuellar, 21, New York*

Noon   Administer anesthesia to patient. On a lighter note, six of us (staff and two doctors) from the operating room discuss what we would do if we won the lottery. $196 million for tonight's drawing.

>   *Fatima Mawji, 54, Texas*

12:00 p.m.   Lunch with the Congressman. We eat and lobby . . . eat and lobby.

>   *Pat Bryson, 51, Oklahoma*

12:13 p.m.   The tyrant queen is home. Not two minutes out of camp and she loses television privileges due to her unfortunate puddle fetish.

>   *Jan Stinchcomb, 37, Texas*

12:13 p.m.   Finally got to talk to Tim, the Cubs trainer. Heck of a nice guy! Carlos, the pitcher, is interested in my personal chef service.

>   *Terry B. Riesterer, 46, Illinois*

12:14 p.m.   Prince, my favorite artist, is singing, "Call my name," and I wish he would scream "Kiki!"

>   *Kiki Carey, 22, Texas*

12:30 p.m.   Wow. Cari (coworker) and Bastard Mike (my counterpart coworker—hate him) ACTUALLY asked me to join them for lunch for once. Hell must have frozen over.

Adrienne Katzman, 24, Maryland

12:45   Stop by the lab to check e-mail. I see something move out of the corner of my eye. Damn it!!! It's a friggin' camel spider.

Angela Montero, 30, North Carolina (serving in Iraq)

1:15 p.m.   On to the *Jassi Jaissi Koi Nahin* Yahoo group where I find my daily needed soap opera fix. Thirty minutes of television mind-numb condensed into five minutes of concise reading.

Henna Budhwani, 27, Alabama

1:20 p.m.   I am amazed at the number of Dunkin' Donuts outlets in Boston. I can see two from where I am standing.

Rosemary M. Corbin, 64, California

1:35 p.m.   Home. Read last week's issue of *People*. Who the fuck are the Olsen twins, anyway? They are both little itsy-bitsy creatures—how can you tell who has the eating disorder? Glad not to be eighteen.

Regina Barreca, 47, Connecticut

2:00 p.m.   I call my twenty-nine-year-old son, Seth, and get his outgoing message and sing the whole happy birthday song.

Leiah Bowden, 59, New York

2:15 p.m.   Write husband a note about candles and lights and atmosphere for the reception. He needs notes . . . no, he disdains my notes . . . no, he really relies on notes.

Joni Axel, 61, Iowa

2:30 p.m.   Daily shamanic journey to center of earth to ask questions from power animals. Have all my business ventures very active right now and lots of decisions to make.

MaryLee Trettenero, 49, Massachusetts

2:30 p.m.   Okay, can someone tell me what the hell all these people are doing in the grocery store in the middle of the afternoon? Seriously, don't people work during the day?

Antonietta Mills, 32, New Jersey

3:21 p.m.   Just cleaned the bathroom. Am doing skip tracing now.

Michelle Dunn, 37, New Hampshire

3:40 p.m.   Finally! We pull into my parents' driveway. Why is it that the moment I pull in this driveway I go from capable adult to becoming someone's child? Dad says I am late.

Jennifer Satterwhite, 34, Texas

4:00 p.m.   I'm holding Mrs. John Hancock's wedding band in the palm of my hand. Yes, that John Hancock!

Sharon Ann Burnston, 58, New Hampshire

4:15 p.m.   Agent phoned. They still don't know if the pilot I did *(Practical Magic)* is going to be picked up for mid-season on CBS.

Shirley Knight, 67, California

4:30 p.m.   I bike by Stan's dairy herd pasture. A cow just had a baby! It is eating the afterbirth, and the new wet baby is on the ground looking innocent.

Marci Penner, 48, Kansas

5:00 p.m. Ah yes, right on time. Standing in the doorway is this wonderful, sexy man looking at me like I was a Tastykake.

Sharon Lambert, 54, Delaware

5:14 p.m. Nicholas has been crying for the past fifteen minutes. He wants me to hold him and pay attention to him. I'm trying to get stuff done! He's driving me crazy.

Ann Ponti, 35, Indiana

5:19 p.m. Ice cream trucks that play music should be outlawed. I can deal with the radio in my head, but if I have to hear "Pop Goes the Weasel" one more time . . .

Nannette Driver, 28, California

5:20 p.m. Afternoon slump, feeling lost. Do I have a nap, snack, cocktail, or cigarette? No, you should do laundry, exercise, pay your bills.

Chaya Thanhauser, 24, Massachusetts

6:00 p.m. Well, three-year-old Elli didn't think Grandma should be resting, so she came in the bedroom so we could talk about our day. We end up having a ticklefest.

Debi Clasemann, 44, Minnesota

6:30 p.m. I see it. Elegant but not overstated. Versatile. Expensive but reasonable given the designer. I slip the skirt on. The lining feels sensual against my skin. It's love. Sold!

Brenda L. Schneider, 58, Michigan

6:38 p.m. Couldn't help but notice the two dead animals left on my doorstep by my serial-killing cats. Burial detail—bummer.

Sheila M. O'Hara, 41, Massachusetts

6:50 p.m.   Treadmill time! This is the third day. (Just got the treadmill Saturday, secondhand for $25. Wow, what a bargain!) Already tired of it.

Nancy Day, 57, Maryland

6:51 p.m.   Hubby and I head out for a walk. We mall walk like the old people, but it's air-conditioned and quiet, unlike the rest of the city.

Mel Edwards, 35, South Carolina

7:00 p.m.   Back in my room in time to watch *The Weakest Link*, then *Family Feud*. Some of the contestants give the worst answers. These shows allow me to think and test my knowledge.

Marion Montgomery, 90, South Dakota

7:30 p.m.   With the flotation device wrapped tight around me, I follow the teacher's instructions for the side stroke—reach for an apple, bring the other hand up to take it, drop the apple in the basket, repeat.

Sande Smith, 41, California

7:30 p.m.   My husband, J.R., won't come to the dinner table yet because twenty-five years of hip-hop is being showcased on the BET Awards, and his thirty-one-year-old ass is sitting in front of the TV rhyming along to the Sugar Hill Gang.

Marci Johnson, 28, Colorado

7:30 p.m.   *Jeopardy* is on! I am hooked on that guy who keeps winning! I wish I could be on. I am a walking warehouse of worthless knowledge.

Kim Olsovsky, 31, South Carolina

7:45 p.m.   I love cookies! I wish being "healthy" was the ideal, instead of looking like a starved supermodel.
Jessie L. Gregorio, 23, New York

7:45 p.m.   After-dinner rounds—a couple of walks to the bathroom and one bedpan later and I'm at the nurses station trying to get some paperwork done.
Mel Andrade, 39, Massachusetts

8:00 p.m.   Stood on my front porch and watched to my amazement as my middle son went zooming up the street on his bicycle. Just a week ago he'd been cautiously braking every time he got up a little speed.
Lynn Pruett, 40, Kentucky

8:00 p.m.   Met a friend for dinner in the meatpacking district. We had a fabulous Thai meal and people-watched. Gwyneth Paltrow drew quite a stir among the patrons.
Elisabeth Röhm, 31, New York

8:00 p.m.   Eoin and I are having a rather heated discussion on the strategic deployment of identity politics and identity descriptives. What kind of couple are we?!
Heidi Ó Nuanáin, 42, Northern Ireland

8:00 p.m.   Watching *Star Trek* with my son, Jason (I don't really like the show, but just want to be near him), while I finish my tea and do some knitting.
Anna Viadero, 45, Massachusetts

8:30 p.m.   Turn on the Red Sox game just in the nick of time to see shortstop Nomar Garciaparra kick around a ground ball for yet another error. Why in the world would I look to the Red Sox as a source of comfort.
Susan E. Cayleff, 50, Massachusetts

9:30 p.m. Wow, what a birthday. I open gifts! Jewelry, note cards, four dessert plates with a picture of a cottage on them, and a bracelet with MGT engraved on it. It is made from a spoon.

Med Tibbetts, 77, New Hampshire

2135 Just stepped out of the shower and suddenly two loud explosions. Red alert!

Tanya AK Williams, 36, Connecticut (serving in Iraq)

9:40 p.m. *Blow Out.* Brandon got fired, and Jen is refusing to do hair at the show that will have leather and fur fashion. Ah, the problems of being a Beverly Hills hairstylist. And it's just breathtaking how they can work in so much product placement.

Mia Consalvo, 35, Ohio

10:00 p.m. We're getting ready to land. No one has been ringing their call bell, no one has been sick, no dogs out of their carriers running down the aisle, and no one drunk. Wish all flights were like this.

Teresa V. Powers, 46, North Carolina

10:00 p.m. We rage a bit about Bush—no night could be complete without that—but feel there are grounds for at least guarded optimism.

Deborah Weinstein, 55, Washington, D.C.

10:04 p.m. Call Mom to let her know I made it home and glance around the house for intruders. Open the shower curtain fast! No one. Under the bed. Clear.

Brittany Baeumel, 25, Idaho

10:30 p.m. Everybody is sleeping. Again to call my husband to see where they sent him. I wish someday he won't need to be a truck driver anymore.

Victoria Martinez, Illinois

10:45 p.m. A hot bubble bath with Johnson's Bedtime Bath. It's really to "soothe fussy babies," but since that's how I feel most of the time, I consider it a bathtime staple.

Joni Autrey, 25, Tennessee

11:15 p.m. I brush my teeth with tooth-whitening paste, three times more expensive and guaranteed to whiten in a month. So far, nothing has changed.

Pam Sexton, 58, Kentucky

11:20 p.m. I put my earplugs in (husband snores). Good thing my husband is a great guy. He has some disgusting things going on, but I love him in spite of it all.

Julie Knutson, North Dakota

11:47 p.m. My new roommate Lindsey, her twin, and their boyfriends just walked in the door with a big cooler of drinks. Looks like the night might just have started.

Natalie Morin, 21, New Jersey

Midnight Soft knock at my door. My thirteen-year-old son asks, Did I know that now there are only twenty-three hours and fifty-nine minutes to the premiere of *Spider-Man 2*?

Melissa Moreau Baumann, 41, Virginia

List of Contributors

**61% of day diarists considered
June 29, 2004, to be an average day.**

~~~~~~

Stephanie Abraham, CA

Krista Ahlers, ND

Tina Alford, LA

Samina Ali, CA

Ivy Alley, MS

Jill Althouse-Wood, PA

Randice-Lisa Altschul, NJ

Connie Linnell
   Ambrose-Gates, NH

Shirley Anderson, SD

Mel Andrade, MA

Cecilia Angell, NJ

Jennifer Armbruster, CO

Jane Armer, MO

Marcia Arnold, NM

Deborah Arthur, NH

Paula Austin, NC

Joni Autrey, TN

Joni Axel, IA

Deborah Ayars, NJ

Katherine Azarmi, CA

Brittany Baeumel, ID

Laurie Ballentine, NY

Paige Balter, OR

Dawn L. Banks, OH

Kristin Banta-Bland, CA

Karen Banuelos, CA

Regina Barreca, CT

DD Bartley, CA

Melissa Moreau Baumann, VA

Rachel Beavers, TN

Paula Begoun, WA

Jean Belille, CO

Soley Belt, AZ

Na'ama Y. Ben-David, TN

Jeannette Beranger, RI

Athena Berkheiser, PA

Brenda Berkman, NY

Terry Besch, MD

Tara Betts, IL

Barbara Bick, MA

Jeannette Bilodeau, VT

Roberta Blain, UT

Mary K. Blanusa, NJ

Tricia Bothun, MN

Leiah Bowden, NY

Rebecca Aldrich Bowen, FL

Susan Bowers, CA

Tana Bradley, LA

Sharon Bragg, TX

Audrey Goins Brichi, CA

Laurel Brightwell, LA

Susan Christerson Brown, KY

Susan O. Brown, FL

Wendy Brown, VA

Jacquelyn C. Bruce, NH

Deborah Bryant, KY

Pat Bryson, OK

Henna Budhwani, AL

Goldie Bulgatz, IL

Susan Burgee, MD

Sharon Ann Burnston, NH

Demetrius Bush, GA

Beverly A. Cabrera, HI

Dorothy Anne Cahill, MD

Linda M. Calhoun, AR

Denise Campbell, CA

Alisa Canillas, NH

Frieda Rapoport Caplan, CA

Marian Carcache, AL

Kiki Carey, TX

Rebecca A. Carlson, MI

Alison G. Carrico, TX

Rosanne Cash, NY

Karin Horwatt Cather, VA

Susan E. Cayleff, MA

Karen A. Celestan, LA

Jen Chapin, NY

Diana Chavez, CO

Lisa Cherry, CA

Debi Clasemann, MN

Doreene Clement, AZ

Lethia Cobbs, CA

Cady Coleman, TX

Taylor Collins, DE

Marie Colwill, SD

Lee Conderacci, MD

Jen Consalvo, VA

Mia Consalvo, OH

Marilyn Cook, IL

Suzie Cook, FL

Ann "Frannie" Coopersmith, HI

Suzanne Cope, MA

Rosemary M. Corbin, CA

Cindi Crain, Kenya

Rachel Crossman, CA

Dona Crowe, KY

Linda Decker Crowe, KY

Vicki Cuellar, NY

Virginia Cueto, FL

Jill Canillas Daley, NH

Lori Daniels, HI

Sheaquan M. Datts, NY

Jymmy Kay Davis, TX

Ruth A. Davis, TX

Elizabeth A. Day, MD

Nancy Day, MD

list of contributors **384**

Ashley Dearborn, NY

Cathy de la Cruz, GA

Laurie Denenberg, CT

Ellen Denham, IN

Annmarie Donnelly, NJ

Joannie Valerie Dooley, IA

Sue Doro, CA

Nancy Dorsey, RI

Michele Dortch, CA

Susan E. Downey, CA

Nannette A. Driver, CA

Jan Dugan, NH

Holly Dunlap, NY

Michelle Dunn, NH

Mary Jane Bradbury
   Duran, CO

Amy Duvall, NY

Melissa J. Dyer, VA

Carey Earle, NY

Jeanette Luise Eberhardy, MA

Rossanna Echegoyén, NY

Mel Edwards, SC

Concepción Elizalde, IL

Normandi Ellis, KY

Alice Elman, NY

Shaletta D. Espie, MD

Alexandra Espindola, WA

Edie Farwell, VT

Judy Fine, NH

Beth Fliehler, IA

Hannah D. Forman, WA

Judi Forman, NH

Susan Forrest, AZ

Stephanie Forte, NV

Jennifer Foth, MN

Louise G. Fradkin, PA

Nina P. Freedman, NY

Patricia Gaffney, PA

Ann Gaillard, NY

Meg Gaillard, RI

Maysel Galiga, IL

Dee Galloway, CO

Beth Garland, AZ

Kimberly Gavagan, NJ

Gina Gayle, NY

Amanda Geary, VA

Marjorie M. German, MD

Stephanie Giancola, NH

Julie M. Gilchrist, MT

Mubina Gillani, TX

Ann Gillard, CA

Debra Ginsberg, CA

Sandra Gittlen, MA

Ginny Goblirsch, OR

Nadine Goldman, MD

Paulina Goldman, NJ

Reid Gómez, CA

liz gonzález, CA

Clare Wilmot Goreau, VT

Ann M. Green, MI

Beth Green, NE

Robin Green, NY

Susannah Green, ME

Amy Greenberg, MO

Jessie L. Gregorio, NY

Deborah Grotfeldt, TX

Jenee Guidry, TX

Kumu Gupta, MA

Jane Winston Gustafson, MN

Trisha Haitz, NC

Pat Halicks, KY

Ruth V. Halloran, NH

Mandy Halpin, Morocco

Jimin Han, NY

Lisa Handman, GA

Sharon Haney, PA

Phyllis Hanlon, MA

Linda Hardesty, CA

Cindy Beatty Harper, MO

Laraine Harper, NV

Heather E. Harris, VA

Cindi Harrison, CA

Charly Haversat, ME

Diane M. Hedler, CA

Frances Field Hemond, MA

Cris Hernandez, CA

Betti-Sue Hertz, CA

Lana Hicks-Olson, VA

Sheila Higgins, AK

I. Javette Jenkins Hines, NY

Jessica Hoffmann, CA

Kathleen Korosec Holmes, KS

Becky Horowitz, MA

Karen Horowitz, MA

Lolly Horvath-Dandeneau, England

Lee Houts, CA

Sarah Hughes, NY

LeAnne P. Hunt, TX

Barbara J. Hutter, NY

Irene "Rocky" Hwasta, OH

Barbara K. Ige, CA

Niké Irvin, CA

Aneeta Jamal, TX

Sindi Jandreau, SD

Bettina Jensen, Denmark

Jonna Jensen, Denmark

Jan Jenson, NC

Lesley Jimerson, NE

Grace Jividen, CO

Marci Johnson, CO

Jackie Joice, CA

Kathleen Juhl, TX

Cathy Kaemmerlen, GA

Robin Kall, RI

Suzanne Kamata, Japan

Ann Karp, GA

Rebecca Lea Kaszubowski, AR

Adrienne Katzman, MD

J. Kehaulani Kauanui, CT

Laura Kaufman, IL

Alexa Kelly, NY

Cathie Kelly, DE

Nataly Kelly, NH

Martha Kimes, AZ

Dottie King, FL

Angela Giles Klocke, GA

Shirley Knight, CA

Julie Knutson, ND

Gail M. Koehler, KY

Jannifer Kotok, NH

Karen Koziol, CA

Tanya Kozlowski, IL

Gertrude Krein, SD

Kate Krile, MN

Sarah Krile, Republica Moldova

Lora Lafayette, OR

Amrit Lal, TX

Amanda Lamb, NC

Sharon Lambert, DE

Barbara Arminio La Mort, NJ

Julie Landsman, MN

Amanda Lape-Freeberg, VT

Polly LaRoche, SD

Laura Stout LaTour, MA

Lillian Lau, IN

Jolee Lautaret, AZ

Marty Lee
Layman-Mendonca, VT

Sharon J. Leach, NM

Mary Eloise H. Leake, AL

Yvonne D. Lemons, TN

Michelle L'Esperance, FL

Batya Salzman Levy, Israel

Hannah Lewis, MN

V. Ellen Lewis, GA

Lin Liedke, NY

Cheryl Lieteau, MA

Michelle Lyle, GA

Ellen Jean Lynch, NE

Alta "Bud" Madsen, MN

Jan Malone, ID

Carol Marino, VA

Vonda L. Marshall, NY

Marta Martin, WV

Gloria J. Martinez, TX

Victoria Martinez, IL

Tori Mason, TN

Fatima Mawji, TX

Carolyn L. Mazloomi, OH

Joan Foster McCarty, GA

Mary McDaniel, KY

Holly McDonald, TX

Nancy Gard McGehee, VA

Sandy McGuire, CT

Marcella McKay, MS

Keith Dockery McLean, MS

Susan "Zan" Meigs, TX

Kelly Raclin Miller, IL

Miriam S. Miller, DC

Antonietta L. Mills, NJ

Sierra Rose Mills, OR

Angela C. Mink, CA

Janet L. Misamore, Russia

Erin Mone, Costa Rica

Angela Montero, NC

Marion Montgomery, SD

Ann Moore, CO

Monica Moore, KS

Julie Moos, FL

Tamara S. Morgan, VT

Natalie Morin, NJ

Priscilla Morrison, PA

Mary C. Moss, OR

Caryn Mower, CA

Sylvia Muhammad, NJ

Jill L. Mullaly, NH

Leigh Sparrow Munsey, NC

Margaret Murphy, SD

Lisa Muth, NY

Pauline F. Muth, NY

Melissa Myers, FL

Catherine Myman, CA

Linnea Nelson, ND

Dawn Neptune, UT

Beth Newberry, RI

Carrie Newton, IA

Anne-Marie B. Nichols, CO

Jennifer Nichols, WY

Jennifer Noonan, ME

Mary Jo Noonan, HI

Tara Nott-Cunningham, MI

Sheila M. O'Hara, MA

Kathryn Ohlerking, CO

Taiye M. Oladapo, PA

Diana Oldenburg, OR

Kim Olsovsky, SC

Maryanne O'Neill, CA

Heidi Ó Nuanáin,
Northern Ireland

Lisa Oppedyk, OR

Maret Orliss, CA

Jeanne Y. Pace, TX

Kristi Padgett, VT

Janet Papazis, VA

Juli L. Parker, MA

Rebecca Parsons, NY

Eve Pearlman, CA

Marci Penner, KS

Marianela Pereyra, NJ

Wendy Pesky, ID

Cindy Phillips, NY

Linda M. Plasschaert, IN

Ann Ponti, IN

Peggy B. Potts, GA

Teresa V. Powers, NC

Amy N. Price, AZ

Diane Elizabeth
Price-Powers, VT

Lynn Pruett, KY

Kristin Putchinski, MD

Sandra J. Quaschnick, CA

Jenine S. Rabin, DC

Tammy Raabe Rao, MA

Sally Jessy Raphael, NY

Paula Raven, VA

Faizbano Rayani, TX

Michele D. Reynolds, MI

Wendy M. Reynolds, MI

Elizabeth A. Rider, MA

Terry B. Riesterer, IL

Véronique Robigou, WA

Jessica Ann Robinson, NC

Christine Elizabeth
Robinson, CA

Pilar Robledo, Pakistan

Sue Rodin, NY

Christine Rohling, OH

Elisabeth Röhm, NY

Lisa Rolls, Kenya

Pauline Romano, CO

Karen Romeo, CO

Valerie Romness, TX

Hollie Rose, CT

Erica Row, NY

Victoria F. Rucker, WA

Lois Palken Rudnick, MA

Lynn Ruehlmann, VA

Maureen Quinn Salamon, NJ

Sherry Salant, MO

Janet Palman
Salzman-Sola, VT

June Samuel, AL

Nan Long Sanders, MS

Cory Sarabia, HI

Jennifer Satterwhite, TX

Kate Savage, IL

Deborah Schenck, VT

Verlene Schermer, CA

Tammy S. Schmidt, MO

Brenda L. Schneider, MI

Amy Ross Schroer, DC

Idalia Schultz, TX

Mary Anne Schwalbe, NY

Darlene Anita Scott, VA

Jennifer Scott, CT

Miriam Scott, UT

Kelly Seigler, GA

Margaret A. Seime, TN

Pam Sexton, KY

Becky Shacklett, KS

Cynthia J. Shafer, FL

Tricia C. Shaffer, WV

Donna Shambley-Ebron, OH

Caitlin Sharbono, CO

Nikki Shaw, OR

Dorothy M. Sheldon, WA

Sajida H. Shroff, GA

Sandra Greenberg
   Silverglade, IL

Jean Simon, SD

Leontyne Sloan, CA

Lauren B. Smith, AZ

Sande Smith, CA

Tamu G. Snow, CO

Heidi Sokol, MA

Midyne Spear, CA

Monica Spears-Lombard, TX

Emily J. Spencer, IA

Rochelle Spencer, GA

Suzanne Spencer-Wood, MI

Kristin K. Sposito, OR

Doris Stallings, MS

Denise K. Stark, NM

Alice Biskey Steele, KY

Julia Litton Steury, MN

Stacie Stevens, AK

Tina Stevens, IL

Laurie Stewart, NY

Jan Stinchcomb, TX

Nicole Stott, TX

Jan Jones Stover, IL

Judith Strasser, WI

Luanne Stuart-Evans, OK

Trudy Suggs, MN

Carolyn Suit, AR

Adeeba Sulaiman, GA

Colleen Sullivan, RI

Melissa Summers, MI

Linda Szeto, IL

Ahoo Tabatabai, OH

Ann Pruett Tahir, TX

Ann Taylor, OK

Jenny P. Taylor, AL

Kathleen Taylor, NY

Pamela D. Taylor, KY

Tayyibah Taylor, GA

Chaya Thanhauser, MA

Samantha Thomas, NC

Kathy Thompson, OR

Kitty Thurnheer, NY

Med Tibbetts, NH

Ann Timmons, VA

Connie J. Tobias, TN

Dawn Marie Tomei, PA

MaryLee Trettenero, MA

Bobbie Trowbridge, GA

Melinda Tsuchiya, Swaziland

Kristen Twedt, MS

Doris J. Underwood, AR

Cynthia Vaughn, IN

Anna Viadero, MA

Suzanne Vold, MN

Janice E. Voss, TX

Chelle Wahlert, CO

Jackie Walker, DC

Vicki L. Ward, CA

Janet Warfield, NH

Suzanne Wargo, CT

Joy M. Watkins, PA

Tanya Abadia Weaver, Afghanistan

Nan Weber, UT

Marilyn Weigel, IL

Marva Weigelt, KS

Megan Weinerman, IL

Deborah Weinstein, DC

Lauren R. Weinstein, NY

Brenda K. White, KY

Muffie White, OR

Jaci Wilkins, ID

Cathy Wilkinson, WA

Crystal Wilkinson, IN

Trish Wilkinson, IL

Dera R. Williams, CA

Holly Ann Williams, GA

Jaye Austin Williams, NY

Niama L. Williams, PA

Tanya AK Williams, CT

Valerie Williams, WA

Lori Windle, CO

Amy Wirdzek, TN

Barbara Wojciechowski, SC

Susan Wolcott, HI

Annie Wood, FL

Karen Wood, CA

Heidi P. Worcester, CT

Keke Wu, NH

Stasia Wussow, WI

Ayla Jean Yackley, Turkey

Susan Yee, MN

Christine M. Young, MA

Susan E. M. Young, PA

Laverne Zabielski, KY

Tanya Zhu, MN

Audrey Zimmerman, ME

Acknowledgments

We owe a huge collective thanks to the 493 women who volunteered their day diaries for this book project. Without them, there would be no *This Day in the Life*. With much appreciation as well to Carrie Thornton at Three Rivers Press and to our agent, Lisa Bankoff of ICM—two women who can make things happen, thank goodness! To our editor, Katie McHugh, thank you for all your wonderful insights. Many other friends and professional associates (often one and the same) also lent their talents and support to this book project, including Nancy Fontaine, James Gregorio, Miki Hickel, Sunta Izzicupo, Alan Joffrey, Nataly Kelly, Bob Myman, Roger Paradis, Cornelia Purcell, John Raven, Nan Sanders, and Judith Seime.

In creating this book, our goal was to gather a true diversity of voices by reaching across experiential, socioeconomic, cultural, and geographic boundaries. In this effort we received support from the following organizations:

Alaska Women's Network; American Academy of Cosmetic Surgery; American Association of Zoo Keepers; American Bonsai Society; American Society of Plastic Surgeons; American University; American Women's Organization of Moscow; Association of Bridal Consultants; Association on American

Indian Affairs; Center for the Homeless; Daughters of Sarah Senior Community; Doulas of North America; Dropzone .com; Empowerment4Women; General Motors Corporation; Hawaii Ultimate League Association; Hawaii Women's Business Center; The Healing Place; Illinois Migrant Council; Indus Women Leaders; International Rescue Committee; Jackson Women's History Council; Kansas Sampler Foundation; MANA, A National Latina Organization; Midwest Dairy Association; Mothers & More; Muslim WakeUp!; NASA Johnson Space Center; New Mexico Wine Growers Association; Oklahoma Association of Broadcasters; Outward Bound; Senior Women Web; Sisters of the Holy Cross; South Dakota Health Care Association; Story Circle Network;Tradeswomen, Inc.; Tuck School of Business at Dartmouth College; United States Army; United States Navy; United States Olympic Committee; US Airways; Women on Wheels; Women's Coalition for Pacific Fisheries; Women's Professional Rodeo Association; Women's Rural Entrepreneurial Network; Write Around Portland; and WritingItReal.com.

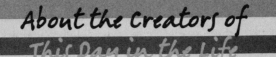

About the Creators of
This Day in the Life

Writer/editor **Joni B. Cole** was having a bad day when she thought up the concept for *This Day in the Life*. Trying to cope with a serious illness in her family, a huge tax bill, and a pre-schooler who refused to wear socks despite freezing temperatures, she wondered if anyone else was feeling so low. Surely not. But what were other women doing and feeling and thinking on this very same day? And so a book was born, out of self-pity, curiosity, and a need to connect. She and her husband, Stephen, have two daughters: Esme, eight, and Thea, six (and a sixteen-year-old dog, Lily).

Rebecca Joffrey is an entrepreneur and marketing executive who, after getting bored selling cat food and credit cards, founded an online mentoring program designed to help women college graduates understand the diversity of paths they can take in life. This program ultimately led to her involvement in *This Day in the Life*. During the creation of the first *This Day* book (published 2002), Becky and her husband, Alan, had a baby girl, Elizabeth. In the spirit of sequels, Becky had baby Dexter in the midst of creating this volume, prompting her to wonder, "Am I going to have a baby with every book?!"

B. K. Rakhra is a writer and part-time professional movie watcher (coding movies for risk behaviors for an NIH-funded study). She left the nine-to-five world of steady paychecks and affordable insurance when she segued from fund-raising to fiction writing (short stories, screenplays, her "memoirs"). As a writer, an observer, and an insatiably curious woman, there was no way she could say no to *This Day in the Life,* a book that would let her ask anyone—anyone!—what her day is like. She is currently testing her theory that no kids + no husband = eternal youth.

The three partners and friends live in Vermont, despite the fact that none of them ski.

For more information about *This Day in the Life: Diaries from Women Across America* and the project that inspired it, visit www.thisdayinthelife.com.